Father of
Racist Ideology

*The Social and Political
Thought of Count Gobineau*

Father of
Racist Ideology

*The Social and Political
Thought of Count Gobineau*

Michael D. Biddiss

Weybright and Talley
New York

Published in the United States by
Weybright and Talley, Inc.
3 East 54th Street
New York, New York 10022

Library of Congress Catalog Card Number: 77-116523

Printed in Great Britain

For my Wife
who helped

Contents

Preface

At the completion of a study of this nature it is a particular pleasure to recollect and acknowledge the help and kindness of many. The debts of gratitude, both academic and personal, which I have incurred in the preparation of this book are beyond full enumeration. But I should like to record here a few of them.

No expression of thanks can adequately repay the officials of the Bibliothèque Nationale et Universitaire, Strasbourg, for all their unfailing kindness and assistance during my work on the Gobineau Archives. I should also like to acknowledge the help given to me in Paris by the staffs of the Bibliothèque Nationale, of the Bibliothèque de l'Institut de France, of the Salle des Communications of the Archives du Ministère des Affaires Étrangères at the Quai d'Orsay, and of the Archives de la Librairie Académique Perrin. In Bordeaux thanks are similarly due to the officials of the Bibliothèque Municipale. Nearer home I should like to mention the assistance given by the staffs of the British Museum Reading Room and Newspaper Library and of the Cambridge University Library.

In thanking the following I wish also to absolve them from responsibility for any failings in this study. In Strasbourg, Professor Jean Gaulmier kindly helped me in a number of ways, not least by allowing access to some of his own work in advance of its publication. Elsewhere in France, Monsieur Roger Béziau of Pau and Father Charles Monsch of the Maison de la Bonne Presse in Paris assisted my researches into certain other sources. In Cambridge, I was privileged to have the benefit of the wisdom and guidance of Professor Sir Denis Brogan in my work upon an earlier draft of this study. There too I incurred a debt of gratitude to the Master and Fellows of Downing College who, while themselves pursuing Truth, showed their interest in this investigation of Error and provided me with encouragement both tangible and intangible.

Finally, my wife has given both time and care in helping to prepare this book for publication. She has lived with it almost as much as I have. Towards both it and me she has shown the most generous patience. To her I have pleasure in dedicating it.

M.D.B.

Cambridge
and Coniston Water
Autumn 1969

Introduction

Centuries of experience prove that the
worst tyranny is that which favours
fictions, for these are by their very nature
unfeeling and pitiless, boundless in their
impudence and their pretensions.

GOBINEAU
Essai (1853)

Introduction

We who live in a world afflicted with growing racial tensions and
conflicts have much reason to study the social and political thought
of Count Arthur de Gobineau. It was he who, in the last century,
elaborated a racial philosophy of history and society that surpasses
in scope and sinister grandeur even the pages of *Mein Kampf*. The
author of this famous *Essai sur l'Inégalité des Races Humaines* was
an enigmatic and complex man, with something about him both of
the polymath and of the charlatan. His career had many facets, for
he was poet, novelist and dramatist as well as journalist, orientalist,
diplomat and historian. As a literary figure he received posthumous
praise from critics such as Gide, Proust and Cocteau, and the
foundation in 1966 of the annual *Études Gobiniennes* has indicated
the current emphasis of interest upon that aspect of his work. Yet,
within the context of the history of social and political ideas, his
fate has been different. There, while being for the present the
victim of comparative neglect, he has been in the past the subject
of excess in reverence, denunciation and misrepresentation alike.
In the era of his greatest fame he had become widely known as the
Father of Racism. Though such a description naturally over
simplified the question of ideological origins, it did at least crystal-
lize his rightful claim to be regarded as a seminal figure in the
history of European racism.

It is superficially understandable that a philosophy stressing to
such large degree the role of race in the formation and destruction
of societies and civilizations should be passed over in our own time
when, particularly with Nazi atrocities in mind, we tend to regard
such systematic racism as intellectually discredited and as the
object of much emotional revulsion. But, only too obviously, racial
consciousness and its political and social repercussions remain
among the most significant concerns of our contemporary world.
Therefore study of the relevant aspects of Gobineau's writings can
illuminate many of the problems still posed by a mode of thought
which, systematically or otherwise, uses race as an instrument of
social explanation and often of political effort too. Race-thinking
was a prominent element in European political theorizing from the

mid-nineteenth century until the fall of the Third Reich. Gobineau
is immediately important both because of his vast *Essai* and on
account of the personal and intellectual links leading from him to
Richard Wagner and on to Houston Stewart Chamberlain and
Adolf Hitler himself. While he remains of relevance to our century,
Gobineau sheds no less light upon his own. In the past the relationship between his race theory and his other contemporary observations has been inadequately treated. But Gobineau provides us with
a lively commentary upon France, Europe and much of the world
beyond in his own time. He reminds us that the nineteenth century
was not entirely dominated by optimism and ideas of democratic-
liberal progress. There is to be considered a vast and disparate
opposition. In its ranks we find Gobineau who, though in so many
ways moulded by the ideas of his age, is characterized above all by
the power of his rejections.

Most earlier discussions of his social and political thinking were
marred by the desire to use his ideas (or a version of them) as
political instruments of racism. Perhaps the most famous 'Gobinist' was Professor Ludwig Schemann of Freiburg who founded the
Gobineau Vereinigung, the society established in 1894 to promote
this particular brand of racist doctrine. Subsequent commentators
must express not only their gratitude for his great labours on the
Gobineau papers but also their awareness of his uncritical obsession with glorifying Gobineau's memory and a form of his racial
thesis. The climate of race-thinking at the beginning of the present
century was unfavourable to any adequately objective assessment of
the significance of Gobineau's thought. The Gobinism of the early
twentieth century was an imperfect reflection of the original
doctrine enunciated in the 1850s. In fact, a bibliography of works
on Gobineau between his death in 1882 and the end of Nazi rule is
less an aid to the study of a man and his ideas than an indication of
primary sources for an essay about misrepresentation.

The desire to use Gobineau for immediate political purposes is
not the only reason for the inadequacy of much previous work.
Since the time of Schemann the available source material has increased significantly. Newly discovered or released information has
given us improved understanding. For example, the present study
is the first to integrate into the general framework of Gobineau's
ideas research upon the entirety of his diplomatic writings. Though
their subject-matter and expression are somewhat circumscribed

by requirements of business and convention they provide none
the less many of his most rewarding insights into societies as
varied as those of Switzerland, Hanover, Persia, Greece, Newfoundland, Brazil and Sweden in the years from 1849 to 1877. This
material has been generally overlooked and remains largely unpublished – the sole major exception being a volume of his reports
upon Persia. We have also examined other sources of information
(such as Gobineau's provincialist writings) which, though available
to others, have been generally neglected. Then, a number of materials used by previous scholars now invite reassessment in the light
of excellent recent editions, such as those dealing with the letters to
Tocqueville or with the correspondence between Gobineau and his
sister in the last decade of his life. The major source remains the
precious collection housed in the library of the University of Strasbourg. These manuscripts, many still unpublished, and the rare
printed materials available there have been fully used in the
preparation of this volume.

Gobineau's work is generally neither entirely systematic nor
completely consistent. We have attempted to use the totality of our
sources to indicate the development and change in his thought and
to dismiss arguments explaining it in largely static terms independently of his evolving experience. For instance, perhaps the most
fundamental contention of this study is that Gobineau's racist
ideology is essentially derived from other and earlier social and
political concerns, and that the interdependence of these factors
(however its details may vary through time) is the key to understanding the later evolution of his thought. Among Gobineau's
published works we have had to distinguish between the semi-
scholarly and the polemical, or, again, between ideas expressed in
any kind of non-fictional work and those more elusively expounded
in novels, verse and drama. We have tried to distinguish in the
midst of a vast number of personal letters the different nuances
revealed in writing to correspondents of various views and degrees
of intimacy. These many sources, remarkable in range, present the
student, whether he be author or reader, with a great critical
stimulus and challenge.

Aided by such fuller material and devoid of any racist intent this
book aims to provide a coherent survey of Gobineau's social and
political thought. It may also serve to indicate to historians and
other students of the social sciences at work in the English-speaking

world that he holds a fascination and relevance greater than has been recognized hitherto in their traditions of study. The following pages cannot claim to solve all the problems. This treatment is presented with a full awareness, annually fortified by the debates of the *Études Gobiniennes*, that we still have much to learn. But its composition springs from the conviction that the time is ripe for generally surveying these aspects of Gobineau's thinking, in a spirit of suggestion and stimulation rather than one of finality and dogmatism. It cannot treat of Gobineau as would-be orientalist, nor as novelist and versifier, nor does it deal with his travels or diplomatic career as such. It is concerned with his curious historical philosophy and with his dubious contribution to the development of ethnological ideas only in so far as these illuminate the central topic, the social and political ideology of racism. It does not claim to provide the much needed rewriting of Schemann's weighty two-volume life history, *Gobineau: eine Biographie*, published in the heyday of Teutonism, at German Strassburg between 1913 and 1916. Instead, this book investigates in detail the social and political ideas of Gobineau, which remain relevant – even if principally by virtue of their errors – to some of the problems of our own world. The diffusion of Gobinism and its absorption into other streams of race-thinking in the late nineteenth and early twentieth centuries will be treated in part of a further volume entitled *European Racism*. It is within the context of that more general survey of the history and ideology of racism over the last two hundred years that such questions of diffusion and absorption can best be considered.

Here, however, we concentrate upon the racist ideology as it appears in the life and writings of one of its most famous, or infamous, proponents. Throughout we are concerned with certain major questions. How did Gobineau's racial theory evolve? How consistently was it held? How does it relate, at various stages, to his thoughts on such topics as Christianity, feudalism, aristocracy, property, liberty, equality, democracy, socialism, industrialization and nationalism? How far are Gobineau's views on these potential subjects of social theory independent of his race-thinking? What is his attitude to the societies of his own time, and how does he view their future? What are the ethical implications of his theories? Again, could his ideas and observations provide the foundations for any sort of political programme?

The first part of this book deals with Gobineau's thought in the period before the formulation of his racist creed around 1850, when he began the *Essai*. The second discusses certain facets of that work, its place in the development of his thinking, and its chief implications for social and political theory. The final part examines the evolution of his ideas in later life. We are thus concerned with intellectual biography – but not as an end in itself. The following pages are intended not only to reveal a fascinating man but also to improve, in some degree, our understanding of the political ideas of race which were so horrifically important in the not too distant past and which are unfortunately by no means irrelevant to our present and future. Moreover, this study may also make some contribution to comprehending the nature of a more general range of political ideas reliant upon unreason and error. Author and reader alike might derive more immediate pleasure from discussing a wiser and more congenial kind of political thinking. But, while there survive dangerous ideas which – striving to conceal their errors beneath the garb of plausibility – continue to be capable of seducing the mind of man and of influencing adversely the conditions of his social existence, it clearly remains necessary to examine their nature and to criticize their conclusions.

PART ONE

The Emergence of Social Pessimism

I have faith in myself! This so obsesses
me that I would scorn all worldly
matters, such as fortune and honours,
because of the awareness I have of a
higher duty to fulfil – that of writing
what is in my heart.

GOBINEAU
to his Father (1838)

As to your talents, it is hard to know
when one observes you just what will
become of them and whether the epidemic
ills of the age, which affect you no less
than they do your contemporaries, will
make them useless. Thus one is
fascinated both by what you could be and
by what one fears you may become.

TOCQUEVILLE
to Gobineau (1843)

1 The Early Years

Arthur de Gobineau was born in 1816, upon the anniversary of the fall of the Bastille, into a family devoted to the Bourbons and to the destruction of the legacies of the French Revolution. His ancestors were prosperous bourgeois of Bordeaux and he always gave great emphasis to his ties with the Gironde, even though his own birthplace was Ville d'Avray on the outskirts of Paris. His paternal grandfather, having stoutly defended provincial rights against royal encroachment before 1789, subsequently showed unequivocal monarchist loyalties until his death in 1796. Arthur's father Louis, born in 1784, joined the royalist forces of Maine around 1799 and remained hostile to the pretensions of Bonaparte. In 1810 he married Anne Louise Madeleine de Gercy, whose father was allegedly a bastard son of Louis xv, and settled in Paris.

Louis de Gobineau's *Mémoires*, written for the benefit of his children, illustrate the atmosphere in which Arthur was reared. They record his activity in the royalist Ordre des Chevaliers de la Foi and his imprisonment by the Napoleonic régime in 1814. They explain how his loyalty was largely unrewarded under the restored monarchy after 1815 and how he was left to make undistinguished progress through the military hierarchy. In 1830 he reluctantly accepted the régime of King Louis-Philippe. Soon the press was criticizing his lukewarm attitude to the new monarchy and he was forced to retire in 1831. The *Mémoires* give views on the state of France which were to be echoed in the son's writings. Louis felt that the Restoration establishment had underestimated his services and talents. He criticized a society in which careers must be bought and where his very penury denied him protection and patronage. The Bourbon failure of 1830 was seen as a despicable loss of nerve on the part of Charles x. Louis had a low opinion of human nature as he found it in the nineteenth century: 'How sad is humanity when we observe it closely and how rare in the world are virtue and honour.'[1] He believed that the valuable ordering of society preserved during the Ancien Régime had been destroyed by the social anarchy of the Revolution and that modern France showed a lack of security and stability, a state of social war in which traditional rules were no longer observed. His recollections are a meditation upon 'the sorry state of France, my own situation as one defeated, my loss of rank and my humiliation that men should see my sword snatched away due to the submission of my princes'.[2] His son was to share such disgust and alienation.

The chief source for the early biography of Arthur himself is the sketch by his sister Caroline (who was from 1867 Mère Bénédicte of the convent of Solesmes), entitled *Enfance et Première Jeunesse d'Arthur de Gobineau*.[3] Its pages put undue stress on the light and joy of these first few years, but Caroline herself saw this essay as 'a very simple sketch of the *real life* of Joseph Arthur de Gobineau from his birth until his entry into society at the age of nineteen'.[4] Still, it reveals very little of the drama surrounding their childhood. The marriage of their parents was unhappy and the family environment was worsened for the sensitive Arthur by the fact that his mother's lover, Charles de La Coindière, was made his tutor and held this position until 1830. It was La Coindière who was to introduce his pupil to that knowledge of German language and scholarship which was to prove so influential in the evolution of Gobineau's interests. In 1830 mother and tutor travelled with Arthur to Switzerland. Four or five months were also spent in Baden at Inzlingen Castle and, in Caroline's view, this experience of the medieval 'always remained for him the ideal of his youthful happiness'.[5]

Shortly afterwards Arthur began more regular schooling at Bienne, where instruction was in German, and it was there that he claimed acquiring his fascination with oriental languages. Soon his parents were finally separated. His mother deserted the family to take up an ever more profligate existence which was marked by scandalous romance, fraud and debt, as well as confidence tricks in the grandest manner of high society, and which culminated in a spell of imprisonment. By the time that he was twenty Arthur had broken off all contact with her, and he remained thereafter sorely embarrassed by rumours of her behaviour. No commentator on Gobineau can afford to neglect this lurid background to his youth.

It would certainly be exaggerated to suggest that these particular experiences fundamentally conditioned the substance of his thought, but they may none the less have made an important contribution to the tone in which it came to be expressed.

Around the beginning of 1833 Arthur joined his father in Brittany, continuing his education at Lorient and then at Redon. It is clear that, while certainly ashamed of his mother, he also reserved a certain contempt for the weaknesses of Louis's own temperament. He may have felt already that his father was a dull product of his class and time and that he himself had a more vital destiny to fulfil, one that would require a greater independence from the conventional shackles of his family environment. Louis's plan that he should enter the military college of Saint Cyr most certainly ended abortively on account of Arthur's greater preoccupation with literature and the Orient. Then, with the pliant Louis's encouragement, he cultivated an interest in history, folk tales and legend. The oriental attraction remained strongest and much later the Baronne de Saint Martin recalled him as he was at eighteen in the following terms: 'All his aspirations were directed towards the East. He dreamt only of mosques and minarets; he called himself a Muslim, ready to make his pilgrimage to Mecca.'[6] Even in the age of the romantics and of the 'oriental renaissance' this was scarcely a normal educational history. At that time Gobineau could almost have said, like a character from one of his later novels, 'I am a product of books alone'.[7] In time social and political experience would complement such book-learning. But Gobineau already clearly possessed a certain cosmopolitan spirit and a mind unbounded by French or even European confines. Within the more limited context of his own continent his main attention had been drawn towards Germany, both by La Coindière's instruction and by his own first direct experience of life and culture beyond the Rhine.

Despite the domestic upheavals a devotion to the house of Gobineau also marked his early development. It was accompanied by youthful prejudices in favour of Bourbon legitimacy and Catholicism. His collection of material relating to the history of his family began in the 1830s. He was proud of his family's noble connections, though the title of 'Count' which he adopted after the death of his uncle Thibaut-Joseph in 1855 was not strictly his. He did not forsake the provincial loyalties so easily nurtured in the

Breton environment and he linked both province and family to the maintenance of the feudal 'liberties' of the Ancien Régime. He accepted the ideals attributed to the golden age of feudalism and was, in the words of Baronne de Saint Martin, 'already an Amadis with chivalrous ideas and an heroic spirit, dreaming of what was most noble and most grand'.[8] Romantic medievalism had even made him especially proud of a christian-name which brought him close in spirit to the tales of the Round Table.

For the adequate pursuit of the studies that most interested him a less capricious education would have been desirable. In the outcome we have, as Ernest Seillière suggested, a figure who was 'self-taught, whimsical, indeed amateur. There lay the predisposition towards an incomplete perception of things and great likelihood of error and partiality. Still, on the other hand, there also perhaps was the most favourable environment for originality of thought.'[9] Gobineau was conscious of some of the drawbacks and was even, just occasionally, apologetic. His self-reliance, enthusiasm and boundless intellectual aspirations were, at once, his weakness and his strength. We shall now go on to see how these qualities and defects were confirmed or remoulded through his experience of Paris, where he came to settle in October 1835.

2 The Orleanist Monarchy

Gobineau's fame is based primarily upon his vast *Essai sur l'Inéga-lité des Races Humaines*, which is regarded as the work of a racist and a reactionary pessimist. But in 1835 Gobineau was no racist, nor was he unduly reactionary or pessimistic. At first the prejudices of his upbringing were reinforced by the influence of his uncle Thibaut-Joseph de Gobineau with whom he began living in Paris. The nephew was to recall with pride the opposition of his tempestuous relative to the Revolution and the Empire. More recently Thibaut-Joseph had broken a close association with Talleyrand when the latter supported the Orleanist usurper in the successful revolution of 1830. Gobineau commented: 'His hatred for Louis-Philippe was unlimited. . . . As for Thiers and Guizot, he could not envisage any scorn that would be sufficient to do them justice.'[1] Although Thibaut-Joseph provided early financial assistance Gobineau resented his uncle's tetchiness, desired independence and soon went to reside elsewhere in the capital.

Gobineau began employment with a clerical post in a gas company but, despite this humble situation, his name and family connections brought him into the salons associated with the politics of Bourbon legitimism. Meanwhile he sought commissions for articles and translations. He wrote thus to Caroline: 'I have ambition and a heart that is proud and resolute – and dare to say so. I shall not be trapped by the dull and stupid pleasures of Parisian life.'[2] Still, despite some journalistic work and his uncle's aid, these first Parisian years were financially lean. They were marked both by the influence of an uncle alienated from contemporary society and by Gobineau's own first taste of personal deprivation and degradation. Certain seeds of social pessimism were ready to germinate.

He was introduced early into the legitimist salon of the Comtesse de Serre, widow of a minister under the Restoration, and was impressed by its elegance, good taste and simplicity. He established a particular friendship with his hostess's nephew Hercule de Serre, whom he was to describe as his *alter ego*. Nothing of the two friends' correspondence has been discovered as yet, but there are many indications that their exchange of letters was considerable until the death of Hercule in 1859. In the same social milieu he was able through the introductions of the German artist Guermann Bohn to enter the circle around the painter Ary Scheffer. There he met Scheffer's niece, the future wife of Ernest Renan. With the German–Dutch Scheffers Gobineau could further his knowledge of German culture. Through their acquaintance he met Charles de Rémusat, then on the threshold of his distinguished political and academic career, and it was probably he who in turn made the highly important introduction to Alexis de Tocqueville.

It was the Comtesse de Serre who aided Gobineau to obtain a situation in the postal service in January 1839. The pay was meagre but the limited hours gave precious leisure. In 1840 Gobineau helped form a small society of young intellectuals called '*Les Scelti*' – the elect. Though it was short-lived it none the less provides us with a probable indication of his fondness for élites. The subjects for its discussions were less political than historical, literary and artistic. He explained: 'The members of the Most Serene Society have three things in common: ambition, independence of mind, aristocratic ideas.'[3] Among its members were Hercule de Serre, Guermann Bohn and Maxime du Camp, a writer remembered mostly for his later association with Flaubert. Despite their élitist aspirations the members remained for the moment poor, and none more so than Gobineau. He felt that financial dependence was a limitation upon his freedom of expression and, as with Rousseau in the preceding century, the humiliation engendered by such dependence became entwined with a form of social pessimism.

From the family letters still in manuscript we can trace Gobineau's growing gloom and his deepening disillusionment with Paris and France: 'How I despair of a society which is no longer anything, except in spirit, and which has no heart left.'[4] Such feelings eventually became the basis for his social and political observations. He was indignant that the criteria for place and promotion should be connections (though he used these himself) and money rather than true merit. For himself he was loath to relinquish complete independence of mind: 'From a gentleman I shall turn myself into a condottiere. The sword that this age has shattered will be replaced by my pen. Light as air, knowing how to eat bread and drink water gladly when necessary, but also knowing how to preserve my independence at all cost, I shall give the lie to all the world – and I shall succeed.'[5]

Gobineau's background had encouraged him to support the elder Bourbon line rather than that of Orleans. His daughter Diane later remarked that Louis de Gobineau 'never allowed my father to serve the July Monarchy'. For herself, she added, 'I was brought up amidst feelings of the deepest contempt for the Orleanist line.'[6] Among Gobineau's earliest judgments on the upstart Louis-Philippe was that he acted 'like a simpleton, or (what amounts to the same thing) like one predestined'.[7] But Gobineau found his own legitimist party condemned by its internal disagreements: 'The big men are there, but like toads plunged into inertia. We are lost and had better resign ourselves to the fact. What is more, we have deserved this because of our torpor ... How I should already have shaken the whole machine!'[8] Viewing the political life of this period he noted the impotence that resulted from the inability of any single group to dominate the Chamber. Factional rivalries were placing the governmental machine under excessive stress. Gobineau explained that his lack of contact with the republicans prevented him from properly assessing their policies, but he was convinced that the legitimists, at least, were for the present incapable of reorganizing French political life: 'I do not know any ten of them who think in the same way, or (what is still more unfortunate) who agree to give mutual aid and support. All the legitimist sects anathematize one another with a hate and rage which is as ridiculous as it is odious when one thinks moreover of their small resources in *men*.'[9] He emphasized their lack of leadership and saw in clerical defection a striking symptom of decay: 'An infallible sign heralds the death of legitimacy. The clergy, that body which always has the habit of fleeing instinctively from expiring forces, is going over to the side of revolution.'[10] He concluded that,

Our poor country lies in Roman decadence. Where there is no longer an aristocracy worthy of itself a nation dies. Our Nobles are conceited fools and cowards. I no longer believe in anything nor have any views. From Louis-Philippe we shall proceed to the first trimmer who will take us up, but only in order to pass us on to another. For we are without fibre and moral energy. Money *has killed everything*.[11]

Gobineau shows here some of the concerns which were to dominate his future thinking – in particular, a perception of advanced social decadence as well as of the aristocratic decline and the materialism with which it is associated.

Central to his disillusionment was his experience of the capital, with its arid political wrangling, place-seeking and corruption. In 1840 he corrected his father's outdated view of Parisian politics: 'You still see parties, but here one no longer sees anything but speculations. You view Paris as it was eight years ago.'[12] Although he criticized the ineptitude of the legitimists he strove to remain loyal to their real principles. Having sent a copy of his poem *Jean Chouan* to Henri Comte de Chambord, the legitimist pretender, he received thanks for 'your honourable sentiments, worthy of your father and your family, whose fidelity and devotion I know and appreciate'.[13] None the less Gobineau's private fear was that, should the Bourbons return, his first duty would be to save them from the incompetence of their own supporters.

In 1843 Gobineau relinquished his position in the postal administration and thereafter, until the revolution of 1848, he earned his living from journalism, primarily in the legitimist press. His correspondence becomes replete with plans for articles and new journals, with promises of commissions and announcements of assignments – though much of this suggested activity never came to fruition. Some of this early work comes close to mere hack-writing and it is now and again difficult to assess where the inspiration of his editors ends and where that of Gobineau himself begins. The matter is further complicated by the need for discretion that was imposed on all French journalistic activity after the restrictve press laws of September 1835. Since a number of the articles in question are unsigned we are presented with some still more direct problems of authorship and therefore, in the discussion that follows, no major points of interpretation have been made to rest on material where there is any serious doubt as to Gobineau's authorship. In general, we have adequate information as to the journals for which he wrote and often in correspondence we have broad indications of his subject-matter or even specific reference to anonymous articles that he had undertaken. Still we must bear in mind that Gobineau probably wrote a number of unsigned articles which are nowhere mentioned and that others appeared under pseudonyms unknown to us.

He collaborated on the *Union Catholique* in 1842 and on *La Quotidienne* from 1843 until 1847. In connection with the latter Gobineau wrote thus to his father in an undated letter of 1843: 'I am regularly one of the keenest contributors to *La Quotidienne*, writing every day and realizing increasingly all the time the laxity' the weakness, the foolishness and – in a word – the pure folly of my cherished party.'[14] Other important work was done for *L'Unité*, of which he was editor for part of its short life from 1842 to 1843; for *Le Commerce*, partly owned by Tocqueville, on literary subjects in 1844–5; and for the *Revue de Paris* on political topics at the same date. With Rémusat's encouragement Gobineau helped found *La Revue Nouvelle*, as a rival to *La Revue des Deux Mondes*, and he wrote there on literary and political topics from 1845 until 1847. Though he also contributed fiction to these and other publications his predominant feeling was that, 'My business is to write on politics'.[15]

The unflattering view of France found in Gobineau's letters is reflected in his public writing. His comments in both must be seen in relation to his hatred of the French Revolution. Much later he wrote, 'My birthday is July 14th, the date on which the Bastille was captured – which goes to prove how opposites may come together.'[16] The articles reiterated his regret at the decline of the French nobility: 'We seek the aristocracy in history. We seek it in the present state of the country. We find it nowhere.'[17] But publicly he was somewhat less critical of the royalist party than privately. The unpleasant truth of past and present was tempered, in this period at least, by the need to provide exhortation for the future. While that need was still felt he could excuse himself from the charge of inconsistency. He reprimanded the legitimists for becoming a mere party. Previously their advantage and chief justification had been that they could transcend everyday considerations of party tactics and that they had embodied consistency and disinterestedness. Gobineau's views imply a clear belief in the ability of an élite to lead towards the fulfilment of a proper conception of freedom. 'The royalists are depositaries of the principles, traditions and customs of the nation, therefore they conserve its rights and interests; and, in a philosophic sense, one could say that they are the nation itself.'[18] He suggests that the party's aim must be to gain support from every class in order to maintain due liberty, order and security for all. In this royalist propaganda he manifests a humanitarian and even vote-winning vein, uncharacteristic of Gobineau as normally depicted. He regards violent change as the enemy of liberty as well as of order and he therefore exhorts royalists to respect tradition and to preserve social tranquility. The best legacies of past centuries are those left by nature rather than by man's presumptuous attempts at drastic change. But he agreed that once such change had occurred it was necessary to take it fully into account. Therefore Gobineau strongly criticized, for instance, the first restored Bourbon, Louis XVIII, on account of his failure to realize the significance of the transformation in ideas and behaviour that had come about since 1789.

It was clear to Gobineau that under the Restoration the opposition factions had not hesitated to disturb public order and security. In his view the 1830 revolution had been a disaster not merely for the dynasty but also for the whole of society. The subsequent Orleanist régime appeared marked by ambition, cupidity and hypocrisy. Under Louis-Philippe the legitimists are regarded by Gobineau as suffering an exclusion from the profits of power – an exclusion sufficiently complete as to be a tribute to their honesty. Their very repudiation is seen as a great incentive towards still keener political activity, in opposition to corrupt government and in support of programmes for the improvement of the whole nation and for the protection of its citizens. To the charge that they were outdated feudalists Gobineau replied in this manner:

There is in the present age a magnificent patronage which the royalists assert. It is the patronage that operates through charity, courage, virtue and intelligence. There is the true feudalism of every age. And the royalists oppose it to the oppressive feudalism of money, that abominable and infernal despotism which we see growing around us and which, within half a century, would have made a serf of the workman, a brute of the proletarian, if our tenets had been altogether defeated by the doctrine of revolutionary force.[19]

Though Gobineau cherished individualist doctrines (for some men of aristocratic nature at least) he strongly opposed any crudely possessive individualism couched in bourgeois terms. He regarded this as 'the leprosy of modern times, the principle of servitude among the ruled and of despotism among the rulers'.[20] He despised its alleged hedonistic egoism and its orientations towards material acquisitiveness and social change.

Gobineau believed also that the foreign policy of the Orleanist régime had humiliated France and led to her diplomatic isolation. England had consolidated a position of dominance and France had become more sterile and devoid of a proper sense of social values: 'Money has become the principle of power and honour. Money dominates business; money regulates population; money governs; money salves consciences; money is the criterion for judging the esteem due to men.'[21] In a prevailing atmosphere of disorder and corruption Gobineau's programme is a call for honesty and royalist order. After 1870 he was to comment again upon French history in this period and at that point he added the charge of a blinding self-satisfaction which allegedly possessed the whole society. He then penned his final obituary on the monarchy of Louis-Philippe:

This was the era when men shouted the most. The sovereign was of the opinion that he must let each man speak and write his mind. Yet it would not do to have the peace disturbed. So there were difficulties. Men spoke of 'Liberty and Public Order', and the National Guard carried the phrase on its banners. Then one fine morning (and without anyone understanding why) that same National Guard knew better than anybody else that the rabble was bringing off a revolution. And there was the régime of 1830 laid low.[22]

Gobineau consistently described this period as one of national mediocrity. Matters were to become still worse after the revolution of 1848. But even before then, his growing pessimism concerning France was gaining reinforcement from his belief that in societies farther afield symptoms of decay were also developing.

3 The German Situation

The territorial structure of Gobineau's Europe had been established at the Vienna Congress of 1815. He was highly critical of the settlement, claiming that ancient rights had been disregarded and that even the supposed defenders of legitimacy had made revolutionary demands. Amidst conflicting ambitions and grievances traditional values had received short shrift. He claimed that subsequently governmental attitudes had shown no significant improvement and that policies continued to bear the stamp of greed. Gobineau takes the German example:

The Spanish revolt, the convulsions in Italy, the progress of liberal attitudes in France, the secret societies (phantoms which later managed to scare them), none of these seemed sufficiently menacing for Prussia to give up its ideas of encroaching upon southern Germany, for Austria to abandon its designs on central Italy, or for the small states to relinquish their ambitious plans. Thus they destroyed harmony, the semblance of which it was important to preserve in the face of the governed, who became daily stronger and more menacing.[1]

Though the Vienna settlement had indeed reduced the number of German states, he felt that further rationalization was necessary and this matter became one of the most predominant concerns of his writing in the 1840s.

Despite the fact that he was less of a germanophile than most of his later followers believed he certainly held Germany in some esteem at this time. He showed a laudable cosmopolitanism: 'Good features are not so common in Europe that each nation can preserve its own without acquainting its neighbours of them.'[2] Gobineau's attraction resulted partly from the marked difference he saw between the French and the Germans – 'a people who, despite being our neighbours, hardly resemble us'.[3] His views on Germany, like those of many other Frenchmen, were affected in one direction or

another by the public controversy between Madame de Staël and
Edgar Quinet. The sentimentalized Germany of the former basked
in a romantic haze of liberalism and cosmopolitanism. On the other
hand, Quinet, though originally he helped popularize in France the
works of German nationalists such as Fichte, Hegel and Herder,
regarded their countrymen as concerned after 1830 with power
rather than liberty. His cosmopolitanism was replaced by a brand
of uncritical French nationalism and by growing fear of Prussian
dominance. Quinet's revised thesis found its most eloquent expression in an article entitled *Teutomanie* which was published by the
Revue des Deux Mondes in December 1842.

To this very article Gobineau soon replied in the pages of
L'Unité, with an essay which was quickly translated and published
in the *Allgemeine Zeitung* of Augsburg and which thus marked his
first literary appearance beyond the Rhine. Though he declined to
accept Madame de Staël's benevolent view and found that he could
accept a number of Quinet's conclusions, he refused to share the
latter's pessimism: 'From that violent tirade, we glean that in the
mass our neighbours beyond the Rhine are species of brutes . . .
that feed upon Frenchmen.'[4] He thought that Quinet had erred in
attacking the whole nation indiscriminately; 'It is dishonest to
insult a whole people because of the stupidity of some individuals.
It is dishonest at such a time to fan the fires of national hatred.'[5]
Gobineau viewed aspirations to unity as a natural reaction to the
artificial complications perpetuated in 1815. There can be no doubt
of his support for German unity as he writes thus of the Vienna
Congress: 'To build what it ought to have created it will be necessary to overthrow what it did . . . Every mind is tense. Princes,
scholars, people, all pay homage to the change which is going to
come. All are working to recreate the unity of the race and to
develop national industry.'[6] We do meet here one of Gobineau's
earliest usages of the word 'race'. But, as yet, it bears no precise
significance and is certainly not fundamental to his observations
upon society and politics.

Gobineau's sympathy with the unification movement stems in
part from his conviction that it is a justifiable attempt to return to
a golden age of true nationhood. In this context he contrasts the
revolutionary methods of the French with the German tendency
towards more gradual change. Coyly refusing to judge explicitly
the relative merits of the two procedures he comments of the latter:

B

'It would not be right to praise or blame such a mode of proceeding in politics. It is the very nature of the national character which is acting thus. We must accept the principle, study the facts, and above all strive to steer the emerging results towards a goal which is useful and legitimate.'[7] This pretension to objectivity scarcely conceals Gobineau's rooted hostility to revolutionary methods, especially as adopted by his own countrymen. He does eventually quite directly commend the Germans for learning the lesson of French excesses: 'They distrust the consequences which have come from our popular convulsions. Being calm lovers of liberty they have no desire at all to fall, before having attained it, beneath the rather sharp sword of some restorer of order.'[8] He allows that the Germans do not always advance by gradualist methods. For instance, in 1844 he commented on the disturbances in Silesia and elsewhere that, 'For some time now the Germans have appeared completely unfaithful to that renown for moderation and patience which they still enjoy among us.'[9] Still, the prevailing conclusions from his observations of Germany in the 1840s are expressed as follows:

The Germans are demanding important, profound and radical modifications in their present mode of existence. But they rely on the justice of their case to obtain these great reforms. They claim neither to make undue haste nor to rush matters. And in the successive development of their institutions they refuse, however dear they hold their aim, to see any cause for civil upheaval.[10]

The key to Germany's comparatively conservative progress, and to Gobineau's general approval, is the nobility's role in controlling its tempo and direction. Whereas the power of the French aristocracy is virtually lost, in Germany the greater nobles have managed to keep a significant degree of influence:

If, as with us, her secondary nobility, the nobility created by princes, has lost its prestige, if Saxon, Bavarian and Prussian gentlemen get no more than lukewarm esteem, none the less the German noble – he whose essentially free race once related to none other than the Holy Roman Empire, he who had the right to style himself the equal of rulers and who, even today, is but half-subject – he enjoys a popularity and esteem great enough for us to take account of the order to which he belongs when we consider the reorganization of Germanic lands.[11]

We encounter here a striking statement of linkage between freedom and German 'race'. The minor nobility are inferior, originating from an entirely different class of imperial subjects. These lesser nobles – whatever the dignities accorded to them in the social ordering of the modern world – are marked not by the quality of truly high birth but merely by the favours of petty princelings.

Gobineau suggested that the greater, and truer, nobility had become the symbols of opposition to Napoleon's designs and had thereby enhanced their popularity. In 1815 they favoured the re-establishment of the Holy Roman Empire, believing that this would restore the ancient Germanic forms of rule. Their desires came to nothing because Prussia was eager to assert her independence and Austria was shunning renewed responsibility. Gobineau wrote: 'It is annoying that at such a favourable moment no great power could find the courage necessary to call frankly for German unification . . . Nothing, or little, was done to bring closer that unity which is the need of modern societies.'[12] In his view it was to the greater nobility of Prussia that Germany must look: In proportion as Prussia grows the federal Diet will emerge from its torpor. . . . The end of all this will be to arrive perhaps at a state of affairs if not better at least more complete than that existing today.'[13] Thus Germany's future might still be guided by an aristocracy imbued with fruitful traditions and able to command the respect of all society. The great question was whether she would so develop, and upon this uncertainty we can centre most of the apparent inconsistencies emerging from Gobineau's comments.

During the 1840s Gobineau tended to prefer Prussian leadership in Germany to that of Austria:

Prussia is . . . a purely German state. Its politics, however clumsy we wish to think them, cannot but be German. But Austria is, on the whole, Italian, Slav, Hungarian. Its most pressing concerns are elsewhere than central Germany, and it has only one thing to impose and to beg of its fellow-states – this is, again, the maintenance of the *status quo*.[14]

Later, when he more fully realized how little there was left to conserve, he was to be less critical of the conservatism of the Austrian statesman Metternich. For the moment he suggested that it was the preoccupation with her Italian, Magyar and Balkan subjects which was causing the decline of Austria's influence among Germans: 'Every day she moves further from the German sphere, and Prussia inherits her influence.'[15] Nevertheless, though her non-membership of the German customs union, or Zollverein, further weakened the Austrian position, he remarked that this showed no fundamental weakness in her economy and that at a more opportune moment her full participation would be generally welcomed. Gobineau did however fear that the Zollverein might threaten Germany's aristocratic survivals. Commercial and industrial growth was enhancing the importance of the bourgeoisie and was menacing the remaining power of the greater nobility in Prussia and elsewhere. He saw this economic revolution as in many ways the German equivalent of 1789. It shows that Germany is falling foul of the false attractions of materialism. The national motto is increasingly *Deutsch macht alles um Geld* and Madame de Staël's vision is progressively more unrealistic. Gobineau writes that Germany's social revolution has 'nothing to lure the imagination, nothing to captivate the eye. This noble Germany is no longer the mystic virgin concerned with praying and chanting that one is wont to depict for us. Today she is a shop-girl.'[16] The greatest social changes that Gobineau witnesses are the result of economic rather than political influences:

It is ... natural that this power is at all points abetting the movement which, through the preference given to material wealth over all other values, is forcibly creating a new social order. Only, in the German case, and unlike our own, this social order has as yet no political formulations at all. It is reduced to commercial results.[17]

In the absence of more adequate political rallying points it is the Zollverein which becomes the symbol of unity. Yet, in so far as this is itself symptomatic of materialist preoccupations and of consequential changes in the social order, Gobineau maintains great caution in his assessment of its desirability. Moreover, he describes the discussions centring upon the further development of the Zollverein as an example of the German predilection for reducing or promoting all practical matters to an inappropriately metaphysical level. Thus, in one of his first striking generalizations about modes of thought in a country which was so widely to adopt the racist ideas he eventually elaborated, he remarks that Germany is the land 'where they love to make spiritual even such questions as import, export and transit, and where their only taste is for the ideal, which, in politics and administration alike, is equivalent to the impracticable'.[18]

We can see that in the 1840s Gobineau is seriously uncertain about Germany's future, but that he advocates in general a greater degree of unification beneath the leadership of Prussia. He is unsure whether the aristocracy will in fact prevail against the encroachments of the more materialistic middle-classes. In an article of 1847 entitled *Institutions Politiques de la Prusse* he traced the historical background to the discussion of Prussia's prospects. He emphasized the latter part of Frederick William III's reign, when Prussia turned from constitutionalist progress towards more reactionary developments. The old king had shared what Gobineau regarded as the marked German desire to theorize from 'scientific' deductions from past history and to shun piecemeal constructions. Gobineau writes that, in calling these developments 'historical' and 'organic', 'Frederick William III proved abundantly just how well he understood his society.' Moreover, concerning his people, 'He adapted innovation to their views and sympathies and modelled it upon what they were used to seeing in action around them.'[19] Henceforth all were devoted to the monarchy and even the revolution of 1830 did not disturb Prussian social harmony: 'Nothing is less democratic than the spirit of the German people; nothing less heated than their supposed antipathy towards the upper classes, towards the princes.'[20] He thought that, since the accession of Frederick William IV in 1840, the pressures towards liberalism had strengthened. There was greater activity in the Diets and a reaction against Russian and Austrian attempts to exert conservative influence. Gobineau derided the utopian brand of conservatism manifested in the king's speech of April 1847. Having summoned a Landtag in February, the monarch then announced two months later that there were to be no paper constitutions to threaten due fealty. Gobineau certainly showed his own distrust of constitutional claims: 'I do not think that Prussia has any need today of the democratic institutions wished for by the most advanced innovators of constitutional frameworks. And, for the moment, I even believe that the system of representation by orders meets its needs.'[21] Yet, except in this matter of representation by estate, Gobineau thought the monarch misguided: 'Without disrespect to the efforts of a wise king, the order of things which he is striving to create is no better rooted in German soil than it is in men's hearts or in the realm of possibility.'[22] For Gobineau the king's excessive romantic nostalgia again epitomized the German love of impractical social constructions.

German liberalism is also seen as a collection of incompatible theories. It is less concerned with freedom than with national independence and self-respect. Liberalism becomes itself the object of national vanity:

> The Prussians very much want to be considered as liberals, extreme liberals, ultra-liberals. But they also expect that we should do them the honour of recognizing that they have themselves invented their liberalism, that there is no model anywhere but with them, and that, if you like, they are copying nobody.[23]

Gobineau himself regards German liberalism as primarily a borrowing from France and England. Being alien to the German spirit it is mainly attractive to a few theorizers: 'The Germanic peoples do not have a feeling for the political principles that today rule the nations of western Europe. In short, they have no predisposition to constitutionalism.'[24] He views German constitutions as playthings at the mercy of monarchs and denies that a theoretically constitutionalist Prussia would uphold representative principles in the federal Diet. Behind the written forms the real power would be balanced in favour of king not people:

> In the event of serious conflict, the Prussian people, however great they may be, would be seen to be treated with no more respect than that shown by those who determine the destinies of the people of Hanover. A charter can give no real serious advantage except in the terms made by any contract, that is by making the contracting party who wishes to violate the agreement liable to a stiff penalty – a condition which is difficult to fulfil anywhere, and which is quite impossible in Germany.[25]

Gobineau emphasizes that unity under Prussia will not be marked by liberalism:

> Prussia is ruled internally after the Turkish fashion. She imposes silence against the complaints of provinces and responds to the universal wish for liberties and guarantees by tortuous and despotic legislation through cabinet-orders. In short, continuing its old policies, Prussia aims to inaugurate its religion of the state upon the ruins of other cults.[26]

Prussian administration is characterized by lack of public responsibility and by oligarchical bureaucratic tyranny. Both bureaucracy and monarchy oppose any reform which might diminish their powers.

We need to reconcile Gobineau's general support for the idea of

German unification under Prussia with his distrust of both the
despotic and the liberal elements in Prussian society. He believes
that the king would have to make future concessions to claims for
representation and yet remain strong enough to resist more extreme liberal demands. Gobineau puts great trust in the strength of
municipal rights in Prussia, since these help to conserve for his
precious aristocracy control over police and the administration of
justice. Yet they by no means assure the greater nobility of
dominance over the minor aristocracy or the bourgeoisie because
political rights are there the adjuncts not of noble birth but of
noble land which all may attain through wealth. There is already
enough uncertainty in Gobineau's thinking on the greater German
nobility to explain his belief, held shortly, that they were after all
declining as a political force. For the moment he looks to Prussia
for leadership because, 'If . . . political liberty amounts to little
there, its communal liberty . . . is vast.'[27] Gobineau's devotion to
decentralization and the preservation of local rights, subsequently
so evident in the contributions to *La Revue Provinciale* that we
must examine in due course, is already clear here. In Prussia he
applauds the increased recognition given by the king to provincial
diets and regards this as a useful brand of liberalism. He welcomes
the possibility of mild concessions on the part of the king and
shows a moderate liberalism alien to his later thought in observing
that, 'The greatest glory for France is that every concession
from sovereigns to their people brings them immediately closer to
us.'[28]

Gobineau would have been happier about the German future
had he been sure that the nation could be shaken out of its love of
obscurity in thought. He hoped that deputies beyond the Rhine
would remember that 'they sit on their benches as national
representatives not to build theories, to discuss principles, to delve
into abstractions, but rather to conduct business'.[29] The history of
the Frankfurt Assembly of 1848 was to justify Gobineau's qualms.
Although he did not see the Germans as especially revolutionary he
felt by 1847 that a major crisis was imminent in Prussia:

A king motivated by very good intentions – though ones marked by a
quite outlandish enlightenment – finds himself confronting a people
which has only a mediocre idea of practical matters but which is uneasy
in its present situation. At such times one can always foresee great
political crises . . . It is impossible to be positive that some morning this

badly driven coach will not swerve and toss its driver and passengers into the rut.[30]

When these words were written such a crash was but twelve months off.

In these years Gobineau is far from being the uncritical germanophile depicted by some commentators. His uncertainties are aggravated by the problem of mass emigration which, though common to many European countries, was particularly marked in Germany. Gobineau's concern is symptomatic of his increasing interest in the movement and mixture of peoples – subjects which were to become prominent in his racial studies. The movement is primarily the result of poverty and of resentment against the organization of property and industry in a manner unfavourable to the lower classes. Gobineau suggests that it is also a search for those political and religious liberties still denied in the homeland. The nineteenth century, in his view, is marked by a thirst for the satisfaction of ideological desires and it is felt that, 'If bread is a necessity then ideas are no less so.'[31] But Gobineau denies that this search for fulfilment has itself escaped tainting by materialism, for he continues: 'The investigation of ideas engenders a burning thirst for independence that is more deadly and hateful, especially in its clumsy aspirations, than worthy of respect or sympathy.'[32] The situation is another justification for demanding more intelligently cautious reform in Prussia.

Gobineau considers that the present migrations have little in common with the heroic movements of the past:

> When our barbaric ancestors left their huts, fleeing from the vanquisher, they themselves marched to conquests; what they went to face was either massacre or dominion ... But the nineteenth-century emigrant scarcely resembles the Teutonic or Sicambrian warrior. He must know that there is nothing heroic about his position and that, very much to the contrary, greeted on his journey like a vagabond, he must bow his head and yield his pride before the mistrust of the different authorities.[33]

This juxtaposition of heroic past and dismal present is an early example of the Janus-like tendency which becomes more frequent in Gobineau, who looks back nostalgically to a golden age while facing the future with darkening despair. The emigrants are already seen as disheartened and degraded. In time Gobineau's racial

theory would provide an ingenious and deeper explanation of the
degeneration that he sensed already.

Many were emigrating with thoughts of reaching and promoting
a democratic and egalitarian society elsewhere. There is a rarer sort
of migrant, a man of worth in Gobineau's judgment, who perceives
the real degradation left behind even if he is unduly optimistic
about his future fate. Such a man's alleged view of Germany – not
merely of Prussia – must stand as Gobineau's own. These men, he
writes,

withdraw angrily from a homeland that is treacherously parcelled out
and timidly oppressed, where, beneath the dull colours of a bogus
aristocracy, a nobility of hirelings is blindly dedicated to fulfilling the
whims of petty rulers who are always trembling, always seeking in vain
to deny the despoiling and revolutionary origins of their power; a
homeland devoid of patricians and full of courtesans . . . Not everyone
puts up with the cult of commerce; many people are alarmed or indignant at it and, as they can change nothing of what exists, they resolve to
move away.[34]

Such sentiments are a certain corrective to any illusion that
Gobineau is an uncritical germanophile.

It is denied in general that German emigration is related to what
later would be called 'imperialism'. The migrants, having striven
to free themselves from the restraints and miseries of Germany,
scarcely wish to continue in her service from afar: 'It is difficult to
understand why those who abandon their country, so ill-satisfied
with the lot it has provided for them, should want to be convinced
that they ought to live and work for it alone.'[35] To this generalization the migrations to Hungary and Transylvania may be exceptions. There, he suggests, 'the German race has the higher interest
of increasingly associating the Magyar populations with its destinies, and of spreading its civilization over half-barbarous lands
contained within its own natural frontiers'.[36] Here, in addition to
the imperialistic implications, we discern a notable willingness to
associate the Magyars with the work of the Germans – a willingness
which eventually found some reflection in the *Essai* where Gobineau
was to stress the Germanic element in the Magyar stock.

Though for long the German states had ignored the dangers of
this human outpouring they are now alerted. Gobineau observes:
'A country without nationhood, such as Germany was before the
Zollverein, scarcely worries over the complete loss of a portion of

its inhabitants, since those that remain cannot even be used in pursuit of any common goal. A constituted nation, on the other hand, misses those vital forces that part company with it, and strives to seize them back, even from the ends of the earth, in order to make use of them.'[37] Yet Germany has scarcely begun to solve this problem and Gobineau's view of the nation is, on balance, pessimistic. Though he has hopes for Prussia, and for the possibility of continued aristocratic influence there, these are limited by threats from the despotism of the monarch on one hand and by the opposing but excessive demands of the bourgeoisie and the masses upon the other. In sum, his conclusions on Germany are hardly more hopeful than those we examined in relation to France. Nor is the gloom dispelled elsewhere.

4 Europe and Beyond

Though in the 1840s Gobineau's main concern was with France and Germany his work also provides more general glimpses to further horizons. He subscribed firstly to the popular view of his compatriots that England was France's major enemy, a belief that enabled him to join in denouncing the Orleanist monarchy's broadly sympathetic foreign policy towards this neighbour. He believed that the revolutionary and Napoleonic wars had not only established British dominance but also had saved her from the growing threat of internal revolution. In 1815, he alleged, Britain showed greed and hatred, failing to respect the much vaunted rights of other nations. She showed as much hostility to the restored monarchy in France as to the Empire itself, and she had feared the growing boldness of French foreign policy in Italy and Greece as well as French designs on North Africa. Gobineau was not surprised that the British government had greeted the French revolution of 1830 as marking the removal of an increasing threat.

The unscrupulousness of the English is shown by their treatment of Ireland. After six centuries of spoliation and murder the Irish are still the subject of commercial exploitation. But Gobineau believes that the day of reckoning is near. The English constitution, famed for its susceptibility to peaceful adaptation, is endangered by the mutual resentments: 'It is Ireland which is pushing England into the abyss of revolution.'[1] He regards it as natural that so many from Britain and Ireland should have chosen to migrate. Unlike the Germans and most other Europeans they are generally able to travel to places where their own flag still flies. Whatever their disillusionment, their usefulness to Britain none the less continues: 'While the mother-country is being relieved of so much of her population, simultaneously they are bringing life and fruitfulness to the sundry parts of her gigantic colonial

empire.'² If this stands to the credit side of the balance of commercial power one must consider, on the other side, the increasing
power of the Zollverein and the growing Russian threat to India.
More hopefully, he notes the considerable degree to which the
English aristocracy have kept their social and political influence even
after the Reform Act of 1832. Still, his greatest stress in the 1840s
is upon the misery of the masses in England and Scotland, and in
Ireland above all. The peasantry of Ireland and Scotland have
reached 'the ultimate in poverty'.³ Gobineau concludes pessimistically that Britain is moving 'towards the gradual annihilation of
its external trade, towards the ruin of its constitution, towards
the secession of Ireland'.⁴

In discussing another major power, Russia, Gobineau emphasizes her essentially Asiatic nature. This is not to deny her
European interests and designs but to suggest the characteristics
which will be stamped upon them. Her internal administration is
harsh, but also chaotic and corrupt. The government has been
eager to attract migrants but, in Gobineau's opinion, wherever the
central authorities have interfered disaster has resulted. Nevertheless he forecasts that Russia will become an even greater power on
the international scene. Already she threatens Germany, the Habsburg fears her appeal to Slav nationality and the British are uneasy
regarding her interest in India. He regarded the British defeat by
the Afghans at Kabul in 1842 as indicative of the changing balance
of colonial power: 'England, an ageing nation, is defending its
livelihood and its existence. Russia, a youthful nation, is following
its path towards the power that it must surely gain.'⁵ Indeed,
Russia's potential vigour is in striking contrast to the general
debilitation of the other great powers: 'The empire of the Tsars is
today the power which seems to have the greatest future. . . . The
Russian people are marching steadfastly towards a goal that is
indeed known but still not completely defined.'⁶ There is already
in Gobineau's mind the foundation for a Slav threat to European
civilization. The very vigour of Russia would then become a cause
of apprehension.

Gobineau certainly recognized Russian designs on Constantinople and on the Greeks, and he devoted a number of articles to
the Eastern Question. He even mooted the (unfilled) project of
launching a *Revue de l'Orient*, and of himself and his potential
collaborators he remarked that, 'To restore Greek, Wallachian and

Slav nationhood – that is our aim.'[7] These liberal attitudes to
Greece, so common in his generation, were clearly manifested in
an essay on Count Capodistrias, the first President after the
achievement of independence, which was published in the *Revue
des Deux Mondes* during April 1841. Gobineau criticizes this
statesman's leaning towards Russian interference in Greece and
also his particular conception of authority, which was unsuited to
the Greek character: 'He appeared to make it his duty to offend
unnecessarily the feelings of the nation. Upon a gay people which
favoured independence he wanted to impose the categorizations
and classifications that he had admired in the north.'[8] His strictures
upon Capodistrias, the artificially ennobled administrator made
ruler, were symptomatic of his general mistrust of centralized
powers operating contrary to valid local susceptibilities. In addition, Capodistrias was guilty in failing to take the opportunity of
wresting the future of the Balkans from the ambitions of the great
powers. Instead of concentrating upon his own aspirations within
the purely domestic sphere he should have paid greater attention to
the more general implications of the Eastern Question. Now, in
1841, Gobineau finds Greece herself increasingly at the mercy of
Russia and of great power manœuvres.

He expresses himself pleased that France, 'the born protector of
small states',[9] should have sympathized with the fight for Greek
independence. But he is ashamed that she has now deserted her
proper interests here, as elsewhere. Greece in the midst of the
depredations of the great powers is a sorry sight:

> By sea, its foreign commerce, limited all about by English, Austrian
> and Turkish tariffs, is made null . . . On land, the mountains and rivers
> behind which we have hidden her, on the pretext of defending her, are a
> prison; and, even though her internal situation may be improved and
> her population may eventually be increased considerably under the
> influence of new laws, the envious looks which the Greeks give to
> Ottoman territory proclaim loudly their desires and their fears. In fact,
> Greece cannot escape from Russian domination except through a drastic
> change in boundaries.[10]

As the temporary friend of Greek nationalism and as a liberal in
this respect at least Gobineau writes boldly: 'May there come a
day when a well-intentioned France will remember that the Greek
revolution, sword in hand, awaits her signal to continue its

course!'[11] Nothing could be more typical of the liberal–romantic attitude to nationalism. In the *Union Catholique* he continued to advocate that France should be proud of her role in the formation of the Greek kingdom and should extend her legitimate interest there with a view to improving the state of civilization – an aspiration which will be seen as especially ironical in the light of Gobineau's later opinions upon the subject of civilization. When he visited Greece as a diplomat in the 1860s intervening events had changed his view of any such civilizing mission.

Even by the end of 1841 his attitude was hardening. He wrote a series of articles on Greek politics since 1833 which revealed a certain disillusionment, and where he emphasized for instance the poverty of the people and the disorganization of the army. After troubles leading to the granting of a parliamentary constitution in 1843 he criticized Greek harshness towards the king, Otto 1 of Bavarian origin. For Gobineau liberalism and nationalism could no longer be identified with one another, and the internal political struggles of Greece could only hinder the nationalist cause he still supported. He felt that France, which could still prove the only honestly disinterested party, should intervene to maintain security and order. Increasingly he showed a distrust of Greek politicians and their public. In 1845 he called them starkly 'a vain people',[12] a criticism with which he later ridiculed their nationalist aspirations and fitness for self-determination. Still, in this decade, his predominant plea is that France should not desert Greece, and yet that she should also beware perpetrating the kind of harmful interference exemplified by the actions of the German states who, with Bavarian Otto on the Greek throne, pointedly make distinction between king and nation, praising the former and denigrating the latter. But, in time, Gobineau himself would be not the least of the denigrators.

In northern Europe Gobineau suggests that the Danes, until recently so peaceful, have been stirred up by the threat of foreign interference, by the appearance of new political doctrines and by growing class rivalries. Inspired again by national vanity the Danish government is wastefully enlarging the navy. Gobineau sees correctly that the provinces of Schleswig and Holstein are her greatest problem. Inhabited predominantly by Germans, their destinies are complicated by uncertainties in the Danish royal succession. Gobineau has no doubt of the importance of Prussian ambitions and of the influence of the German Zollverein upon Denmark's future. Already Gobineau's future obsession with the decline and death of societies appears as he comments of the Danish monarchy that, 'No more than so many other states in Europe can she escape that fatality which seems to make dissolution inevitable.'[13]

Spain is another example of weakened monarchy. There anarchy and chaos concerning the kingship and political liberties were rife and Gobineau could come to no decisive conclusion about the conflicting claims of the rival factions. He merely castigated a nation which rejected 'a firm and natural authority, a power rooted in national liberty'.[14] Without such authority theories of liberty are worthless:

The fatal delusion of our age is to imagine that peoples may do without rules and that liberty itself may do without law. This produces a thousand conflicts of opinion, fierce struggles bloodying every faction, apalling anarchy in which everything perishes – laws both old and new, morals public and private alike, honour, fortune, indeed the strength of the whole nation.[15]

The basis for the practice of any political theory must be the reality of security and order. The alternative, thought Gobineau, was that 'some mule-driving corporal' would seize power and rule despotically: 'That is the inevitable upshot of all purely anarchical revolutions, those which are made outside the normal developments in the morals and ideas of a people.'[16] Spain is sick, but the cure is not through any further instability: 'There where we have greatness, there also is liberty. Shame is only the preparation for servitude.'[17] At present the energy of Spain is dissipated by exploiting adventurers and, if this continues, she will either suffer military despotism or else fall 'quite exhausted beneath some constitutional charter'.[18] The latter would be unfortunate because it would not be a judicious concession from a monarch but a scrap of paper unrelated to the natural evolution of liberty, authority, order and customs within the society.

It is scarcely surprising that Gobineau's censure of Spain (and, by implication, of Portugal) should be extended to Latin America. Both Iberian countries, and their former colonies, have made sacrifices in pursuit of an illusory liberty. Gobineau asserts:

The destruction of their agriculture, trade and finances, the inevitable consequence of long civil disorder, did not at all seem to them a price too high to pay for what they had in view. And yet who would want to claim that the half-barbarous inhabitants of Castille or the Algarve or the gauchos on the River Plate really deserve to sit as supreme legislators, in the places which they have contested against their masters with such pleasure and energy.[19]

The mass of migrants to South America should be warned of the political and social disillusionment ahead. Of Brazil in particular he warned that, 'The life of the migrant is threatened every day. Moreover, if he presents himself to a government as rudely formed as that of Brazil, he must expect the most baleful hazards.'[20] We shall see eventually Gobineau's curious alteration of attitude in this particular case. But, for the moment, his denunciation was unqualified.

Gobineau's main interest beyond Europe was naturally the United States of America, at that time the great symbol of political progress in the eyes of European democrats and liberals. A man's view of this so-called great experiment was frequently the touchstone for his general attitude to politics and society. As with Latin America, Gobineau's first approach was by way of the migrant question – but the implications were broader. He juxtaposed the utopian America envisaged by the Bavarian peasant with the reality that would confront him across the Atlantic. The contrast is a key to Gobineau's views on still more general issues.

The prospective migrant seeks, he suggests, virgin land, favourable climate, and certain ideals of which equality and political and religious freedom are the most basic. The prevalent belief is that these requirements are fulfilled in the United States. Who does not know, asks Gobineau,

that the New World knows nothing of kings, princes and nobles? – that on those semi-virgin lands, in human societies born yesterday and scarcely yet consolidated, no one has the right or the power to call himself any greater than the very least of the citizens? If there is any superiority in that country, it does not derive from birth – nor indeed from renown. Genius, talent, knowledge give their possessors no advantage over coarse labourers or ignorant and jealous traders. The only greatness is that of wealth, and as everyone can acquire this its ownership is independent of any of the qualities reserved to superior natures.[21]

To this equality of opportunity and this release from the bonds of the old social heirarchies is added the hope of political and religious freedom. Sometimes these expectations receive an encouraging degree of fulfilment but, for the majority, the great experiment is a failure. The immigrant is preyed upon by agents in the pay of capitalists exploiting the supply of human labour. Amidst the wild speculation and the economic and social insecurity of the United States Gobineau observes that,

There real estate gives only chimerical guarantees, thanks to the frantic land speculation. One recollects the position of the banks and the depreciation of the paper money; and one must dwell on the difficulties of the local authorities, the incurable weakness of law-enforcement, the impudence of those who are subject to its administration, and the impotence of the law to create respect for goods and persons.[22]

The fate of the poor is worse than in the old world for, whereas in Europe the government and upper classes habitually contribute to relieving distress, no one in America has time to turn from the heartless pursuit of material wealth. Gobineau thus dismisses the picture of an America providing equality of opportunity, or of one realizing conceptions of social and political freedom adequate for men, least of all those of 'superior nature'. It is an essentially acquisitive society, breeding hatred and jealousy, which follow necessarily upon the lack of order and security. Without these later foundations liberty is inconceivable. This account is not merely the story of the disillusionment of the immigrant. It reveals too Gobineau's own disenchantment with the claims made for liberalism and democracy.

Gobineau's outlook on Europe and some of the world beyond in the 1840s is characterized by gloom. Of migration from the old continent he writes: 'Our world, which is said to be old, is returning in a thousand ways to its primitive misery and suffering and it can no longer retain its inhabitants.'[23] But even the so-called New World shows no improvement. The elements of Gobineau's despondency concerning his contemporary world are already evident. They await elaboration in a theory that will give a coherent diagnosis of the whole disease and a fuller explanation of his deepening pessimism.

5 Literature and Society

Gobineau's many-sided activity during these years in the more purely literary field – as critic, novelist, poet and dramatist – remains in need of adequate study from students of literature. But here we can discuss these aspects only briefly and simply in so far as they impinge directly upon the evolution of his social and political thinking. It seems unnecessary in the present context to reach any firm conclusion as to whether he was a literary romantic, and, in any case, such an investigation is complicated enormously by the amorphous nature of 'romanticism' itself and by Gobineau's own brands of originality and inconsistency. In his literary work both creative and critical before 1850 we can discern conventionally romantic features, such as vitalism and the cult of energy in the hero, resentment against artificiality and mediocrity in modern society, the Byronic attitude to Greece, and the oriental influences. But he detested association with any particular literary clique or school. In substantial essays for *La Revue Nouvelle* in 1845, entitled *Une Littérature Nouvelle, est-elle possible?* and *Des Buts Techniques de la Littérature*, we have his most sustained commentary upon the rivalry of classicism and romanticism. He rejected the restraints of the former and yet found the latter also unsatisfactory, not least in its extension into the domains of social thinking.

It was his opinion that literature might prosper even where religion, politics and manners exhibited corruption. As he wrote in the *Littérature Nouvelle*, presaging one of the contentions of his *Essai*, 'Virility in public morals does not make virility in books.'[1] He contended that, though his country had possessed no single literary genius to rank with Ariosto, Shakespeare, Cervantes or Goethe, no other nation could match the overall standards of sustained literary talent associated with France. Still, his remarks were not unequivocally complimentary. For instance, he thought that contemporary France provided an undiscriminating audience: 'Today's *reading public* is such that, for all its disdainful airs, it is incapable of taking pleasure in any but the products of mediocre literature.'[2] Some years before he had commented still more caustically:

When I stoop to consider this present century I see men who are doubtless talented but who are without love for what they are doing, without respect for beauty and form, who are gnawed by ambition and replete with self-esteem . . . These are things which so disgust me that, had I not for long already detested humanity, I should have done so at this point.[3]

We see here Gobineau's literary appreciations severely limited by his unflattering view of human nature. It was a view which, in time, would become an essential component of his political and social theory.

Critics have frequently made comparison between Gobineau and Stendhal, about whose work he was enthusiastic and in whose activity he could see obvious parallels with his own writing. In an essay on Stendhal Gobineau wrote as follows:

He is a novelist who, if not a philosopher, is an observer rather than a poet, and the qualities of his style, like those of his mind, act more directly upon the intelligence than upon the heart. Perhaps there, after all, is the greatest cause for the lack of popularity that his name has won hitherto. Yet, at the same time, it is a further reason for the critic to make it his duty to praise a writer who can speak in so powerful a fashion to that part of ourselves which is the most difficult to arouse and move to sympathy.[4]

Although these words were written at the beginning of 1845 they largely hold good as a commentary from Gobineau upon his own writing and its reception during the next thirty-five years. He saw himself primarily as a philosopher, whether his passing medium happened to be fiction or criticism or history or the discussion of contemporary affairs. Moreover, he was continually to attribute his lack of public recognition to the debasement of his age. Objectively speaking, such perceptions were certainly mistaken but they tell us much of Gobineau's self-image.

The most striking similarity of attitude between Stendhal and Gobineau relates to Renaissance Italy and to the vitality, energy

and heroism they found there. As early as 1838 we read privately of
Gobineau's attraction to Renaissance studies. In 1841 he wrote thus
to his sister: 'I am going to begin the history of the Italian Captains
of the sixteenth century. There will be something good to do on
that subject. To start with, there are the most beautiful hues in the
world to convey and an agitation, a life of independence that I should
depict with enthusiasm, for the condottieri have always fascinated
me.'[5] He set to work upon a study of the condottiere Bartolomeo
Alviano – all that emerged for the moment from his broader project. In this essay, published in L'Unité in 1843, he expressed his
fondness for the vigour of the Renaissance and declared that it was
a golden age followed by one of rapid decline. He concluded as
follows: 'Shortly after the condottieri disappeared everything that
had lived and flourished with them went too; wealth, gallantry,
art and liberty; there remained nothing but a fertile land and an
incomparable sky.'[6] Both now and in his later study of the Renaissance he strove to concentrate on individuals of spirit. Life, art,
freedom and personal independence could only flourish through
the physical and mental energy of great men. The isolation of such
figures becomes symptomatic of the general degradation of society.
Two other works of this period centre on such heroic characters –
the tiresome verse-epics Les Adieux de Don Juan (privately published in 1844) and Alexandre le Macédonien which was being considered for presentation at the Comédie Française in 1848. The
revolutionary events of February ruined any such opportunity of
performance, as indeed they cut short Gobineau's work in the
genre of the serialized roman-feuilleton.

This was the form in which his novels of the 1840s first appeared.
They generally deal with events set against a background of French
history. We find Gobineau moralizing from historical developments and there is particular stress on the influence of class
considerations upon the behaviour of his characters. This is evident
even in the least historical of the works, Mademoiselle Irnois (1847),
where the heroine's financier father is a target for Gobineau's
hostility to the corruptions of modern materialism. Nicolas
Belavoir (1847) and Le Prisonnier Chanceux (1846) are novels set in
the period of the French religious struggles of the late sixteenth
century. Gobineau's interest in the Middle Ages contributed to the
production of the Abbaye de Typhaines, a work composed before
the 1848 revolution but not published until 1849, and one acclaimed

by Prosper Mérimée as 'a chapter from Froissart'.[7] It illustrates Gobineau's great concern with the history of French communal liberties and it deals with the twelfth-century conflict between the town of Typhaines and its abbey, as well as with the rivalries between the Crown, the nobility and the Church. The author treats harshly the commune of Typhaines. It is described as lacking the aristocratic influences which were essential in Gobineau's own defence of provincial rights and it was controlled by bourgeois unable to perceive any interest other than their own. In depicting this commune he is referring equally to the mob of 1789. He suggests that before that date it would have been difficult to appreciate the accuracy of such a picture but, 'today, when we know so well what the people may do when aroused, we have less difficulty in depicting the interior of a communal council, even in those remote periods of history'.[8] One of Gobineau's numerous unflattering descriptions of its inspiration and principles is this: 'It was inspired, at one and the same time, by war-like ardour, ardour for liberty, ardour for trade and profit, ardour for distinctions and social honours, as well as ardour for the novelties and other risky excitements that are so dear to insurgent peoples.'[9] Gobineau denied that mere love of liberty was enough. Liberty as the instrument of vanity, purblind chauvinism or materialism was not freedom at all.

His revulsion against the French Revolution is still more explicit in two other works. In 1846 he published a verse narrative, *La Chronique Rimée de Jean Chouan et de ses Compagnons*, which described the peasant revolt in the Vendée against the Revolution. The burden of the argument is contained in these lines:

> ... Paris, la capitale,
> Frappait de coups mortels l'autorité royale,
> La traînait dans la boue, et brisait à la fois
> Et la croix des chrétiens et le sceptre des rois.
> À Paris, on voyait l'immortelle Assemblée
> Courber sous ses décrets la patrie accablée,
> Et répoussant l'ancien pour placer le nouveau,
> De destins inconnus commencer l'échevau;
> Au monde épouvanté montrer la république;
> Faire de nos parens une race héroïque;
> Édifier, enfin, sur mille droits brisés,
> Nos vingt ans glorieux, nos trente ans méprisés.

> Dans ce profond chaos, pleins de lueurs sublimes,
> Le paysan manceau ne voyait que les crimes.*[10]

The provincialism of these peasants is certainly healthier than that of the bourgeois of Typhaines. The province here seeks to correct the excesses of a peccant capital and to base freedom upon respect for tradition. Gobineau's account shows striking consideration for the common people when they are possessed of such ideals.

The novel *Ternove* (1847) depicts the sad consequences, for one noble house, of the Revolution and the subsequent wars. Set in the period of the Napoleonic 'Hundred Days' it presents a banal romantic plot against the background of events experienced by Gobineau's father. Gérard, like Louis de Gobineau, is a hapless retired soldier who combines resentment at the degradation of himself and his house with a contempt for the men and events of his own time. Gobineau hastens to the defence of the émigrés:

These poor men have been greatly reproached for not recognizing that times had changed and that a nineteenth-century monarch could not be a perfectly exact copy of an eighteenth-century one. Blame is easy; but if we consider that the Girondins, the Feuillants, the Dantonards, the Montagnards of all kinds, the supporters of the Directory, those of the Consulate, those of the Empire, and, later, those of the Restoration, were all deceived, we may then be disposed to much indulgence towards these other men who have paid for their errors with their fortunes, their happiness, and often with their very limbs, and who received from a deep past and from ancient custom the command to be unequivocal in their old ideas.[11]

Ternove is also a cautionary tale about the need to maintain the purity of the aristocratic stock. It elucidates the ill-effects that flow from the betrothal of Octave de Ternove to a cousin who is the product of marriage between his émigré uncle Gérard and a mere miller's daughter. Then, again, the feelings of one of the characters seem clearly those of Gobineau himself: 'Monsieur de Marvejols would think of himself, and of all members of the nobility, as of a

---

* Paris, the capital, struck mortal blows against royal authority, dragged it in the mire and shattered at once both the cross of Christians and the sceptre of kings. In Paris one saw the immortal Assembly crushing and overwhelming the country with its decrees, thrusting aside the old and replacing it with new, taking up the thread of unknown destinies, showing the republic to a fearful world, making of our forbears an heroic race, finally, building upon a thousand broken rights our twenty years of glory, our thirty years of scorn. In this deep chaos, full of rays sublime, the peasant of Maine saw nothing but crime.

race apart, of a superior essence, and he believed it criminal to sully this by mixture with plebeian blood.'[12] As yet Gobineau had not systematically converted such an opinion into the foundation for a historical and social philosophy, but its elements were certainly in the process of formation.

In the light of Gobineau's own family relationships *Ternove*, with its commentary upon misalliance, has an additional and ironic element of interest. On one hand, his profligate mother had been descended from a line of European settlers in Santo Domingo; on the other, Clémence Gabrielle Monnerot, whom he married in some haste in 1846 (under circumstances which might just possibly have been connected with some breach of her sexual honour by Hercule de Serre), had actually been born in Martinique. Some commentators have taken the latter to be a creole, in the sense of of being a half-caste, and have thus launched into flights of fantasy about this inconsistency of Gobineau the racist. Clémence was, of course, a creole, but only in so far as that description is also correctly applied to any European who is native to such parts. There was no question of any immediate Negro ancestry. Yet it is not inconceivable that Gobineau, with a mother of whom he was ashamed and a wife whom he eventually came to detest, might have concluded by believing that the lines both of Gercy and of Monnerot had become tainted in the deeper past with some element of Negroid miscegenation. If there is any truth in this suggestion – and by the time of *Ternove* the thought could well have arisen in regard to his mother at least – it would add a further important element in the evolution of the convictions behind the *Essai*.

In concluding these few remarks on the literary activity of the 1840s we should take some account of Ernest Seillière's conviction that Gobineau was a social romantic on account of his 'extreme individualist reaction against the encroachments of a society increasingly clamouring for material progress'.[13] Gobineau did look back to a better past and, in that at least, he superficially resembled Rousseau. But he came to reject any form of significantly democratic thought, whether inspired by Jean-Jacques of Geneva or by anyone else, and it was this more liberal stream which was to dominate French romanticism both in politics and literature after 1830. Therefore we have to bear in mind a further remark of Seillière, that Gobineau was 'a romantic of 1820 rather than of 1830'.[14] His was increasingly the romanticism of reaction rather than of reform. While he might agree with the liberal romantics' judgment upon many of the symptoms of malaise in society – for instance, the materialism and mediocrity of bourgeois values – he was ever more unlikely to concur in their remedies. Gobineau has been seen too readily as a social romantic because he faced problems similar to theirs. We shall appreciate increasingly that he and his responses defy such labelling and that social romanticism's new order was to have no place in his philosophy.

6 Religion and Morality

So far Gobineau is revealed as a young man of modest attainment and considerable promise. His talents were not long concealed from Alexis de Tocqueville, who moved in many of the same social circles and who in his first known letter to Gobineau wrote that, 'You have wide knowledge, much intelligence, and the best of manners'.[1] Their correspondence, invaluable for the investigation of further aspects of Gobineau's thought, is embodied in over eighty surviving letters. These fall into three clear periods: in 1843–4 they debate the history of social morality, from 1849 to 1852 most of the letters concern Gobineau's views upon democracy in Switzerland, and between 1853 and Tocqueville's death in 1859 much of their discussion centres upon the nature and reception of the *Essai*.

Tocqueville was undoubtedly one of the first to be struck not only by Gobineau's genuine charm – to which many testify – but also by his ability to rearrange many of the ideas of his time and to present them in new and unexpected combinations. Although Tocqueville's ancestry was vastly more distinguished than Gobineau's they shared a love of nobility, connected to moral conceptions of quality and independence, and this encouraged mutual respect even in the midst of their differences. In the summer of 1843 Gobineau wrote of the distinguished author of *Democracy in America* as 'one of my best friends, though with a certain distance between us of course'.[2] In the 1840s Tocqueville was a critical Orleanist and Gobineau a critical Legitimist. Eventually their divisions were to go still deeper and then their conflict would come to represent, in John Lukacs's words, a debate 'between those who like Tocqueville, love liberty more than they dislike democracy and those who, like Gobineau, dislike democracy more than they love liberty'.[3] Still more exactly, it was to represent a disagreement over the meaning of liberty itself. It is not however our purpose here to enter into any full-scale comparative study of these two figures and primary attention will be directed towards Gobineau's contributions to their debate. In itself this may be a useful corrective, since previous treatments of their confrontation have not merely dealt with Gobineau as too much the minor character but also have sometimes conveyed his arguments only by means of Tocqueville's interpretation of them – a procedure which is particularly unfair in regard to the first phase of the correspondence. In addition commentators have tended to neglect the active evolution of Gobineau's ideas or to characterize it wrongly or inadequately. Yet it is crucial to understand, for instance, how the eventual rejection of liberal romanticism, at which we hinted in the preceding discussion, is all the more significant in the light of the genuine attraction which certain of its elements had earlier possessed for Gobineau. For purposes such as that the first phase of the dialogues with Tocqueville is indispensable and, for the present, it is that stage upon which we shall concentrate.

The principal subject-matter emerges as the relationship between religion and morality. Tocqueville had asked Gobineau to collaborate on what the latter termed 'a large work about the state of moral beliefs in the nineteenth century and about their application to politics and administration'.[4] It was a project which quickly took on both historical and religious dimensions. The excited Gobineau announced to Caroline that his first task was to provide a summary of the historical progress and transformations of moral ideas and social habits. Tocqueville was relying particularly upon Gobineau's help with the potential sources in German which he himself felt unable to master. The basic question posed by Tocqueville was: 'What is there that is *new* in the works or the discoveries of modern moralists?'[5] The problem was thus slanted towards finding novelty. Ironically enough, while Gobineau the self-professed Catholic was stressing the benefits derived from eighteenth-century innovations in the field of moral perceptions, Tocqueville the self-confessed agnostic tended to accentuate the valuable moral revolution produced by Christianity. Tocqueville demanded a link between morality and a positive faith, whereas Gobineau discerned and partially defended a new morality independent of religious belief. Thus the general debate upon the relationship between religion and morality became particularized primarily in terms of the relative virtues of the Christian and the rationalist Enlightenment views of man and society. It is moreover significant that in Gobineau's insistence upon denying to Christianity any significant civilizing power we have advance indication of one of the key components in the framework of the *Essai*.

For Gobineau's early religious history we again have to rely heavily upon the testimony of his sister. His relations with her show throughout that he was careful to make some display of religious orthodoxy for her benefit. She, especially after joining the convent of Solesmes, tended to believe of him what she wanted to believe. Her evidence is therefore to be treated with great caution. She declared that when he left home for Paris he had 'inclinations that were pure and upright, and ones to which religious feeling was not foreign. He spoke little of them. But he himself, speaking of that period of his life, said that he had kept the Faith of his first communion.'[6] Yet she was also obliged to note concerning his religious education that, 'Unfortunately it was not very effective, especially upon an extremely penetrating and meditative mind in which reason needed to be fortified against frequent domination by the imagination.'[7] From his letters to Tocqueville there emerges a coherent hostility to Christian moral teaching. In his public writings about the same time his disapproval was concealed by his genuine desire to support the Catholic Church, not as the purveyor of truth but as a social bastion. In this he shared Tocqueville's pragmatism and he declared, for instance, that in Prussia the replacement of Christianity, even in its Protestant forms, might involve an unfortunate weakening of traditional political as well as religious institutions. We are confronted with the picture – not uncommon in the mid-nineteenth century – of a Catholic without faith, a believer in the value of the Catholic Church as an institution who is simultaneously a critic of Christian morality. Louis Thomas, an antisemitic commentator upon Gobineau writing in the Vichy era, provided in his otherwise worthless diatribe a sentence of at least some truth relevant to this very point: 'In minds of this sort . . . Catholicism is often a means of protecting oneself, in part at least, from Christianity.'[8]

In this correspondence it is Gobineau's contention that a truly new morality has emerged in Europe since the last years of the eighteenth century. He describes it thus:

It is not a body of doctrines firmly bound together and vigorously defended by a central principle, as is the case with Christian morality. It is rather a quite incoherent assemblage of consequences drawn from principles that are, for the most part, still badly defined . . . It is as yet more visible in reality than on paper.[9]

If some of the inspiration for the new morality comes from Christianity this is so only in the same sense that Christian teaching is indebted to certain forms of Greek and Judaic thought. Gobineau denies that Christianity originally had any theoretical concern with mercy and charity. Its nature was dictated by practical necessity. It was the creation of the oppressed seeking gentler rule. It taught love not for the sake of altruistic charity but out of self-interest: 'There was the starting point, there the basis of Christian morality – personal interest, instinct, feeling, rather than any pondered and reasoned conviction as to what should have been.'[10] Gobineau suggests that Christianity, though it extended protection to all men, had the unfortunate effect of seeming to justify the existence of pain by its belief that suffering was in some sense holy.

The new social ethics dissociate the elements of morality and sectarian belief. Their linkage was for Gobineau one of the greatest flaws of Christianity, which subordinated charity and kindness to the all-important assertion of faith: 'With everything made to rest upon faith all other powers of the mind were struck down into a kind of relative insignificance.'[11] He accuses Christianity of encouraging withdrawal from society and of undervaluing social participation. Yet he does so in words that could be used against himself when, in his last years, he spurned corrupt society: 'Salvation could not be obtained more surely anywhere than in secluded retreats where, without either temptations or social duties, men had few opportunities of helping their fellows.'[12] This asocial tendency is, for Gobineau, typical of the negative nature of practical Christianity, which stresses the avoidance of evil rather than the promotion of good. The new morality, separating relations among men from those between man and God, emphasizes purely social considerations. It is the morality of no one sect or religion and, because it asserts the disjunction between views of earthly and heavenly organization, it does not invite interference and thereby is able to provide the basis for a new kind of tolerance. This is not the semi-tolerance of the ancients who could frequently accommodate a new god in the Pantheon. It is the fuller toleration which follows the separation of social virtue from religious belief. This development is 'nearly new in the history of the world' and Gobineau praises it as 'a great and fortunate innovation due to the spirit of our age'.[13]

The new emphasis is shown in the Enlightenment's concern with the world for its own sake. Gobineau's praise here for eighteenth-century social philosophy contrasts with the criticisms he made later. For the moment Voltaire is a humanitarian hero, under whose influence men have studied in a new way varied social questions. For instance, Gobineau sees the conscience-salving charity of the Christians replaced by a deeper concern for humanity: 'People no longer desired to feel compassion for Man; they concerned themselves only with Humanity . . . Suffering is no longer holy. Like the plague, like every scourge, it must be extirpated.'[14] In this mood Gobineau even supports some state action for humanitarian ends, though admittedly the degree of intervention is never defined.

He favours the Enlightenment's assertion of rights. Of the growing belief in the right to work – as opposed to work considered merely as a painful duty – Gobineau comments: 'The strength and dignity which morality has gained from this principle are beyond question.'[15] He holds a similar view of the right of the poor to education – a point of interpretative interest for the future of his thinking. He approves the recognition of the human rights of criminals:

Men now agree with Voltaire that a hanged man is good for nothing and that they are seeking a means of making criminals good for something. In this difficult task people have been guided, as in everything else, by a firm desire to improve the lot of humanity upon earth; in the upshot, they have been more moral, more kind, more merciful than Christians could ever have been.[16]

Preferring Voltaire to the Christians, he believes that the eighteenth-century achievement shows the progressive nature of our ideas on morality. Yet the contrast is made by a figure who was shortly to write a work attacking ideas of progress and implicitly bringing into doubt the existence of a meaningfully common humanity and of its human rights.

Like Christianity the new morality derives partially from considerations of interest, but not however those of self-interest alone. The Enlightenment is seen as contributing a conception of interest

which is not concerned with the material fruits of virtue for the
individual but with the benefit to humanity in general. It is also
separated from Christianity by its greater indulgence towards
human passions. The Enlightenment's purely social preoccupations free it from the restrictive attitude of Christianity:

> The sphere of the doctrine of interest is now hedged about with con-
> siderably fewer difficulties. Anyone motivated by the influence of com-
> mon ideas and living in an environment resembling that of the majority
> will indeed have less difficulty than before in adapting himself to a
> morality which is more indulgent to natural inclinations. Even so we
> must admit that this morality has become no less severe in regard to
> everything that might harm peaceful and innocent relations with other
> members of the social body.[17]

All this testifies to Gobineau's humanitarianism. But one is also
struck by his simplification and idealization of the Enlightenment.
By the time that he published *Mademoiselle Irnois* early in 1847 he
was capable of writing a passage stigmatizing the shallowness of
eighteenth-century humanitarianism, but, for the moment, Gobineau's only major reservation was that the new morality had not
yet provided itself with a solid basis. It was wrong to connect it
closely to Christianity and it was too much of a simplification to
relate it solely to Voltairianism. Gobineau remarks that, 'It is clear
enough that ancient religions found it simple to ennoble morality
by putting it under divine aegis. Now it has been brought down to
earth and we have not yet been able to discover its sources.'[18] But he
is able to conclude that,

> The results are quite evident and I think that it is very often proper to
> show satisfaction with them. But, as with everything that is just begin-
> ning, we have not yet defined at all happily what has been discovered and
> remains to be assessed. These are virgin territories, with limits still
> unknown and with heartlands yet to be explored but this is soil which
> already yields a harvest.[19]

Gobineau declared to Tocqueville that all judgments on this must
be provisional: 'You might perhaps conclude from this that the
time may not be altogether ripe for hastily writing a history of
endeavours which are still in their infancy, especially a history
which has to stop at 1830, a moment at which ideas took a particularly great stride forward and since when they have made such
real progress.'[20] This contains the significant implication that the

1830 revolution has encouraged the progress of morality in a manner of which Gobineau approves – a view which is irreconcilable with his subsequent observations.

Particularly notable is his comparatively optimistic underestimation of the threat from socialism. He agrees that its roots are similar to those of the new morality, but he opposes socialism on the ground that it is 'too hazardous'.[21] What is more surprising is that he should write of the future of socialist ideas with so little disquiet: 'It does not seem to me that we really need to concern ourselves greatly. Adherents of these very advanced doctrines are quite rare, and none of the programmes they support appear to be winning them many more followers for the future.'[22] It was in this same vein that, as late as 1847, Gobineau derided the Duc de Valmy for his belief in a possible 'invasion of communists'.[23] The events of the following year abolished such complacency.

Tocqueville's argument was that Enlightenment philosophy had the perennial symptoms of thought in any age of declining religious faith. He accused Gobineau of erecting moral laxity and religious disbelief into a system of ethics. The latter refused to shift his basic position, though he made some deferential remarks suggesting that he might have been unduly extreme in his assault upon Christianity. He continued to affirm that it had added no moral teaching of significance to that of Socrates, Plato and Aristotle. He tried to clarify his attitude to the gospels:

You misjudge me in supposing that a reading of the gospels leaves me cold. I am neither Voltairian in the dry and hateful meaning of the word nor sceptical in so far as they impinge upon the heart – at least, I hope not. I acknowledge that the gospels form a book, a code if you like, well suited to enthralling the world and to guiding its progress for a long time. I consider, doubtless like yourself, that this popular format for the wisdom of thinkers and great men has – so to speak – breathed life into truths that were recognized only transcendentally and in realms beyond the practical. But I do not go so far as to believe that the contents of the gospels emerged fully fledged from the mind of Christ.[24]

Gobineau, with his oriental interests, stressed – here at least – the competing merits of other world religions. Christianity, if practised to the letter, could be the foundation for a most satisfactory society, but, he added with an exceptionally accommodating religious relativism, 'No religion is harmful if properly observed; all of them are morally pure; all want man to perfect himself through a conception of duty; finally, all have an immensely sincere desire to seek what is good'.[25] Gobineau was probably unduly generous to the bulk of his contemporaries in also suggesting that they believed a Muslim might have a moral character as laudable as that of the most devout Christian hermit. It was certainly too generous to Tocqueville who harshly attacked the social consequences of Islamic belief. In time, as we shall discover, Gobineau himself would launch a somewhat similar assault.

Gobineau discerned religious pragmatism and relativism in Tocqueville too. He compared him to Cicero in his concern with the social utility of religion, but added sceptically that he thought it was 'a utility which we might sometimes doubt – I believe, it is true, that fear of the Lord has been capable of stopping the theft of a few loaves, but I question just how many murders it has prevented'.[26] Such doubts were only occasionally voiced. Generally, like Tocqueville, he upheld religious institutions – the Catholic Church above all – as conservative forces. From this first exchange of letters we see that Gobineau was not a Christian in any conventional sense and that, moreover, he declined to see any of the world religions in terms other than those of secular utility.

The projected collaborative work never appeared, but we do possess a number of Gobineau's notes. Most valuable is an essay entitled *Coup d'Oeil Général sur l'Histoire de la Morale*,[27] which attempts a historical summary of his conclusions. Gobineau asserts that an agreed moral law is an extremely desirable bond in all societies, but that its nature will change according to time and circumstance:

> Morality, like all institutions and all human beliefs, has not kept any inexorably stable character through the ages, and in fact, even if some of its prescriptions (including the most important ones) have never ceased to be applied, its principles, its roots and even its most subtle applications have often varied.[28]

He describes such a moral law as operating at first with the limited function of maintaining peace within society and unity against hostile forces without. In the West the story is one of development into 'an absolute generosity and an innate love of humanity'.[29] Gobineau agrees that religion and morality may sometimes support each other but urges that this is not a complete necessity.

The universal scope of Christianity is seen certainly as

revolutionary but, in the outcome, an obsession with dogma paralysed its activity in the social sphere. Yet again Gobineau tends to minimize, if not to deny, the importance of faith. He writes of Christianity: 'It had hardly emerged from persecution when it began to fragment. The energies that had once been promised in order to ameliorate the lot of humanity were henceforth taken up – even if not exhausted – by sectarian quarrels, the struggles of Catholicism against dogmatic heresy.'[30] Moral activity waned as the criterion of virtue became faith. Gobineau asserts that those, such as women and the poor, who had looked to Christianity for the fulfilment of social promises were deceived. It is only with the development of post-Christian morality that women, for instance, have received due respect. A marked improvement in their treatment becomes an essential symptom in Gobineau's diagnosis of social progress. It is 'one of the newest and most solid foundations upon which to rest the moral conceptions accepted in modern times'.[31] To the theme of female dignity Gobineau frequently returned.

In this historical survey he shows that the moral revolution of the eighteenth century, though it is the greatest one, is preceded by two others. The first resulted from the so-called barbarian invasions. These were to figure crucially in Gobineau's racial philosophy. He asserts that these barbarians 'brought into the western world most of the ideas that still mould our political existence'.[32] He allows that it was in conjunction with Christianity that the invaders achieved the social renovation he perceives in the post-Roman era. Together they provide the twin foundations of early medieval Europe: 'Christianity and barbarian ardour had an almost equal role in the task of renovation.'[33] Of the barbarians he comments:

What is certain is that Life began to spread in Europe only with their arrival. The principles of absolute liberty touched those of absolute despotism and reduced them to dust. The emperor, who even as a Christian had always been the object of virtual adoration, fled before the elected chieftain of the Goths or Lombards, and a clergy composed of barbarians, even while spreading ignorance in every cloister, did much to reinvigorate those customs that had been enervated in the shadow of the sanctuary.[34]

The second great movement is the Renaissance and the rebirth of platonic philosophy. Their greatest contribution is alleged to be the

c

assault on the link between faith and morality – the conjunction finally severed by the Enlightenment. At the time of the Renaissance it was the immoral conduct of the champions of faith, the clergy themselves, that nourished religious doubts:

People were surprised by everything that was allowed to happen in the name of religion. They held it answerable for the orgies of the Vatican and for the monstrous political behaviour of the princes. Then, with more indignation than justice, more feeling than reason, they quickly turned from the sorry spectacle presented by the morality of the time in order to throw themselves in rage upon the fabric of its beliefs. It is for this reason that only after a long effort did humanity reach the point of putting a proper valuation upon morality. Before the sixteenth century Christianity constantly erred in subordinating this valuation to belief.[35]

Since the Renaissance secular philosophy has continued its conquest and, eschewing the foundations of faith, it is free to attend to needs and ideas previously neglected:

From the sixteenth century onwards, and especially since Cartesianism, Christian activity has gradually subsided. Great men, still battling in its name, have not succeeded in holding back the philosophic movement. Thus it follows that morality, even when at depth Christian, is modified by all the systems that divide the minds of men.[36]

It is however difficult to reconcile Gobineau's statement of moral progress from Renaissance to Enlightenment with the gloom of the conclusion of the article on Alviano in which decline was said to follow upon the great age of the condottieri.

In Gobineau's description of Jeremy Bentham we have his view of the outstanding characteristics of the eighteenth-century social philosophers – 'cool, calm, reasonable, essentially positive and attaining the utmost kindness via channels strongly indicated by knowledge and thought rather than by the natural passions of the heart'.[37] But Gobineau considers that the Enlightenment preoccupation with earthly life does encourage an unpraiseworthy tendency to materialism. Benthamism, again, exhibits this:

This new school attacks Christianity in a very special manner. Quite differently from philosophical battles, it does not make a frontal attack – it even conserves the enemy. But, by establishing in one context after another certain rules – whether the liberty of thought and expression, or the necessity of having differing opinions, or even some moral principles favourable to luxury and well-being – it strikes much more palpable blows against Christianity.[38]

Increasingly Gobineau was to attack the materialism of his own century and he regarded this as the least desirable result of the defeat of Christianity. He saw the new morality growing in strength. Still uncertain of its foundations he commented that, 'It presents the world with the spectacle of being a recognizable force, even though its origin is difficult to establish'.[39] He was soon to retract his favourable assessment of Enlightenment thought and it was then to be attacked as the fount of materialism.

The collaboration with Tocqueville had great educational value for Gobineau. He had been required to examine the working of charitable institutions, savings banks, plans for public relief and its administration. Tocqueville also encouraged him to study governmental efforts to promote popular instruction. We now have the summaries that Gobineau prepared on the thought of Kant, Fichte, Schelling and Hegel. Though these fragmentary notes are factual and reveal almost nothing of Gobineau's own assessments they are useful as indications of the scope of his own reading. As to British writers, there are notes on William Godwin and Joseph Priestley, as well as brief summaries of Bentham on punishment and usury and of David Hume on political economy. A number of notes on various other books read by Gobineau for the proposed work have been discovered.[40] The range and variety of these background studies give some idea of his knowledge of recent social thinking.

It has been suggested by some that the project failed because Gobineau did not succeed in procuring enough usable material. It is difficult to judge that particular point, but certainly his initial excitement waned. Towards the end of 1843 he wrote to Charles de Rémusat: 'You commend moral science to me. Alas you must commend me to something quite different, for I am beginning to fail to see with any clarity through all the principles, precepts, dogmas, obligations and so forth that I have the honour of labelling.'[41] The strains caused by divergences of opinion began to show. In October 1844 Tocqueville wrote that, 'I think what we are doing wearies you.'[42] It is even possible that Gobineau came to despise completely Tocqueville's standpoint. Many years later, in 1868, he wrote of him to the Comte de Circourt: 'From no point of view was he a philosopher.'[43] It is difficult to know when such feeling set in, but it may well have originated in their first philosophical disagreement a quarter of a century before.

It has not been sufficiently noted in most accounts that, despite the crudities, simplifications and inaccuracies in Gobineau's arguments, he manages to hold his own in this discussion, as well as to score some palpable hits against the failings of Christianity as applied historically in social practice and to produce some comments of continuing relevance to debates upon the 'new morality' of any age, including our own. Gobineau had perceived Tocqueville's essential pragmatism, and its limitations. The latter could only conclude that their differences were as follows: 'You have greater ambitions than I have. I limit myself to seeing new consequences where you wish to reveal completely new principles. Your need is to change the world and you will not be content with less. I am more modest.'[44] Eventually Gobineau was to give up hope of any such change, but, with respect to the scope of his intellectual ambitions, these remarks (however true already) were certainly to be ever more accurately applicable in the years ahead. Though friendship was maintained till Tocqueville's death in 1859 the intellectual divergence became greater. In this first encounter it is essential to realize that it is Gobineau who is still the more sympathetic to the progressive aspirations of his age. He seems scarcely shackled by conventional religious belief and is more hopeful than his distinguished mentor about the present state and future development of morality. When the two men entered upon another great debate ten years later, across the pages of Gobineau's *Essai*, the situation had changed. By then Gobineau had formulated fully certain less liberal and less progressive ideas into a system for the explanation of history and the description of society. The more generous feelings, which flourished so freely before, were then scarcely discernible. Tocqueville had feared something similar all along. There is no more striking monument to the prescience of the great social philosopher than these words in his first known letter to Gobineau:

As to your talents, it is hard to know when one observes you just what will become of them and whether the epidemic ills of the age, which affect you no less than they do your contemporaries, will make them useless. Thus one is fascinated both by what you could be and by what one fears you may become.[45]

7 Revolution and Reaction

The concept of 'the turning point' is a stock historical cliché. It is of some value, but it must never be used uncritically. It has been applied nowhere more lavishly than in assessments of the epidemic of revolutionary activities that swept the European continent in 1848. Still, however excessively facile many of its applications to that context may be, a discussion of Gobineau's reactions to the events of 1848 will reveal that for him at least they were indeed just such a turning point.

We have noted already his hostility to revolutionary methods and to the civil strife which he regarded as their necessary concomitant. His praise of the Greek revolution had been exceptional, and he was eventually to recant that judgment. In the mid-1840s his view of the possibilities of European upheaval was ambiguous. In 1843 he declared that in France 'revolutions are the work of a few days'.[1] But, as late as 1847, in the text of his article on *Institutions Politiques de la Prusse*, he expressed the view that his own country had acquired a greater sense of responsibility than previously. We have already seen his underestimation of the socialist threat. Now he added that developments in commerce and industry made susceptibility to revolution less likely. We shall note that eventually Gobineau was hostile to the social effects of urbanization and industrialization, but, in this one article at least, we find him regarding such progress as a check upon revolution. There he suggests that since 1789 the masses have become more aware of their social responsibilities:

> The bulk, the mass of the population, disinherited from any participation in the public wealth, were not, as today, aware of the operations of business; they were not, as today, attentive to the movement of assets and they were, furthermore, deeply ignorant as to how far peace and quiet are indispensable to well-being. Today there are few

people, even in the less favoured classes of French society, who do not understand the harm that the smallest social disturbance brings not only to the general prosperity of the State but also to the very least individual.[2]

After 1848 Gobineau never again showed such optimism about the good sense of the masses in France or elsewhere, or about the desirability of their having such a stake in society.

On the eve of revolution he seemed more concerned about Germany where previously he had been stressing gradualist inclinations. In March 1847 he had indeed written that, although they were desirous of profound changes, the Germans would avoid any undue haste or any danger of civil upheaval. Nevertheless two months later he could conclude that Prussia at least was in a revolutionary situation. Gobineau apparently considered that the commercial and economic progress which had brought greater sense of responsibility to the French was acting differently upon Germany. The alleged reason was that the Germans were 'a people with only a mediocre idea of practical matters'.[3] Such inconsistencies are partially explained by Gobineau's inadequate conception of the meaning of revolution:

There are two kinds of revolution – political and social. The former is produced by sudden, accidental and irregular factors as well as by causes that are meditated and calculated. The latter manifests itself through the slow and progressive workings of human society which derive from a succession of gradually modified requirements.[4]

Gobineau was uncertain about the German situation because he was unclear about the interrelation of the two brands and because he overemphasized the slowness of social revolution.

The events of 1848 – so influential upon European intellectuals in general – banished any further doubts on the part of Gobineau. His immediate reaction to the revolutionary coup of February in Paris was not eloquent. He wrote home: 'We are quiet enough. The provisional government has been set up. I cannot tell you any more about it today. Besides, you will understand that this is not the time to talk politics and that there is much else to do after such big events than to bother oneself with theories.'[5] In an undated letter of the spring he talks of the spread of revolutionary activity through Germany: 'Things are going pretty badly ... I do not mean the dismissal of the princes – that was deserved. Their cowardice and lack of political faith make them scarcely interesting. But the peasants, there they are nearly barbarous. There is pillage, and burning, and massacre – and we are only at the beginning.'[6] Henceforth the combined themes of contempt for kings and fear of the mob were recurrent in Gobineau's thought.

In the autumn he maintained an air of detachment from the French political scene. He wrote of the presidential elections, held at the end of the year, as follows: 'I have no personal preference. Only, I do believe with Falloux, Cazalès, Kerdel, Fitz James and all the men of honour in the party, that the greatest disgrace for the legitimists is to serve as the pedestal for the ambitions of a Bonaparte. The rest may be dangerous, but that would be dishonourable and disloyal.'[7] As the son of a persecuted father Gobineau could have little enthusiasm for the first Napoleon. He had denounced the Emperor's ecclesiastical policy as despotic, he had criticized his contempt for intellectuals, and he generally regarded the imperial régime as an unfortunate extension of the Revolution. In *Mademoiselle Irnois* he had depicted the corruption and degradation of society under Napoleon. He was thus naturally hostile to the Emperor's nephew, who was elected President of the Second Republic by universal manhood suffrage in December 1848. Although Gobineau saw this, from one point of view, as the triumph of the provinces over the degenerate capital, he continued his bitter opposition for a time, particularly as the President showed no sign of significantly enlarging provincial rights. In April 1849 he wrote despairingly to Caroline:

I maintain that we are going to be like America. No man who is in any degree at all honest, proud and capable will want to give himself up to the vile whims of this pack of imbeciles . . . Legitimists accepting the name of Bonaparte! You have to live in the nineteenth century to see such scandals! . . . I yielded to the republic in very good faith and if it had been able to get along without Bonaparte I should have thought nothing against it.[8]

The truth of Gobineau's reluctant republicanism is borne out in a letter to his father the previous spring, concerning the candidates in the local election at Redon: 'I hope and wish that there may be two honest republicans, and if they are workmen or foremen the choice is fine. Do not give us . . . any centre-left bourgeoisie.'[9] Any such benevolence to republicanism was in recognition of its overthrow of the despised Orleanist régime of bourgeois virtue. But during 1849 Gobineau became more consistent, linking republicanism to revolution and stressing that France's greatest need was order. Disillusioned with his own party he saw that his immediate course should be to support a Bonaparte who, though for the moment accepting a republic, was a representative of order above all else.

There was also a very strong element of personal self-interest in Gobineau's decision to support the régime. In the summer of 1849 Tocqueville became Minister of Foreign Affairs, thereby suppressing some of his own distrust of Louis Napoleon Bonaparte. He invited Gobineau to become his official secretary and, at the age of thirty-three, the Minister's former collaborator concealed his scruples and seized the opportunity. He had indicated in his earlier family correspondence some interest in a diplomatic career and, now that a number of the journals for which he had written had foundered in the turmoil of revolution, such a change of occupation must have appeared doubly attractive. Tocqueville's gesture testified to the strength of a friendship and to an intellectual respect which was surviving their increasingly serious differences in political and social thinking. In 1860 Gobineau wrote as follows to the Comte de Circourt: 'I was very fond of Monsieur de Tocqueville who, I think, reciprocated this feeling a little. But the proof of esteem which he showed in choosing me as his secretary made me all the more proud in so far as, I believe, we thought differently upon all topics, except the matter of conscience.'[10] Gobineau was acutely aware of the break with family tradition. Nearly twenty years after his appointment he wrote to a German acquaintance Adelbert von Keller that, 'My grandfather never served either the republic or the First Empire, nor did my father or uncle. I am thus the first in my family to have accepted the new state of affairs.'[11] Gobineau's acceptance of any such order could be no more than partial. Bonapartism was for the moment a convenience, and the least imperfect of the practicable options. Gobineau declared that, whatever his success or failure in Tocqueville's office, 'I shall have had the sterile joy of being something in my life.'[12]

He thus approached his new position with an odd combination of lethargy and curiosity. Most of his time in the secretariat was devoted to the diplomatic problems that had arisen for the French government, in its role of Catholic and Papal protector, during the period of the revolutionary Roman Republic of 1849. Gobineau probably had little realization that this was to be the commencement of a diplomatic career that would last until 1877. During nearly thirty years, as the official of three régimes, he was to remain critical of France and of her degenerate governors. The original post was not held for long, since Tocqueville lost his position upon the fall of the Barrot ministry at the end of October 1849. Gobineau's own interests were preserved at this juncture by the fact that the Marquis d'Hautpoul, the interim director of the Foreign Ministry and indeed Barrot's successor as Premier, was a former comrade in arms of Louis de Gobineau. On 9 November Arthur was nominated as First Secretary of the French Legation in Berne.

In his subsequent family letters we find Gobineau's growing reaction against the events of 1848. In February 1850 he wrote from Berne:

I cannot see that the political atmosphere is becoming either very pure or very calm. Germany is gangrenous and the rivalries of its princes certainly do not contribute to restoring peace. I should certainly be most interested to know how things are going at your end and how from Brittany the situation in France is assessed. The papers tell us that the socialists are making frightening progress in the east.[13]

In April he declared: 'We are being delivered up defenceless to demagogy! I doubted its triumph a year ago. Today I doubt it no longer.'[14] Elsewhere he wrote that, 'I am favourable to quite a tough little despotism* as an urgent necessity and as the sole refuge for the future.'[15] Late in 1851 he prophesied the re-election of Louis Napoleon. When Bonaparte forestalled this by his coup of 2 December Gobineau showed his own primary concern with the preservation of order: 'What is certain is that the socialists have been led a merry old dance, which is always very good. As to constitutions . . . the best I can say about them is nothing – we have had virtually seventy years of them making trouble everywhere.'[16] Gobineau was now less than ever one of those second generation romantics who saw romanticism as liberalism in literature and who supported Victor Hugo's eventual strictures upon the President – indeed upon the Emperor, as he became in December 1852.

* The French text refers to 'un petit despotisme bien *corsé* (tough, full-bodied)' – here, additionally, a pun upon the Corsican origin of the Bonapartes.

Tocqueville resented the coup of 1851 and his protégé's toleration of it. He met Gobineau in July the following year and gave Gustave de Beaumont this important account:

> I said to him point-blank: 'How can you explain that the President, who has spent all his life in free countries, should at this juncture destroy liberty in ours?' For myself, I added, 'what will always prevent me from rallying to his government is still not so much the Second of December as what followed.' Gobineau agreed with embarrassment that it had surprised him too, and that one had gone much too far. He assured me that he would not despair of a return towards liberty.[17]

1848 stimulated Gobineau to recast quickly one work which, although it was a literary failure and was not published in his lifetime, is most germane to our studies of the evolution of his thinking. This creation, the epic poem *Manfredine*, is preserved for us only in its final version. In some respects the acquisition of the earlier drafts would be for students of Gobineau a matter second in importance only to the discovery of a manuscript of the *Essai* itself. The work is significant as an indication of the effects that the year of revolutions had upon the author and those effects have to be elucidated via an investigation of the chronology of *Manfredine*'s composition. The title-page of the final manuscript gives us some demarcation of the stages in the work's preparation:

> Conceived in 1838. Begun in the spring of 1842 . . . Taken up again in 1844 after a quite long interruption. Finished in its first draft in 1845, but not corrected. Resumed in 1848, under the influence of events and realized then in a manner that was broader, clearer and more absolute in its convictions. Until that time I did not know what I wanted.[18]

Though it remains difficult to distinguish those parts which were added or adapted in the light of Gobineau's experiences of 1848, some clarification can be derived from the fact that the poem was originally titled *Masaniello*. The epic deals with the mid-seventeenth-century struggle of the Neapolitans against their Spanish oppressors and into this context we must fit the figure of the plebeian fisherman Masaniello, a leader of popular national revolt and one who was quite likely to have proved a literary hero attractive to Gobineau in his comparatively more liberal phase of the early 1840s. One may therefore offer the fairly well grounded suggestion that the epic's final revision chiefly took the form of moving the emphasis away from Masaniello and towards the character of Manfredine, who is depicted as the daughter of a Neapolitan lord and who comes to dominate the work both in title and in much of its substance. The change of stress is probably revealed, for example, in a passage of some five hundred lines devoted to her Scandinavian ancestors which bears signs of being an artificial insertion into the fabric of the story. In the light of the earlier title and of Gobineau's general lack of concern with the sustained discussion of racial matters in any other context before 1848, it seems reasonable to conclude cautiously that it is the element of explanation and justification by reference to race that is the most significant novelty in the work as freshly conceived after the revolutions.

We may certainly see the whole finished creation as the literary manifestation of Gobineau's revulsion against those events. It becomes indicative of the kind of relationship that exists between Gobineau's social and political experience on one hand and the emergence of his racist ideas on the other. For we have in *Manfredine* the first more than fragmentary indication as to any of his opinions upon the influence of race. Hitherto this sort of topic seems to have been only on the very periphery of his interests. It is true that even as early as 1838 we may read in the journal *France et Europe* some remarks of his about the permanence of intellectual and moral traits among certain oriental peoples. Yet, typically enough at that point, the discussion is not couched in explicitly racial form. Even now in *Manfredine* the account of racial influence is not systematized. But we do have there, in the poem's final yet still uncompleted version, the first sustained linkage – however imperfect – between his views on race and his reactionary opinions on society. Together they provide the first significant manifestation of Gobineau's own peculiar form of social protest.

Manfredine's heroism is that of her Scandinavian-Norman ancestors. These belong to the Aryan family that is alleged to have been represented in Europe by *les Germains*, the so-called barbarians of the Dark Ages and the men of the North. Gobineau describes them unequivocally as a master race:

> Et les Germains, montrant leur chevelure blonde
> Que portaient leurs aïeux, dans tous les coins du monde
> Paraissent pour régner. Neptune et son trident

Servent l'Anglo-Saxon, leur dernier descendant,
Et les déserts peuplés de la jeune Amérique
Connaissent le pouvoir de ce peuple héroïque.
Mais Romains, Allemands, Gaulois . . . Pour en finir,
Ce qui n'est pas Germain est créé pour servir.*[19]

Notable here – apart from the sudden, and isolated, rhapsodizing about the American scene – is the contention that *les Allemands*, primarily the inhabitants of modern (rather than more historic) Germany, are no more born to rule than the Latins or the Gauls. Though Gobineau was to reiterate the point often enough it was one that many of his later admirers chose to ignore.

Good breeding is characterized by intelligence as well as physical vigour, and both these virtues are inherited from generation to generation. We find,

> . . . dans les nations et l'âme et le visage
> Éléments principaux de l'humain héritage,
> Se transmettant partout avec fidélité
> Des auteurs de la race à leur postérité . . .†[20]

But the preservation of blood-purity is most difficult and the fates of different branches of the Aryan stock have varied. Even among *les Germains* there are differences:

> . . . Au premier rang de ces tribus germaines,
> Splendides diamants dans les races humaines,
> Il en est deux surtout qui par leur majesté
> Dominent tout le reste avec autorité.
> Les premiers sont les Francs . . . Ils sont morts!
>   D'autres braves
> Qui ne leur cèdent rien, ce sont les Scandinaves . . .‡[21]

---

* And the Germans, displaying the blond hair of their ancestors, emerged to rule in every corner of the earth. Neptune and his trident serve the Anglo-Saxon, their last descendant, and the peopled deserts of young America know the strength of this heroic people. But as to Romans, Alemanni, Gauls . . . to put it briefly, those who are not German are created to serve.

† . . . among nations both soul and form, the principal elements in man's heritage, being everywhere faithfully passed from the founders of the race to their descendants.

‡ In the first rank of these German tribes, splendid jewels of the human race, there are two especially which by their majesty dominate all the rest with authority. The first are the Franks . . . They are dead! The other brave breed, who yield to them in naught, are the Scandinavians.

Manfredine's qualities are thus described and praised:

> Sa beauté, sa vertu, sa valeur souveraines,
> Manfredine du sang qui coulait dans ses veines
> Tenait tout! Et c'était aux trésors amassés
> Sur d'antiques aïeux, gloires du temps passés,
> Qu'elle avait en naissant pu prendre avec la vie
> Tant de perfections, dignes de tant d'envie.*[22]

To Tocqueville he had denounced the alleged Christian equation of virtue with faith. Now, without appreciating the irony, he appears to equate virtue with blood. Such virtue must be a delicate flower since blood-purity is difficult to maintain and ethnic degeneration, once begun, cannot be reversed:

> Quand un peuple est déchu, rien ne le régénère
> Ni la prospérité, ni l'excès de misère,
> Ni même les efforts d'un maître généreux.†[23]

Gobineau is thus describing in this epic the elements of his race-theory: the qualities of heroism and intellect in the Aryans, the need for blood-purity, the vulnerability of the stock and the inevitability of complete decline once degeneration takes hold. These were to be elaborated and systematized, with an attempt at lengthy historical substantiation, in the *Essai*.

But *Manfredine* also gives us insight into the social alienation which is inseparable from the emergence of Gobineau's race-thinking. His admiration for the purity of noble blood is complemented by his contempt for the degenerate and impure mob. The epic begins thus:

> Je ne renierai pas ce que j'ai voulu faire.
> Je hais mortellement le pouvoir populaire,
> Et dans tous ses excès, dans toutes ses fureurs
> Je l'ai voulu montrer sous de justes couleurs.
> C'est un monstre aviné, courant à l'homicide
> Et d'autant plus hideux encore qu'il est stupide,

---

* All the supreme beauty, virtue and worth of Manfredine derived from the blood that flowed in her veins! And it was through this hoarded treasure of ancient ancestors, the glories of bygone ages, that she had been able to assume, with birth and life, such numerous and enviable perfections.

† Nothing can revive a fallen people – neither prosperity, nor excessive poverty, nor even the strivings of a generous ruler.

> Et que dans ses dédains comme dans ses amours
> On peut bien affirmer qu'il se trompe toujours.*[24]

In the light of his attitude to Louis Napoleon it is of particular interest to note his account of the normal progress from popular revolution to despotism:

> Oui, le peuple est stupide; en sa sottise extrême,
> Sa manière d'agir reste toujours la même:
> Au début du combat, il se gonfle d'orgueil,
> Ferme les yeux, s'en va battant sur chaque écueil,
> Puis, tout désemparé, comme un méchant navire,
> Mis à l'eau sans patron qui le sache conduire,
> Après avoir jeté ses biens par-dessus bord
> Échoue aux pieds d'un maître, y demeure et s'endort.†[25]

And Gobineau adds, quite explicitly, that the upshot of all this is the death of liberty in the arms of a Bonaparte. Whichever Napoleon was here referred to, this is the very charge that Tocqueville had been making in the conversation reported to Beaumont. But so great was Gobineau's hatred of democracy by 1852 that he could consider the rule of Louis Napoleon as a lesser evil. Still, it was a reluctant acceptance. Gobineau's embarrassment upon such points may explain why *Manfredine* never reached completion and was never considered, so far as we know, for publication.

The motto for the epic might well be the words of the old priest describing the will of God:

> Il défende, il est vrai, même envers les tyrans,
> Toutes rébellions, aux petits comme aux grands,
> Et voulut, puor marquer combien il les déteste,
> Que ce fût, aux États un remède funeste,
> Plus féconde en malheur qu'il n'en peut extirper.‡[26]

* I shall not deny what I am wanting to do. I have a mortal hatred of popular power and, in all its excesses and all its rages, I have wished to show it under its proper colours. It is a drunken monster, rushing to murder, and all the more hideous for being stupid. We can well assert that, in its loves and hates alike, it is always mistaken.

† Yes, the populace is stupid. In its extreme folly its mode of conduct is always the same. When battle begins it fills its sails with pride, closes its eyes and crashes into every rock. Then, as with an ill-fated vessel in distress which has put to sea without a skipper who can steer, its cargo is tossed overboard and it runs aground at the feet of a masterful figure. And there it stays, to sleep.

‡ In truth he forbids to great and small alike any rebellion even against tyrants. And to show how much he detests it, he wills that for States it should be a fatal remedy cultivating more calamities than it can uproot.

Even taking into account the poetical exaggerations, we can state firmly that *Manfredine* remains a work fundamental to the understanding of the *Essai*. It indicates something of the nature of the relationship between Gobineau's original political concerns and his race-thinking, suggesting the manner in which the latter derives from the former. In 1865 he wrote to his brother-in-law Jules Monnerot: 'It is *Manfredine* that is my great monument.'[27] The finest summary of the significance of the year of revolutions for Gobineau appeared in a letter to Tocqueville of 1856: 'When I saw revolution with my own eyes – no longer just in the mind – all those filthy shirts disgusted me to such a degree and so exaggerated (if you like) my ideas of what was true and proper that, had I not been married. I would have been capable of becoming a monk in order to take the very opposite road.'[28] Gobineau's reactions to the events of 1848 were expressed fairly immediately in two further forms. We must therefore discuss firstly his views on decentralization in France and then consider his comments upon democracy in Switzerland.

8 Decentralization and Liberty

Gobineau's upbringing in the provinces naturally encouraged an interest in local liberties. His provincialism and his advocacy of decentralization are inseparable. Local rights had already been a theme in the *Abbaye de Typhaines*. For France Gobineau advocated greater decentralization, but he did not necessarily argue this elsewhere. For example, although he encouraged local feeling in Prussia, he realized that in general Germany's greater need was unity and enlarged central control. This was also his attitude in relation to Switzerland, where the problem was to preserve, or even to create, national unity – and this was a standpoint he took with regard to the administrative chaos of Russia as well.

Yet, in the case of France, his insistence on a greater measure of local autonomy is clear. He was not the first to be faced with the situation of a marked divergence between the theory and practice of decentralization. In recent French history provincialist devolution had been perennially favoured largely by those deprived of power at the centre. Despite a number of ameliorative plans, governments once in power tended not to act upon Louis de Bonald's assertion that, 'The commune is the real political family'.[1] Decentralization was a prominent issue in the thinking of Tocqueville too, and Gobineau was to praise highly the attempts made in *Democracy in America* to survey the problems involved. Tocqueville saw that, with the growth of democratic societies, centralization was a natural development and that henceforth the preservation of local liberties would need to be contrived in the face of the dangerous trends to uniformity. For both Gobineau and Tocqueville the period after 1848 was crucial. They agreed that revolutions tended to centralize power, and they shared a belief in the value of local initiative and participation for their beneficial social, intellectual and moral results. But they disagreed as to who should participate. Tocqueville saw local rights as valuable in controlling the excesses of democracy; Gobineau's more aristocratic theory asserted the desirability of decentralization without such clear reference to democracy. But he had trouble in remaining consistent since his pleas for participation sometimes seem to amount tacitly to a claim of political rights for all. Gobineau also diverged from Tocqueville by rejecting federalism as a solution, but he agreed with him that one should attempt to distinguish between the essentially governmental and the merely administrative sorts of centralization. The first related to the enactment of properly national laws and to the conduct of external relations. The second represented an encroachment upon matters of more purely local interest. It was upon this latter, never adequately separated from the concept of the former, that both men concentrated their attacks.

Gobineau's ideas were published in his own journal, *La Revue Provinciale*, which lasted a year, appearing monthly from September 1848 to August 1849. In July 1848 he wrote thus to Jules Monnerot: 'I would like to establish in Paris a journal ... the whole concern of which would be, beyond all party politics, to call for moderate decentralization.'[2] His collaborator, and the source of the necessary finance, was Comte Louis de Kergorlay, a boyhood friend of Tocqueville. He was an arch-reactionary of whom Gobineau could say: 'He is much too legitimist for my liking.'[3] Gobineau saw some inconsistency in advocating decentralization in a Parisian journal and wrote to Richard Lesclide: 'In order to do it I should prefer to be, as I am by *birth*, a writer from the provinces rather than a writer from Paris.'[4] The journal carried articles on governmental and administrative affairs, on history and culture, on agriculture, industry and economics. All these were linked by emphasis upon their relevance to the relations between centre and periphery in the French state. The publication aimed particularly at stimulating the provincial press, and Gobineau contributed a major article to nearly every issue.

The review's prospectus, signed jointly by Gobineau and Kergolay, proclaimed its aim – to advocate institutions that would give France both order and liberty. The present system, centred on Paris, provided neither:

Until now stability has been created in spite of our various governments. The reason for this surely lies in the deplorable fact that liberty has been neither equally real, nor equitably spread, nor properly implemented over all the different areas of the nation. In short, while excessive centralization has been putting authority at the mercy of successful risings within the walls of Paris, the whole of France has been deprived of the power to defend the State against haphazard violence.[5]

Gobineau refused to separate freedom and authority. He was shortly to write that, 'Political sense suggests that liberty and authority should come together without mutual exclusion and that, one with the other, they should create proper modes of procedure that would clearly be beneficial to the governed'.[6] He held that a judicious increase in local liberties would encourage order and suggested that further centralization would bring either disorder or absolutism: 'Centralization, political absolutism, these are two branches from the same tree.'[7] Increased central control would leave France merciless before the turbulent passions of its capital. The power of government should not belong to a single city. In their prospectus the editors stated their fundamental credo as follows:

It is of the utmost importance that our system of centralization be replaced by freer action and by greater flexibility of institutions and, consequently, of attitudes. In brief, henceforward it is necessary that public life, in so far as it is noble and exalted, should extend through the whole of our country, and that, from the humblest rural commune to the capital itself, true liberty in all its most necessary and useful applications should exist equally everywhere.[8]

The revolution of February 1848 had made such a change indispensable and the *Revue Provinciale* was meant to study the question, not only in its administrative aspects but also as applied to education, economics and commerce.

Gobineau charges that French administration is designed to make the exercise of authority more rapid and to stifle dissent. It takes no account of regional differences and of the needs of individual provinces. Centralization strengthens the national government but is harmful when it brings neglect of public opinion beyond the capital. Centralizing bureaucratic despotism not only annihilates the moral unity of the nation but also negates liberty:

One questions how a people has been and is able to be so irresponsible as to allow, alongside a political constitution that is free and is often jealous of prerogative power even to the point of a most dangerous puerility, the existence of an administrative structure which owes its completion to the warrior Emperor, in whose eyes the departments were solely a mine for gold and a nursery for soldiers.[9]

The political and administrative domination of Paris is accompanied by her economic growth which attracts provincials to the capital. Beyond Paris is increasing desolation: 'For all France's great population, the provincial towns are for the most part deserted, with weeds growing in the streets, and nearly everywhere agriculture is short of labour!'[10]

Cosmopolitan and rootless Parisian society offended against Gobineau's desire for the preservation of tradition and order. There in the capital he saw in microcosm the breakdown of French society. He considered the family as basic to social cohesion and saw danger in the fact that so many people in Paris lived for the most part 'outside families and in an isolation which results in debauched habits, the normal training-ground for those who dream of organizing or disorganizing society'.[11] Naturally such alienated and isolated men have no respect for property and the family, and they are particularly susceptible to socialist ideas:

Paris alone is really troubled by the efforts of the most ardent innovators, and the rest of the country is simply irritated by their doctrines. Paris is troubled, because it is no more socialist than the provinces. But its frantic centralization has made it the headquarters of a floating population, one devoid of traditions and real homes alike, and one which, heeding only the signals of the leaders whom chance provides for it, henceforth keeps Paris, and with Paris the whole of France, at the brink of endless calamities.[12]
... Paris has no traditions ... Paris, the city for everyone, is the city of none.[13]

Demagogy and socialism seem inseparable, and the latter especially is regarded as an attempt at subjecting individuality to the omnipotence of the state.

Gobineau was insistent about the attraction of such extreme ideas for the alienated man and the déraciné. He did however fail to appreciate to just what degree he too was both. His daughter later wrote this: 'Our family was not numerous. We were, in short, déracinés. Had the Gobineaus, Joseph and Louis, gone back to Bordeaux after the Revolution they doubtless would have rediscovered all those cousins and so forth who had issued from the course of many centuries. But in Paris they were isolated, save for some families of distant cousins.'[14] None the less it was within this context of perceiving the dangerous rootlessness of others at least that Gobineau was to enjoy some interesting posthumous praise from fellow-countrymen of right-wing convictions, such as Charles Maurras and Maurice Barrès. For instance, in 1907 the latter, with an eye to what he alleged to be the contemporary scene, commented as follows: 'Gobineau saw the place that is held in France by the déracinés and recorded how they work towards our decomposition.'[15] On one side Gobineau put family, property and a social order strongly rooted in tradition; on the other he saw social disruption embodied in the ideas of rootless socialists. In February 1849 he wrote of them thus in the *Revue Provinciale*:

At a time when the enemies of family and property can unite so well and band up against the social order, all honest men, all true Frenchmen naturally find themselves forced to come together, to reach out for one another, to join hands and form a group to repel the invasion of Vandals. See how those who call themselves socialists agree and unite! From Paris they thrust themselves through all the land . . . Look at them as they strive to ensnare France in the midst of their web and to set up centres of discontent and instantaneous insurrection even in towns where no one was aware of the identity of any local agitator.[16]

This was Gobineau's considered reaction to 1848. True liberty begins at home, with the family and the local community, their property and traditions.

In his journal Gobineau undertook a historical exposition of centralization in France, primarily in two articles entitled *Études sur les Municipalités*. He claimed that under the Romans the Gauls enjoyed a form of municipal right which, if it failed at all, erred only in allowing local administration too much independence of the central power. The Franks more clearly appreciated the need to separate governmental from administrative control. Of the feudal age Gobineau writes: 'That period of terrible organization merits neither the zestful anger that has been lavished to curse it, nor all the unfair wiles that were once employed in defending it.'[17]

Feudalism did not destroy local liberties. These were defended in the greater towns, but the latter were animated from the outset with a haughty and unpatriotic spirit: 'The medieval communes were not communes. They were political bodies supplied with every sovereign right and ones which, had they been given the time, would not have failed to make of France what the imperial cities made of Germany and Italy – countries without any possible unity.'[18] Such attenuation of central power in itself is not Gobineau's aim. His emphasis throughout is not upon the emasculation of centralized government but upon its happier harmonization with the justifiable claims of the localities.

Gobineau held consistently that a centralizing reaction had begun around the time of Philip the Fair, at the beginning of the fourteenth century, and that this heralded increasing encroachments by the royal power until the Revolution. The sole advantage of these developments was that, by limiting the excesses of the communes, they contributed to the creation of a strong and unified France. But the encroachments also caused harm and in the perennial confusion of political and administrative issues no great progress could be made: 'To have separated two such different elements would have been best; to have disentangled them, one from the other . . . there was a task that wisdom would have applauded.'[19] Although the events of 1789 had a long pedigree, of which the movement towards greater centralization was a major strand, it was not until the Revolution itself that provincial life and liberties died: 'Provincial life was only to expire completely on the rostrum of the Constituent Assembly.'[20]

Gobineau's account of the eighteenth century is one of centralized monarchical exploitation. It is also the tale of the encroachment of Paris upon the political, social, economic and intellectual life of France. The men of 1789, though frequently of provincial origin, were Parisians in outlook, so devoid of respect for tradition that they were altogether more revolutionary than similar elements elsewhere. They had 'none of those hidden ties which made it so difficult, even so impossible, for the revolutionaries of all other countries to detach themselves from their nation's past and to launch themselves into the future by kicking aside the remains of their ancestors'.[21] The Revolution marks the growth of federal ideas supported by the Third Estate. Gobineau denies that these have any foundation in the feudal or monarchical history of

France. They were yet another of the *a priori* conceptions of 1789. During the revolutionary period the municipalities simply offered themselves in servitude to successive Assemblies.

The Empire was, if anything, even worse, and with regard to the imperial prefectorate and mayoralty Gobineau mentions 'the despotism of which they were the organ and the utter absolutism that they represented'.[22] Gobineau describes the failure of attempts at decentralization after the Restoration. In 1831, under Louis-Philippe, a law was passed improving the municipal electoral system but Gobineau viewed this progress as insufficient and suggested that the legislation contributed more to a desire for local liberties than to their actual attainment. Recent history he regarded pessimistically:

> Since the last years of the eighteenth century we have lived with plans, projects and utopias which, in short, their sponsors threw down for discussion by the handful without having thought about them. And what remains of this vast outlay of inventions and systems? Nothing, except a pile of ruins to serve as a basis, amongst which we are still fairly fortunate to find – alas not intact, but rather more secure than all the rest – those ancient edifices of the family, of property and of religion which the innovators have not yet completely succeeded in razing to the ground.[23]

Though Gobineau looks back to a happier past he insists in these articles upon the impossibility of constructing a better future system automatically from any historical knowledge of local liberties. His traditionalism is here modified by the assertion that, because of the long confusion of political and administrative rights, history can provide no neat models for the future.

In these writings Gobineau is undoubtedly willing to accept some form of parliamentary government. Indeed, he appears to advocate that provincial power should be increased so that there may be more effective representation of the people. Here at least Gobineau speaks like a democrat: 'To study the developments of which municipal liberty may be susceptible is to do nothing less than seek the solution of a great problem and strive to give a really useful meaning to that declaration of our political law which puts supreme sovereignty in the hands of the whole people.'[24] In doing all this governmental and administrative realms must be distinguished. Elaborate theory must give way to what is practical. France cannot continue to exist 'flying like a shuttlecock off the racquets of a thousand more or less liberal or despotic theories'.[25] Though there was to be some shift in his position with regard to a federalist solution in the years after 1870, here at least he was adamant in his opposition to it. As he remarked of one proponent of a French federal system, 'He has copied the Anglomaniacs and, without investigating more closely whether we were not organically different from the Anglo-Norman peoples of North America – in race, traditions, customs or geographical situation – he has thought up for us the yoke, which he sees as attractive, of a purely American constitution.'[26] The basis of a federation must be the equality of the contracting members, whereas the feudal system was founded upon submission. Medieval French unity was based upon common admission, by the subjects, of the king's sovereignty: 'Feudalism resembles federalism rather less than monarchy ... resembles a democratic republic.'[27] Gobineau argues that French federalist theory is really the invention of the revolutionary Brissot and is inspired by the contempt for tradition that was shown by him and his followers in the first Assemblies after 1789.

In seeking a better solution Gobineau surprisingly found some comfort in the more recent revolutionary happenings in France. In November 1848 he declared that, 'One of the most obvious results of the February revolution is a certain leaning towards the application to the departments of a more liberal régime than formerly.'[28] In January 1849 he interpreted thus the recent presidential election: 'All took fright, all drew back, all bowed to the will of the majority of Frenchmen, and the tenth of December saw the radiant provinces bringing in their candidate.'[29] It is only in such a context that we can still discern a democratic tinge in Gobineau, seemingly supporting a suffrage which by sheer numbers gives power to the provinces and overthrows the rule of Paris. It can only begin to be reconciled with his other thinking, especially after 1848 itself, if we suppose that he believed, as he had done earlier in the case of Germany, that some degree of aristocratic influence might still remain available in the localities in order to guide the provinces. Only after that qualification has been made could we agree with Janine Buenzod in suggesting that he was advocating 'a conglomeration of small direct democracies after the fashion of Rousseau'.[30] In any event, Gobineau soon registered his disillusionment and realized that the President, once in power, was no more inclined than his predecessors in government to dispense with centralization.

In his exhortatory vein Gobineau refused to see the struggle for decentralization as one of party:

> Even if the protests are inspired by varying motives, with hatred of Parisian instability making some speak out while love of liberty alone spurs others, at least all are united in the same profession of faith that the establishment – or if you like it another way, the development – of local liberties is the first principle to invoke in order to arrive at any real understanding of the voice of the people.[31]

The decentralist issue should have this position outside the normal sphere of party disagreements because of the place that Gobineau attributes to communal liberties in the history of the origins of society: 'Communal liberty derives no small strength from the strong advantage of being logically anterior to any form of government, whether republican or monarchical, and of constituting the first idea of fairness, of universally agreed administration, that the mind of man ever brought to fruition.'[32] Gobineau saw its very weakness as its ability to be recognized in theory and ignored in practice. To ensure its full recognition he suggested the following: 'It is no longer enough to be a decentralizer because the political party one supports has managed to have the wisdom and merit of accepting the dogma. We have to be decentralists independently of any other opinion and for the sake of the thing in itself. It is necessary to be so because we must love true liberty, because we must love the land where we were born.'[33]

This patriotic concern is strong in Gobineau's writing on decentralization. It is worth emphasizing – at least at this point in his intellectual development – because of the unqualified assertions of his lack of patriotism that one may find in some discussions about his thinking. His article *Du Renouvellement de l'Esprit Public*, dating from December 1848, is animated throughout by his love of country – not merely the provinces as such, but also France taken as a single entity. He suggests that, though centralization has sapped their spirit, his countrymen are fundamentally patriotic:

Among the French people we find consistently in all ages three convictions, three passions, one could say, of the most elevated, noble and genuine kind that could be conceived: firstly, a deep attachment to unity and national glory; next, a wise mistrust of rash innovation; finally, a generous desire for freedom and progress. Who would dare ask for more before declaring that a people thus fashioned is sincerely and deeply patriotic?[34]

In the light of much that he had suggested hitherto – and of nearly everything that he was to say on the subject henceforth – we may suppose that this represents a mood of assumed optimism, born less of conviction than of a pressing need to exhort some action. He declares that he will not despair for the future or prophesy a period of decadence. At this point – perhaps for the last time in Gobineau's intellectual history – the future is open:

It will be gloomy and full of misfortune if the provinces do not solidly establish new institutions upon the foundations of their independence; it will be prosperous and glorious if the laws can make a reality of what has been hitherto a fiction – the right of the departments to move forward as the equals of Paris.[35]

Those words were published in January 1849. But pessimism was not far off, and in the following month we read: 'It is a matter of averting the ruin of France. . . . It is a question much less of being sure today how France will be administered than of knowing, in fact, whether she will even live.'[36] But at least we have here none of the explicit indications found in the *Essai* that there is no remedy to discover. Gobineau's plans to achieve greater administrative decentralization and to restore public morale have their institutional basis in proposals for the foundation of provincial committees. And, of existing institutions, it is the *conseils-généraux* especially which must be strengthened, to make their members 'the first figures of the department, the judges upon local matters, the guides, the controllers of action by the prefects, in short, the strong and respected representatives of the electorate who will act, with full authority under the guarantee of law, in all the matters which are definitely closest to the citizens' interest'.[37] Decentralization must be linked to such a spirit of true patriotism lest otherwise one simply fosters a movement towards social fragmentation.

The last sentence of the prospectus issued by Gobineau and Kergorlay in September 1848 had read: 'It is impossible that a conscientious, practical and patriotic venture should fail to take root in France.'[38] A year later Kergorlay was bidding farewell to subscribers and announcing the review's closure. It had not succeeded in establishing any large circulation and funds were exhausted. Its failure to attract public enthusiasm – no less than that of the *Essai* itself a little later – doubtless confirmed Gobineau's opinions of the triumph of mediocrity in French society. The review's end was also certainly hastened by Gobineau's new preoccupation with the Foreign Ministry secretariat, and the valedictory address was signed by Kergorlay alone.

Still, Gobineau's opposition to centralization continued. In April 1850 he wrote home about Paris: 'This wretched city, and the vital energies of France, seem to have become dizzy, and I believe that we are being delivered up defenceless to demagogy! I doubted its triumph a year ago. Today I doubt it no longer.'[39] Later, during his diplomatic mission to Greece, he complained that the great powers had centralized the kingdom's administration to no good effect: 'We have brought about the disappearance of communal organization, the only institution that is understood and useful here in Greece.'[40] In 1871 the English poet and traveller Wilfred Scawen Blunt visited Gobineau and wrote in his journal that, 'He thinks the best chance of regeneration for France is that the provinces should disunite and govern themselves.'[41] If Blunt understood him correctly then it was indeed a sorry ending to all the patriotic hopes of the *Revue Provinciale*.

In 1848–9 Gobineau had sought to encourage other forms of social and political organization beyond those of the over-centralized state. He still had a programme and a belief that by publicity and action improvement might be achieved. The impotence of political action asserted in his future racist theory was not yet triumphant. He was pleading still in practical political terms for the rights of the individual and of certain associations against those of the state. His hope was soon replaced by disillusionment. As early as the end of 1849, and still more clearly by the close of the following year, desperation was in the ascendancy. By then he had concluded that in France the rootlessness of the capital was prevailing inexorably over familial and provincial loyalties.

To understand an important connection, for the moment only implicit in Gobineau's own thinking, between these considerations and a racist social philosophy we might note, in conclusion, some comments by Robert E. Park. In a classic pioneering study on the sociology of race relations he made the perceptive suggestion that racial tensions are instances of the conflict 'between a society founded on kinship and a society founded on the market-place, the conflict between the folk-culture of the provinces and the civilization of the metropolis'.[42] It was this tension that was intimately felt and manifested in Gobineau's provincialist writings. There, both in the commentary upon the conflict and in the gathering pessimism of the conclusion, further foundations were being laid for the formulation of his own racist theory.

9 Diplomacy in Switzerland and Germany

Gobineau was First Secretary of the Berne Legation from November 1849 until January 1854, and it was during this posting that he composed the bulk of the *Essai*. Although it was only early in 1853 that he had any real opportunity of presenting official reports upon political matters, none the less from the time of his arrival he was charged with supervising the commercial work of the Legation and with providing formal commentaries on the economic situation in Switzerland. He had arrived at a particularly interesting time, following the war of the Sonderbund and in the turmoil accompanying the influx of political refugees after the 1848 revolutions elsewhere. Though his first impressions of Switzerland were not unfavourable he soon became obsessed with the evils of Swiss democracy. He followed in the wake of reactionaries such as Antoine Cherbuliez who had despised radical influences on Swiss politics. In 1836 Tocqueville had written in Berne that, 'The two great factions, aristocratic and democratic, that divide the world are just as much present here in Switzerland.'[1] In January 1848 Tocqueville discussed Cherbuliez's book on Swiss democracy before the Académie des Sciences Morales et Politiques and, while criticizing the author's excesses, he supported his idea that Switzerland was a particularly interesting and highly dangerous example of the operation of democratic processes. There is no evidence that Gobineau read Cherbuliez, but he was certainly acquainted with Tocqueville's assessment of his work.

Gobineau's reflections are nearer to the spirit of Cherbuliez than to that of the more moderate Tocqueville. The young diplomat asserted that, 'I am tempted to regard this country as the prototype, as the very ideal of democracy, if you like, but even more still of *self-government.*[2] To Caroline he wrote of 'the intrigues . . . of these big, fine and quite stupid democrats, who are very tame when they need your help and very violent when they do not'.[3] Both Tocqueville and Gobineau were fearful that democracy would level down men into mediocrity. Gobineau writes to the former that the Swiss Confederation 'does not produce, in intellectual terms, a single man who rises above the common level to any significant degree, and I believe that this levelling out – about which you remarked in *Democracy in America* – could well be the inevitable and fatal result of some law inherent in the nature of popular governments'.[4] He reported to Paris the insufficiency of Swiss education above the primary level and claimed that the ill-educated Swiss were especially susceptible to deception by cosmopolitan demagogues, had become irreligious, contemptuous of authority and (because of their continual unprincipled coalitions) lacking in any adequate political morality. He saw the power of Swiss public opinion as excessive and as frequently directed towards deplorable ends.

Gobineau depicts a society moving in the direction of extreme conflict. The attempted abolition of titles and decorations had done nothing to turn egalitarian fictions into reality. But the fiction itself could arouse hostility, for, as he suggests to Lesclide, 'Out of these equal rights which are harmed by the lack of intelligence there arise in the heart of the people a secret violent hatred for any superiority whatsoever.'[5] Gobineau examines these conflicts in terms of classes and of the corresponding parties. The patricians still have some influence, but more on account of past than present power. Gobineau suggests that they are not unduly wealthy and considers that it is the peasantry who are collectively the richest. Patrician ambition appears limited: 'It seems to me that not even the most ambitious of them gives the very least thought to seizing back the exclusive control of government.'[6] Again, he writes: 'The patricians have fears which are all the more lively in so far as they know that, in the case of any alliance supposed on their part with foreigners through diplomacy, public opinion would flatly abandon them to the vengeance of the radicals.'[7] It was naturally with this patrician group that Gobineau had the greatest social dealings. He wrote lightly to Caroline: 'I gather from all sides that I am indeed very popular with the patricians, with conservative aristocrats of every kind, with ultramontanes, with Jesuits and with others who are

much behind the times.'[8] Next, Gobineau saw that the conservative
party, previously independent of the patricians but now lacking
leadership of its own, was drifting towards alliance. These conservatives were 'small in number, certainly since the advanced
liberals moved out of their camp'.[9] Gobineau regarded alliance
between conservatives and patricians as possibly successful, and he
added that no political convictions would be harmed since nobody
in Switzerland had any to which they were thoroughly committed.
The conservatives were looking to support from the rural areas
which were afraid of the radicals and would ask no more of politicians than the reduction of taxes.

But it is to a third group, these radicals, that Gobineau gives the
most attention. He discerns two kinds: 'those who are already
satisfied with what they have obtained for themselves, and those
who are not yet so – and naturally the latter represent what are
termed the most advanced ideas, that is to say, a communism
derived from Germany and compared with which ours is but child's
play'.[10] However wild their theories they are in practice compelled
to be more moderate, particularly since the Swiss are great
defenders of their own private property. The radical party has also
moderated its views on centralization:

Through proclaiming that Switzerland needed a fuller concentration
of its energies by means of the creation of a more vigorous central
power, the radicals implanted a principle between themselves and their
opponents which clearly separated them from one another. Today, the
central power that they established has no more violent adversaries than
they themselves.[11]

Gobineau emphasizes that the radical party, though small in active
membership, is strong in lawyers and intellectuals and that many
of its most influential members are German and Polish political
refugees. Its importance is greater than its numbers might seem to
indicate: 'The profound apathy of the Swiss regarding everything,
except issues of profit and its conservation, surrenders them to a
very small number of daring radicals.'[12] For the present the conflict between patricians, conservatives and radicals is limited by
this indifference to many subjects. But in matters of material
enjoyment the Swiss, like other democratic nations, are prepared
to do battle. Gobineau does not find it easy to side with the con-
*servatives who, in the case of Berne for example, frequently show

themselves no better at government than their rivals. In 1853 he concluded that, 'We shall never see as ministers in Switzerland any but rascals. . . . All of them behave the same, being as weak in their minds as they are strong in their pretensions.'[13]

Gobineau asserts that, whatever moderation remains for the present, greater social conflict lies ahead between patricians and conservatives, on one hand, and radicals, on the other. He is convinced that the political refugees of 1848 who found haven in Switzerland form the hub of an international conspiracy against the forces of order in the Confederation and elsewhere. Of this small country he comments: 'In regard to Europe she is becoming a place of rendezvous for all those who are dangerous.'[14] Whether in official dispatches or in private letters Gobineau is passionate on this topic. The geographical and political situation of Switzerland has made it 'a permanent club for those who are most hostile towards us, towards Germany and towards Italy'.[15] It is 'a kind of promised land and mother-country which revolt and treachery need but touch in order to regain their strength'.[16] Gobineau writes of the refugees as 'these emeritus professors of revolution'[17], and suggests that 'to act clearly against the refugees would be to strike at the very nerve of the radical army and to decimate its body of officers'.[18] He is convinced that the Swiss government has neither will nor power to prevent their influx. The chief role of the Swiss in history has been to export themselves as mercenaries and they are now putting their services at the disposal of Europe's revolutionaries.

Switzerland itself, alleges Gobineau, is a land where continual revolution is seen as a solution to political and economic problems. 'The rulers of Switzerland are men born in insurrection and reared upon its doctrines.'[19] Nothing can be established there and the so-called conservatives are scarcely less to blame than the radicals. Gobineau's general conclusion, offered in similar terms both to the Ministry and to Tocqueville, is that, 'Switzerland is organized in such a way as to demonstrate, by its mobility, permanent revolution. She can never offer any guarantees to neighbouring powers. She is always ready for upheaval.'[20] Confronted with conflict and disruption on all sides Gobineau gives strong support to the Swiss Catholic hierarchy as a social bastion, describing himself – admittedly to the pious Caroline – as 'a zealous and unflinching defender of the Church'.[21]

In the light of his activity on the *Revue Provinciale* it is not surprising that in the Swiss case Gobineau should give considerable attention to the conflict between the cantonal and federal systems as a fundamental cause of strife. He believed that Switzerland unlike France, suffered from weakness at the centre. He regarded the cantonal spirit as fundamental to the Swiss mentality. Writing to the Ministry he commented that it is to this that,

Switzerland owes all that it has hitherto preserved – its equality of rights, its freedom, the sympathy of its neighbours and that neutrality which is the most precious, though most derided, of its possessions. Still, the cantonal system does not do for everything, It isolates the various states too completely and, notably in economic matters, it has often displayed an impotence for which the federation has been forced to compensate.[22]

But Gobineau suggests additionally that even the cantonal spirit is insufficient because, as he writes to Tocqueville, 'If the Swiss much prefer the canton to the Confederation, they have no less a preference for the commune over the canton. Properly speaking, that is their only true homeland.'[23] A very excessive local spirit, encouraged by ignorance and blind to the value of federal co-operation, has paralysed necessary reforms such as those of the tax and postal systems, the army and the currency. Gobineau is keen to emphasize that the Swiss patriotism which does exist has no significant application to internal affairs. The federal council possesses neither troops nor money except as allowed by the cantons. The radicals have weakened it by their newly found hostility to centralization. The council can act usefully only by avoiding conflict with local interests and by playing upon an unhealthy national vanity projected against the world outside. Of this Gobineau remarks: 'The vanity of the Swiss is that of all small nations – it is implacable and limitless.'[24]

Gobineau perceived that, once allied to Switzerland's further democratic vanity, this could be a potent force. He prepared for the Ministry a long memorandum on the Swiss army – a report that impressed his superiors considerably – in which he wrote:

It was beneath the sway of active nationalist ideas that Switzerland, after 1848, busied itself in reshaping its military organization. It seemed to her indispensable that she should bring this into line with the views of European Demagogy, as well as with the feeling of national pride developed since 1815.[25]

Gobineau concluded from his military study that, 'Even if the Swiss are not really warriors ... they are very much soldiers, mercenaries. They love payment ... Devoid of imagination and initiative, they greatly cherish that irresponsibility which cloaks men under arms once they have obeyed the orders of their superiors.'[26] He decided that the Swiss military system was not only internally disastrous but also was capable of threatening the stability of other European countries to a degree well in excess of that indicated by the comparatively small number of soldiers involved.

The most disturbing results of Swiss national vanity are seen as the resentment against her own neutrality and the distrust towards foreign states. As members of communes the Swiss sometimes show political wisdom; as members of the nation they have inflated ideas of Swiss power. Their attitude to France is described as follows: 'Continual assaults against our dignity and our interests – that is what we experience constantly from the Confederation.'[27] Since he perceives a similar attitude towards other countries Gobineau concludes that, 'The whole of Switzerland's foreign policy is simply an unfortunate web of senseless provocations and real failings – God alone, and then only by a miracle, can prevent all this from coming to a very bad end.'[28] He recommends a programme of moderate economic sanctions as a suitable response to these attitudes. This Swiss foreign policy is a reflection of the mixture of deception and over-excitement notable in her internal affairs. Gobineau's disquiet as to the domestic consequences of harbouring the political refugees is projected into his considerations of her external policy. Most European powers were indignant at the Swiss refusal to arrange for the expulsion of the fugitives. Gobineau's official judgment is that, 'The refugee question is less the cause than the simple effect of the fact that Switzerland is so badly disposed towards the countries around its borders.'[29]

Gobineau's chief official undertaking was a lengthy report on the Swiss economy, covering topography, communications, agriculture, industry and commerce in general. He considered the population, rural and urban, in terms of religion and language. In October 1850 he was writing to Tocqueville of the increasing difficulties ahead for Swiss industry and by the beginning of November he had prepared his final conclusions for the Ministry, in a document that was largely instrumental in ensuring his appointment as Chevalier de la Légion d'Honneur the following

D

February. He emphasized firstly the instability of institutions and the mediocrity of ministers. He was alarmed that economic vitality should be so concentrated upon three towns and that beyond Bâle, Neuchâtel and Geneva there was such comparative stagnation. The symptoms of this were the rapid growth of 'needy classes' and 'the appearance of a proletariat, a pest still unknown less than thirty years ago, which is relentlessly gaining ground, especially in eastern Switzerland, and which is bringing in its wake all the demoralizing effects that are seen planted elsewhere'.[30] Men of intelligence were lacking, and as yet there was no solution. Gobineau's pessimism about the interrelation of politics and economics in Switzerland continued throughout his stay. In 1853 he described it as a country,

where there exists only suffering agriculture and mediocre industry, where governments, without power or prestige, have no means of containing the passions of the masses, from whatever source the agitations may spring.
. . . It is quite evident that such a country is ruled by the poor, and that there the poor will welcome with alacrity all the theories that appear to promise them relief in the present or the future. And that is why Switzerland belongs to the radicals, and why its sorry economic state is the prime cause of the permanence, the intensity, and perhaps the incurability of the political ills which torment it.[31]

This passage brings together his political and economic observations and concludes, with the now customary pessimism, that the ills of political democracy and economic failure are linked and beyond cure.

Gobineau detested his Swiss sojourn and it is easy to see that his descriptions were biased and that his passions entered (not for the last time) into his official writings. It is instructive to appreciate that this was the social and political experience that Gobineau was undergoing during the writing of the *Essai*. He never repented of his views of Switzerland and his fundamental revulsion against its society was to be expressed intermittently throughout the rest of his life.

Before his transfer to a post at Frankfurt Gobineau's diplomatic work also provides notes on Piedmont and Hanover. He visited Piedmont in 1851 and was impressed by its beauty and wealth. An account given to Tocqueville shows that Gobineau understood the limitations of the pre-1848 régime, but at the time of his visit he could still write thus to his family about the country: 'It is a

tailpiece to the Ancien Régime, which makes for an agreeable people
... We were like that when 1789 dawned. The bourgeois is as yet
unaccustomed to rights and to success. Here people will still say
quite simply that someone is "as dumb as a bourgeois".'[32] It was
his opinion that Piedmont was fortunate in deriving its prosperity
primarily from the land: 'As industry is still of little significance,
nowhere have there been created those manufacturing centres
which, by spreading misery and demoralization among the lower
classes, encourage the development of revolutionary feeling.'[33]
He nonetheless appreciated that Cavour was coming to the fore
and he feared the social and political consequences that would
flow from the industrialization schemes increasingly mooted.

Gobineau has more detailed observations on Hanover, where
he was Chargé d'Affaires in the autumn of 1851. The kingdom was
then at the centre of the debate on German unification and the
reign of Ernest Augustus was obviously drawing to a close.
Gobineau showed his admiration for the old monarch:

> The wisdom that the king embodies, the successful support that he
> gives to his ministers, the deep calm, the well sustained development of
> material interests, of agriculture, commerce, shipping and industry –
> and of the public works which must be, indeed are, the consequences of
> all the rest – all this attracts from afar the attention and agreement of the
> other small sovereigns of Germany, who are in varying degrees threat-
> ened as regards their forms of internal organization by the attitudes of
> the two great Germanic monarchies.[34]

Gobineau made the additional comment to the Foreign Ministry
that, 'The Hanoverian character is little inclined to be led astray
and is foreign to sudden bouts of defiance and anger, rather being
practical and dogged.'[35] There at last he found traces of real
nobility, in the king and his court, and not least in the philosopher-
heir. It was to the latter, when he had succeeded to the throne as
George v, that Gobineau was to dedicate his *Essai*. As the author
explained to Caroline it was a gesture that the new king acknowledged 'in the most affectionate and flattering terms'.[36]

From Hanover Gobineau observed the rivalries of Austria and
Prussia. In the year after the pact of Olmütz had seemingly
reasserted the diplomatic predominance of the Habsburg in German affairs Gobineau tended to reverse his prediction of the 1840s
with regard to Prussian superiority. He had already suggested to
Tocqueville from Berne that, 'Austria ... appears to be enjoying

something analogous to the state of those convalescents who, having recovered from an acute crisis, hunger and thirst to move and make use of their faculties.'[37] This is the predominant theme of a dispatch, dating from November 1851, which gives an overall picture of Hanover and northern Germany.[38] In Hanover he stated that he was impressed by 'the remarkable character of the race of men who live in this kingdom and the particular nature of the generally independent tendencies which they have always shown – qualities which make them conspicuous among other Germanic populations'.[39] He emphasized that the Hanoverians had no time for theories of equality. For instance, the army's obedience was owed directly to the sovereign and the court itself preserved a noble character:

The court is accessible only to the nobility. To be qualified for court . . . or not to be, is a distinction which exercises an influence over all social intercourse. A noble must not – cannot – associate with the middle classes without losing his position, without exposing himself to suspicion, to attacks from his friends and relations, and without creating a highly artificial situation.[40]

The bourgeoisie were kept firmly in their place in a carefully ordered society. In explaining this – even in an official document – Gobineau now freely resorts to racial explanation:

Fundamentally it is that there exists in the race of Lower Saxony – in this Germanic branch that is the most closely related to the English nation of any that survive on the continent – an instinctive preference for hierarchy and an innate aptitude for dealing with the consequences of this state of affairs. There liberty is loved . . .but, as for equality, it fails to charm or tempt them. It is not even understood.[41]

He approved of the Hanoverian idea of liberty as a matter essentially of local and provincial freedom. But developments in Germany were endangering the autonomy upon which this conception now had to rely for its survival. Whatever his previous personal feelings about the desirability of German unification he discreetly refrained in his official writings from pressing any such convictions against the official French policy of maintaining the divisions beyond the Rhine. Yet Hanover did provide him with an example from which to illustrate some drawbacks that he very genuinely saw inherent in the unifying process. It was evident to him that the national movement might well endanger Hanover's praiseworthy social order. There upon the road to unification the interests of aristocracy and bourgeoisie would decisively diverge: 'For the supporters of aristocratic ideas it is virtually a dogma to cling to the locality, to cling to the spirit of the race – I should almost say of the tribe – that is still so strong even among the masses.'[42] On the other hand, the middle classes wished to widen the horizons of commerce and the professions, and the liberals opposed the preservation of the existing system of local sovereignty in northern Germany.

Gobineau suggested that since 1848 Austria had regained her predominance in Germany and was now an effective conservative force with few ideas of aggrandizement. Now it was of Prussia that he wrote harshly:

Being without traditions, without common history, without geographical homogeneity, it is conquest and, even more, the treaties resulting from the transitory requirements of policy that have enlarged her without providing solidity. And Protestantism, which once bound together provinces stripped of any other tie, has lost all its energy and everything that made it a new principle of government.[43]

He described the liberal resentment against Prussia, but also had to add that, 'Men with aristocratic ideas are protesting against the fickleness of a government which, as it springs moreover from an innovating source, seems to them ready to return sooner or later to revolutionary paths.'[44] The Foreign Ministry was presented with the conclusion that Austria was again in the ascendancy, that she had no intention of seizing for herself what she could now restrain Prussia from acquiring, but that Germany must remain for a time in uncertainty and turmoil.

Just over two years later, in January 1854, with two volumes of the *Essai* already published, Gobineau was appointed First Secretary in Frankfurt, the seat of the federal German Diet. We have no record of any dispatches sent by him during this posting, nor are there on file any significant official references to his activities. But his own private correspondence reveals that he was not impressed by the Diet. As he wrote to Tocqueville, 'The Diet is a business office for the German bureaucracy – it is very far from being a real political body.'[45] He confirmed that it was disregarded on all important matters by the two major members, Austria and Prussia. His shifting view of their rivalries was influenced in part by his assessment of their representatives. He disliked the Prussian Otto von Bismarck and was resentful of his alleged advances towards Madame de Gobineau. On the other hand, the Austrian representative, Anton von Prokesch-Osten, became a lasting friend. He was, like Gobineau, a diplomat with pretensions to historical and orientalist studies. He valued aristocracy, hated democracy and revolution, and was convinced of the decadence of modern Europe. Gobineau enjoyed henceforth with Prokesch-Osten a degree of fellow-feeling that was no longer possible with Tocqueville, and his correspondence with the Austrian over the next two decades is a valuable source of information about the further development of his thinking. His encounters with Bismarck, on one hand, and with Prokesch-Osten, on the other, doubtless aided him in reaching the conclusion expressed in a letter to Tocqueville: 'If the visible changes in Germany are occurring in the North, the deeper and determining forces seem to me to reside rather in the South. . . . It is from there that the drive seems to come at the moment and, so long as the North shows such increasing reluctance to yield, this becomes all the more worthy of note.'[46]

The first two volumes of the *Essai* appeared in 1853; the second two were finished, after much rewriting, in the autumn of 1854 and were published the following year. Thus we can appreciate the potential importance of Gobineau's diplomatic experiences in Switzerland and Germany in this period. Prokesch–Osten appeared on the scene too late to influence the fundamental thesis, though he may have had some effect on the composition of its last pages, a gloomy survey of the modern world. He could by then merely confirm the author's impressions and prejudices. These, in turn, had been nourished by experience of democratic excesses in Switzerland, by realization of the dangers of industrialization in Piedmont, by fears for the future of the virtuous kingdom of Hanover, and by disillusionment with Prussia, confirmed at Frankfurt.

The years we have examined reveal Gobineau's increasing conviction as to the decadence of contemporary Europe. He regretted the passing of an older order, marked by respect for family, hierarchy and aristocracy, and he resented the intrusion of newer ideas of equality, democracy and materialism. Gobineau's traditionalism is that of the aristocratic conservative, seeking to mould society with the utmost caution to fit changing needs. He loved, but did not idealize, the Middle Ages. Though his concept of liberty owed much to feudal ideas he thought it pointless to advocate the simple preservation of feudal institutions in the modern world. Despite the fact that he sees the movement from feudal hierarchy to democratic equality as a decline we should beware at this point of over-emphasizing his *féodalisme*. The latter was indeed, as Jean-Jacques Chevallier suggests, a form of 'intellectual revenge and psychological compensation',[1] but we shall hope to demonstrate that in the *Essai* feudalism is itself a symptom of earlier social decline.

While supporting aristocratic property rights Gobineau endeavoured to avoid the charge of being himself materialistic. For him such ownership of property as an essential means towards the maintenance of order and the exercise of social responsibility was a matter far removed from the selfish aspirations of bourgeois materialism. Gobineau viewed the rootless trouble-makers of the capital as those who had thrown off the continuity of family connections and who, lacking well-established property in land, had no respect for an ordered material basis to society. The prospectus of the *Revue Provinciale* had stated that, 'It is more crucial than ever, in these difficult times, that the family be armed with every legitimate means of defence.'[2] Concern with the family was not merely a symptom of conservative inclinations but also one of the keys to the problem of Gobineau's transition to racial thinking. The stress on descent and blood-ties was then simply generalized, and research upon his family history was regarded as complementary to the study of races.

Gobineau's thinking was already marked by élitist ideas. The romantic conception of the *homme supérieur* had found general intellectual expression in the '*Scelti*' and had then taken a more overtly racial form in *Manfredine*. The decline of the European aristocratic élite preoccupied him. In Switzerland, Hanover and Germany generally he feared for its fate. In France he despaired of it already. His provincialism was essentially aristocratic but he came to realize the futility of his appeals. In 1839 he had written. 'Where there is no longer an aristocracy worthy of itself a country dies.'³ With such a criterion he could only conclude by 1850 that France was moribund.

Family, property and aristocracy were all foundations of order. It was this that Gobineau sought in the turmoil of mid-century – order, both in the sense of hierarchy and in the sense of stability. Although his correspondence with Tocqueville embodies a rejection of the social claims of Christianity there is no doubt that he was himself pragmatic in his attitude to the Catholic Church as an institution providing social rather than religious authority. Tocqueville may have found it ironic to read in the *Revue Provinciale* his correspondent's view that, 'In the first rank of the elements of order and progress we put religious liberty and the dignity of the priesthood.'⁴ Even order was sought not for its own sake but as the prerequisite for a certain conception of liberty. Gobineau stressed repeatedly that order and authority were indispensable adjuncts to freedom and his writing on provincialism in particular is a gloss on their relationship.

Gobineau as champion of liberty seems a strange figure until one remembers that his idea of freedom differed from that of more progressive contemporaries. His version owed much to the conception of feudal 'liberties' which, as restricted privileges, were far from being the universal rights claimed by conventional liberalism. For Gobineau liberty began at home, by the aristocratic fireside. It was the privilege pertaining to family and locality, and in mid-nineteenth-century France such an idea was linked necessarily to a plea for decentralization. He felt that too much had been heard of a liberty that was divorced from proper considerations of authority: 'We must realize that the source of all our misfortunes is not that we have too much independence but that we have given poor attention to power and obedience.'[5] Real liberty could not be unlicensed independence. Speaking of the greatest wrong that can be done to freedom, he declared, 'It is not that of being embraced by some despot or other but that of being adopted by some demagogue.'[6] It was this idea of liberty which puzzled Tocqueville when he contemplated Gobineau's comparatively tolerant attitude to the régime of Louis Napoleon after December 1851.

Such opinions naturally brought Gobineau into conflict with ideas of liberalism, equality and democracy. Liberalism was dangerous because it encouraged lack of respect for social order. But his attitude had not always been so stern. For instance, his article on Capodistrias was highly critical of the statesman's authoritarianism, and the early correspondence with Tocqueville displayed approval of the moral progress made possible by eighteenth-century rationalism and nineteenth-century humanitarianism. In 1843 he could write to his father: 'While preferring the Right, I do not scorn the Left.'[7] In 1847 he was speaking of 'that sublime summons of reason and enlightened courage whereby man, acting consciously and armed with moral grandeur, is moved to claim the full exercise of what he knows to be his rights'.[8] But the predominant voice is one attacking the pretensions of rationalistic liberalism and championing a conservatism based upon respect for tradition. For example, we noted earlier Gobineau's opposition to any calculated constitution-building in Prussia, where he favoured the continuance of traditional representation through the various 'orders' of society. There the true liberty of order and hierarchy needed to be opposed to the illusions of liberalism. After 1848 this was to be Gobineau's unequivocal position.

Privileged liberty was naturally threatened by the egalitarian ideal which had grown at the expense of feudal order. Any real equality among men was regarded by Gobineau as a myth – and he was pleased that the Hanoverian authorities at least had realized this. He also rejected any attempt to treat men as though they were equal. In any case, such a policy could only succeed fully under the rule of terror and despotism when all were equal in their debasement. It was illusory to suppose that equality could be achieved in a liberal-democratic society where, whatever the law, social pressures would bring discrimination. He saw the migrant's picture of the United States as an optimistic mirage for this very reason.

While rejecting equality Gobineau developed a parallel attack on democracy. Here he was consistent except when he discussed decentralization and participation in local affairs. In such a context he could write approvingly of 'supreme sovereignty in the hands of the whole people'.[9] The writings in the *Revue Provinciale* sometimes noted the value of political participation to the individual. But Gobineau was never perfectly clear as to who should participate. If this lack of precision leaves open the possibility that he flirted with democratic ideas then it was at most a passing fancy. He decided finally that democratic means to achieve local liberties would destroy the end itself by creating a state of disorder where freedom could not flourish. He saw that democracy itself encouraged centralization and state control. The mob in *Manfredine* became subjects of a consistent attitude, summarized in the line 'I have a mortal hatred of popular power.'[10] Connected with this was the development of his view of socialism, which passed from complacency over its prospects to a stage of acute fear. The mob and its disorder were his most vivid memories of 1848. He now perceived fully the threat of demagogic government and he spent his time in Switzerland elaborating its dire consequences. Gone was most of the earlier humanitarian concern for poverty amongst the masses. Henceforth it was replaced by fear of their rule.

In 1843–4 Gobineau had suggested to Tocqueville that the new morality of the century was still lacking foundations. By 1850, to his chagrin, he had discerned these in the materialism he observed around him. Naturally he recognized that a degree of material satisfaction was necessary for the maintenance of order and on occasion he even appreciated the tendency to stability which greater distribution of wealth might bring through encouraging more people to have a responsible stake in society. But generally he was distrustful of increasing commerce, both because it produced a powerful bourgeoisie to disturb the social hierarchy and because it encouraged the furtherance of materialistic moral values. Commerce and industrialization represented movement and competition in society, thereby threatening the stability established by aristocratic order. They were not in themselves a guarantee even of prosperity. In 1844, for instance, Gobineau wrote of Germany:

'Everywhere that industry is dominant poverty is created.'[11] Four years later he could already point sorrowfully to parts of the French provinces where 'industry daily devours morality by destroying the family spirit'.[12] The accompanying urbanization was also resented. He claimed that historically the growth of towns had been connected with the attrition of noble rights. Gobineau was convinced that the most valuable political institutions evolved naturally from aristocratic governmental practice in the provinces and he despised the artificial constructions of urban phrase-makers. Of local liberties he commented:

They will have the honour, the unparalleled good fortune, of being the sole political institutions in our age that have not emerged from the artificially excited brain of a Legislator, but have sprung spontaneously from the very mind of the nation. They alone will have roamed the fields before going into the towns and then into the political assemblies. They alone will have traversed France before reaching the threshold of Parliament.[13]

He regarded cities as seats of disorder, 'that strange and pressing desire of the populace in great cities'.[14] When the racial theory was elaborated it was in such cities, with their rootless inhabitants, that Gobineau discerned the largest susceptibility to the miscegenation which brought in its wake degeneration and new disorder. The flux and movement in society, to which commerce, industry and urbanization all so powerfully contributed, were perhaps most evident in the great migratory movements within and from Europe. In the growth of Paris as a city and in the development of the United States into a would-be nation Gobineau saw the same rootlessness and rejection of tradition. Miscegenation was to be henceforth the mark of both.

Gobineau began with a benevolent attitude to nationalism. Romantic influences were strong in his feeling for Greece and they also had some effect upon his opinion of Germany. The *Revue Provinciale* was characterized by national, as well as provincial, feeling. His articles show that he regarded the communal spirit as essential to the health of the nation as a whole. He suggests that the Greeks and the Slavs have been fortunate enough to preserve their national spirit through their love of local institutions. In the case of France Gobineau's essay on the *Renouvellement de l'Esprit Public* is in essence a patriotic tract based upon the assertion that,

'Lack of patriotism together with frivolity in matters of national interest are vices that deeply stain the character of a people.'[15] He refers to France as 'that fine and powerful country whose extent still excites our imagination'.[16] We are here far removed from the anti-patriotic tone of Gobineau's later writing. But already he is wary of the dangers of an unenlightened and crude nationalism such as that with which the Russians appeal to other Slavs. He counsels the Prussians against 'a national pride oversatisfied with itself'.[17] It is such exaggerated nationalism that becomes the national vanity he despised in the Swiss. Increasingly he saw this vanity as the basis of modern nationalist movements and attacked it particularly because of its special attraction to democratic societies with their taste for demagogy and their boundless arrogance. He perhaps failed to realize why nationalism had no place in his emerging racist ideology. National feeling is not, as is frequently thought, the necessary ally of race-thinking. Though they may sometimes co-exist they are also frequently opposed. When patriotism is the mark of a clearly defined territorial society it may have little relevance to an essentially ethnocentric and potentially supra-national philosophy such as Gobineau was to develop. As his concern with race deepened so nationalism as such could be dismissed as unworthy of respect.

We may by now appreciate that Gobineau was not always a confirmed pessimist. We have seen, for instance, that the provincialist writings presuppose a future that is still open. It is admittedly probable that, in his desire to exhort, he is there more optimistic on paper than in reality. Even so, one is struck by clear declarations such as this: 'There are no grounds for despairing of the future and for fearing the imminent danger of a period of decadence.'[18] Shortly he was to express this very fear concerning the future of France and Europe alike. As early as 1845 he had commented that thousands were migrating from a continent that had returned 'by a thousand paths to its primitive misery and sufferings'.[19] Although at that stage such elements of pessimism were not triumphant they were by 1850 undoubtedly predominant. Gobineau, confronted by a chasm between his aristocratic desires and the miserable gratification that his world could give, was as alienated from European society as many of the migrants – and much more dangerously so. 'Mediocrity' was the word which he used repeatedly to castigate bourgeois society about him. His loss of Christian faith was a further encouragement to pessimism. When in the *Essai* he reached dark conclusions about the future of society and the impossibility of saving civilization he had no concept of divine intervention or heavenly salvation to provide consolation. As he described in *Manfredine*, the process of degeneration was irreversible. Henceforth his references to decadence would be part of a systematic theory.

Having clarified the roots and development of Gobineau's pessimism we must still suggest how race enters centrally into the picture. Until now it has been generally and – with hindsight – strikingly absent. We have explained that *Manfredine* was conceived in 1838 and begun in 1842, though probably not in a predominantly racial form. More generally, Gobineau's concern with race, like that of many others, receives encouragement from conventional generalizations about national character. These are generously spread through his earlier writings. In 1843, describing German gradualism in politics, he had written with exaggerated detachment: 'It would not be right to praise or blame such a mode of proceeding in politics. It is the very nature of the national character which is acting thus.'[20] A further example, dating from 1848, embodies still broader generalizations: 'A kind of organic defect seems to be connected with the political framework of each state. Italy has its lack of unity; Germany, so well-disposed towards theories, is manifestly unskilled at the practice of affairs; England errs with glory in taking over more than she can maintain.'[21] Again, we have seen for instance how the Foreign Ministry was instructed upon the Hanoverian national character – and such examples could be greatly multiplied.

The evolution of racial pessimism from social despair was aided once more by lack of religious faith. Gobineau's rejection of the transcendental allowed him to concentrate upon the material. The race-theory was to emphasize body and blood rather than mind and soul. Though some Christians – and even Gobineau himself at times – try to reconcile the tenets of Christianity with those of racism the alliance is always unsatisfactory. By rejecting Christianity – except when outward forms of religious observance dictated otherwise – and by dismissing more secular forms of humanitarianism as well, Gobineau cleared the ground for his racist assertion that the body is dominant over the spirit of man.

When Gobineau first uses the term 'race' it has no strict meaning. But in connection with the contribution of the barbarian invasions to the development of European morality or with the ancestry of the German nobility, the usage soon becomes both more exact and more important. In the most complete version of *Manfredine* race can no longer be equated with nation. Gobineau there discusses the Aryans and their branches, describes the transmission of racial qualities and enters into an account of racial degeneration and of man's impotence to prevent it once begun. The greatest distinction between this verse-epic and the prose-epic of the *Essai* is the degree of systematization in the latter. In *Manfredine* we still lack a coherent theory of historical and social development. Nor does it unequivocally reveal the power of the pessimism that by 1850 dominated Gobineau's thinking. When he writes to Caroline, on 28 February 1851, of 'a large book that I am doing on the Human Races'[22] he mentions for the first time the work which was to contain the racist expression of his social pessimism. The next part of this study will be devoted primarily to the implications of the *Essai*'s racist ideology for social and political thinking. Yet such a discussion will need, by way of preface, some remarks indicating why it is understandable that race should have been chosen as the key to social and political explanation.

PART TWO

The Theory of Racial Determinism

No one has ever been given the talent
to publish four volumes completely
free of error.

GOBINEAU
on Villemain (1846)

An author is known only for a
single product of his mind, to
which the laziness of his public
reduces all his complexity.

GIDE
Journal (1931)

1 The Intellectual Context

The word 'racism', a coinage of the 1930s, was unknown to Gobineau and its use in connection with him is, in a sense, anachronistic. Yet the retrospective attribution is justified because he does provide a strikingly systematic and early example of Race used as the sole or primary instrument of historical, social and political explanation, in the pseudo-philosophical manner that subsequently was to become all too familiar. This we term 'racism', thus seeking to distinguish it from related but more reputable studies, such as the sociological investigation of inter-racial relationships or the attempt to classify mankind into population groupings according to criteria derived from biological science. Though it has claimed to describe social reality, racism deals rather with political symbols, and with ones peculiarly suited to the cultivation of intense group loyalties. It provides a point of effective emotional union yet, being but a symbol, its doctrines tend to elude empirical investigation, and although they can change society they cannot properly describe it. Racial theorists must start, unwittingly or otherwise, from the fact that race, however defined, relates to a group. The latter will be self-conscious, will endow itself with an idea of its racial 'personality' and will then tend to oppose this to the similar concepts of other race-groups. On an allegedly biological basis it will cultivate a feeling of group superiority. The idea of biological unity by descent and blood ties will be projected from family to tribe and then on to the more amorphous aggregate of race itself.

There can be no question of entering here into any sustained discussion of the prehistory of racism. But it is essential to note briefly the contribution already made to its understanding by the debates and findings of group sociology. We have to recognize that the long history of group ideas helped to create the environment in which racism could flourish in more recent times. The race-group concept, applied to political theory, has a certain kinship, in terms of function, with that of the Greek polis or of the medieval Mystical Body. The tendency to fragmentation within the Christian community, which we associate particularly with the Reformation, and the increasing secularist emphasis, particularly evident in the eighteenth century, created a vacuum which new group ideas could fill. To put the matter simply and broadly, the nineteenth century discovered these primarily in the secular concepts of class, nation and race.

It seems at first paradoxical to imply that racism drew strength from an Enlightenment famed for its rationalism and cosmopolitanism. But this stream of eighteenth-century thinking, taken as a whole, is not altogether accurately epitomized by Rousseau's denial of innate inequality or by Voltaire's scepticism at the pretentious ancestries devised by his contemporaries. Indeed, with regard to the Jews at least, a strong case can be made for suggesting that Voltaire himself was among those of most limited vision. The rationalism of the Enlightenment too often evaded the moderating forces of its own fundamental relativism and scepticism, and it could indulge in a dogmatism and intolerance of its own. For many the widening horizons suggested not the oneness of humanity but rather the profound cleavages among men. The century which culminated in great pronouncements of human equality was also the age which realized that, for descriptive purposes, forms of inequality were no less demonstrable or relevant. The Declaration of Independence spared precious little of its egalitarianism for the slaves of the New World, and the French Declaration of the Rights of Man and of the Citizen stood for a time in danger of proving just as irrelevant to the condition of the Jews. Despite its cosmopolitan pretensions the Enlightenment's vision of civilization was predominantly ethnocentric, concentrated upon a White world. No less than those representatives of more conventional intolerance and superstition against whom it was pitted, it bequeathed to the nineteenth century a generally tacit and uncritical acceptance of the primacy of the European peoples. Here was a legacy of ideas about apparently self-evident supremacy that were to be of great importance in the creation of an environment for racism.

In addition to speculations about racial differences and to allegations of inequality wrongly derived therefrom, we must also place in context the related but distinguishable question of conflicts between such groupings. Here we need to remember that Gobineau's racism originates from his revulsion against a society that had rejected the virtues of nobility and that his social pessimism begins as fundamentally a matter of class-consciousness. Such a link between class conflicts and racial thinking was not new, and least of all in France. As Jacques Barzun has elaborated in a work titled, with conscious irony, *The French Race*, it had a long historiographical tradition connecting these ideas. The ancient rivalries of Gauls, Franks and Romans – all readily endowed with racial vices and virtues – and the relationship between their conflicts and the class structure of contemporary France were well established subjects for historical debate. This type of interpretation might even be traced back to Caesar and Tacitus, but the theme was certainly developed frequently and very explicitly from the sixteenth century onwards. It was then, for instance, that Hotman described a league of Gauls and Germans in defence of their common liberty against Roman tyranny. Successors, such as Adrien de Valois, made the more generally recognized distinction between the Gallo-Romans and the Franks. In the early eighteenth century Henri de Boulainviller provided the classic exposition of the aristocratic version of this argument. Like Gobineau he took up the cause of the disappointed nobility and, while holding no particularly favourable view of the monarchy, he opposed himself utterly to the encroachments of the lower orders. He maintained that the Franks, having conquered the Roman rulers of the already vanquished Gauls, had come to form the French nobility and to hold their property and superior position by right of a conquest that was itself the outcome of racial virtue.

With this in mind Hannah Arendt has suggested that Gobineau 'must be regarded as the last heir of Boulainviller and the French exiled nobility which . . . feared for the fate of aristocracy as a caste'.[1] Although such a link is not to be denied it is none the less noteworthy that Gobineau was loath to give explicit credit to a predecessor whom he accused of excessive simplification. In the *Revue Provinciale*, where as we have seen Gobineau was keen to stress the unity of the nation, Boulainviller was accused of disfiguring history by too crudely dividing France into two nations. Rather more significant are the remarks in an unpublished preface (to the proposed second edition of his family history) dating from the very last years of Gobineau's life. They constitute a more judicious and less grudging assessment of Boulainviller's contribution to these historiographical debates. The text does however contain the opinion that, 'He had not the least understanding of the idea of race'.[2] On balance it seems fair to suggest that Gobineau's indebtedness was as real as his ingratitude.

After Boulainviller the elements in this tale of class and race were permutated yet again by Dubos, who described the conquests as largely illusory and suggested that the Franks came to Gaul as the allies of Rome. Montesquieu and Mably also played down the divisive issue of conquest, but at the Revolution the Abbé Sieyès was happy to reverse Boulainviller's argument and to justify the superiority of the Gallic Third Estate over the Frankish aristocracy by reference to the recent triumphs of the oppressed. Even the patriotism aroused by the revolutionary and Napoleonic wars was not sufficient to stifle the argument over race and class. Though such writers as Montlosier, Chateaubriand and Augustin Thierry emphasized harmony among the racial elements, the historical fact of conquest remained unshaken and was still at hand for use by a latter-day Boulainviller. Thus for centuries the elements of the French nation and their past rivalries had been evoked in support of contemporary polemics. It was not unnatural that Gobineau, when the class with which he identified himself was being assailed by the mass of society, should find inspiration in this source of racial historiography. But, in his case almost alone, there was, as we shall discover, a refusal to use this as an instrument of meaningful and positive political action.

The broadening horizons of the nineteenth century revealed material beyond France itself. We have noted already that Gobineau had been attracted early by the general renaissance of interest in the Orient. India, in particular, offered for western contemplation a civilization which was both different and alive – a past living on into the present. Its caste system proved of special significance to Gobineau in his concern with the relationship between race and class. When Michelet pondered upon India he was confirmed in his conviction of the identity of all mankind. Gobineau was to reach opposite conclusions – but they stemmed from the same interests. It was in particular the languages of the Orient which had the greatest effect on the development of racist thought. Once Sir William Jones had established in the 1780s a connection between the Sanskrit, Greek, Latin, Persian, Celtic and Germanic languages and their common indebtedness to an 'Aryan' mother tongue, it was a short (though illogical) step to the belief that a single race must correspond to this linguistic family. Thus the idea of the Aryan race and the particular myth of blood associated with it came into existence. Henceforth scholars competed to discover the stock's place of origin, its patterns of migration and settlement and its achievements in culture and civilization through the ages. The automatic link with language continued to be made with disarming facility. Gobineau's *Essai* was to use linguistic evidence freely and to include a chapter entitled: 'Languages, being unequal among themselves, are completely linked to the relative merit of races.'[3] This sentiment, echoed elsewhere in the work, remained for a time a highly misleading platitude of scholarship, one that was certainly not limited to Gobineau or to France alone.

Such speculations on the Aryans were closely connected with more general attempts at classifying mankind in relation to the natural order. Gobineau appears late in the history of the 'biological revolution' which was the prelude to Darwin as much as it was the result of his work. The progress of biology brought a reaction against the myths of fabulous peoples which had filled, delightfully if not accurately, the notebooks of earlier travellers. From the late eighteenth century the sciences of anthropology, ethnology, and prehistorical archaeology, aided by zoology and geology, devoted much of their energy to divining the racial groupings of man. By 1850 there was still no agreed criterion by which to judge human divisions. The common ground of all was the desire to establish order in the description of the human species. This need had still to be satisfied when Gobineau came to ponder on the problem. Discussion was inevitably complicated further by the religious repercussions that such studies produced. When Gobineau began the *Essai* there was already considerable pressure to regard the Bible as part of the great primitive poetry of mankind and Genesis, particularly, as an allegory rather than a literal description of human creation. The questions of monogenesis and polygenesis were of crucial importance to any discussion of racial differences and inequalities and, as will emerge, Gobineau took pains to reconcile the fundamentally polygenetic implications of his racial theory with traditional Christian teaching on creation. Observing his intellectual convolutions on this point we should bear in mind J. L. Myers's remark that, 'Each thinker's own view of the nature of society went far to determine his imagination of its origin; and . . . his view of its nature was itself suggested by the political stresses of his own time.'[4] There was such political stimulation for Gobineau, primarily from his own class consciousness but also, more generally, from the ever more intense debates then being waged over the issue of American slavery.

Among still more generalized influences on the intellectual context for race-thinking was the amorphous movement of romanticism. This moved away from the rational and encouraged, for instance, Kant's association of soul and landscape, Schelling's attraction to myth, Balzac's concern with insanity and Hugo's fascination by the occult. Romanticism cultivated not only the Orient but also the world of the Scandinavian and Celtic north where it could again manifest its growing interest in the primitive origins and purity of peoples as embodied in myth, saga and legend. Thoughts of a return to nature were accompanied by fascination with primitive instinctive barbarism. Thus with Aryanism was associated a Teutonism which found eloquent expression in German romanticism. In Fichte, for example, there was a strong connection between race, language and nation. Again, there are firm links to be made between Gobineau and Rousseau, one of the founding father's of the romantic imagination. For instance, Rousseau's revulsion against contemporary society is similar to the feeling underlying the racism of Gobineau. Both had a vision of a utopian past: in Rousseau it belonged to all humanity, in Gobineau to the Aryans alone.

These remarks may help us to understand to what degree Gobineau and his racism are typical products of a context which Jacques Barzun has characterized as the age of Darwin, Marx and Wagner. Racism, with its concern for the physical aspects of man, was a natural part of the environment of speculation which culminated in 1859 with the publication of Darwin's *Origin of Species*. Between Wagner and Gobineau there was much later a personal friendship but, already in 1850, the composer believed that race held the key to artistic creation and had produced his antisemitic polemic *Judaism in Music* to explain the forces working towards the downfall of Teutonic culture. The connection with Marx can be traced through Gobineau's ultimate concern with the attractions, repulsions and conflicts between classes and races, through his own hostility to industrial capitalism and (despite his attacks on materialism) through his obsession with the material physical world. In Gobineau's *Essai* a form of the Marxist class war is translated into tribal terms. Both men provide theories encouraging collective hostility: one optimistically champions the proletariat, the other pessimistically defends the declining nobility within a racial guise. They shared the experience of a chasm between gratification and desire, and they dealt less in individuals than in social abstractions and typologies. Gobineau, for example, attacked those who tended to judge moral issues in terms of isolated individuals, but did not question how such matters could be meaningful except in those terms.

Like Marx, Gobineau had become obsessed with deterministic historical explanation in terms of a single idea. Both propounded 'ideologies' according to the meaning that Hannah Arendt has given to the term in writing that, 'An ideology . . . is the logic of an idea. Its subject matter is history, to which the "idea" is applied. . . . Ideologies pretend to know the mysteries of the whole historical process . . . because of the logic inherent in their respective ideas.'[5] In these cases, whether the historical law be racial or economic, its working is inexorable and deterministic. Such ideologies cannot be separated from the context of the societies whose needs they attempt to satisfy. Marx and Gobineau together provide different explanations of similar stresses and conflicts. What class struggle was to one the mixture of races had become to the other – the fundamental key to social interpretation. Again we see the connection between class and race, here associated in their identical function as secular symbols of group loyalty in an age when political ideas needed to be no longer the servant of the city state or of the Church or of a dynasty. The major works of Marx and Gobineau, directing loyalty to class on the one hand and to race on the other, are in essence varying responses to the same crisis – that of alienation from the social, economic and cultural state of contemporary Europe.

In the context of the history of racism Gobineau's great contribution was the attempt to reconcile primitive Aryan unity with its modern diversity by means of the systematic treatment so attractive to positivists and romantics alike and the endeavour to link the anthropological racial studies of scholars such as Blumenbach with the historical racial ideas of writers such as Augustin Thierry.

There was an increasing desire to synthesize rather than to observe and analyse piecemeal. Seeking to give evidence of this Gobineau's *Essai* was well buttressed with references to the scholarship of his day. Some of the most frequently acknowledged sources can be enumerated as follows: Abeken on ancient Italy; Boettiger on mythology; Burnouf on Buddhism; Dieffenbach on the Celts; Ewald on the Jews; Alexander von Humboldt on the New World and on central Asia; Keferstein on the Celts; Lassen on ancient India; Movers on the Phoenicians; Karl Otfried Müller on the Etruscans; Ritter's geographical studies; and Schaffarik upon the Slavs.

Quite apart from Gobineau's own production, these years of mid-century were marked by a veritable spate of studies with racist implications. For instance, in the English-speaking world, there came in 1850 from Scotland Robert Knox's *Races of Man* and four years later from the United States Nott and Gliddon's *Types of Mankind*. The latter appeared too late to affect the structure of the *Essai*, and it seems that the former was also at the time unknown to Gobineau. One relevant German work with which he was certainly acquainted had been published by Karl Gustav Carus at Leipzig in 1849 under the title *Ueber ungleiche Befähigung des verschiedenen Menschheitsstämme für höhere geistige Entwicklung* ('On the Unequal Capacity of Different Races for Further Cultural Development'). Gobineau was to concur in this essay's judgment that such capacities were indeed unequal. But he could not share the author's willingness to accept racial intermixture as an instrument of social progress nor his fundamentally optimistic belief that, inequalities notwithstanding, there remained for any race at all great potential towards improvement.

As a final example it is worth noting that through the previous decade, from 1843 to 1852, there had been appearing in Leipzig, in ten volumes, another potentially relevant work but one which Gobineau claimed that he had not to hand while composing his own book. This was the *Allgemeine Cultur-Geschichte der Menschheit* ('General Cultural History of Mankind') of Gustav Klemm, which precedes Gobineau's work in a number of its assertions. In particular we have Klemm's claim that miscegenation between active races on one hand and passive races on the other produces a dissolution of the former as a distinct grouping and ultimately encourages the creation of a more unitary and egalitarian society.

Yet, whatever the similarity in diagnosis up to that point, Klemm none the less propounds a completely different set of value judgments relative to these supposed facts. As a liberal-democrat he welcomed the end of the old régimes and hailed with enthusiasm nineteenth-century movements towards equality. If we take this in conjunction with the opposed attitude of Gobineau we can appreciate how far the 'facts' of the race-theorist may be twisted to support highly variable political standpoints. Though Gobineau referred to his own racial theory as 'well demonstrated mathematical truth'[6] and as 'moral geology'[7], the results of his allegedly scientific method were much more the product of a fertile imagination reminiscent of the romantics. The revolution in the scope and depth of historical study was not lost upon Gobineau. But if he was a modern in his scope he was, as we shall discover, frequently a primitive in his method.

The *Essai*, first mentioned in February 1851, was completed in the autumn of 1854. The original plan envisaged two volumes but there was an early realization that larger coverage would be necessary. As a result two volumes appeared in 1853, followed by two others in 1855. The work comprises a theoretical exposition in the lengthy Book One, and the alleged historical substantiation of this in Books Two to Six.* Though any such venture must contain both inductive and deductive arguments, in the *Essai* it is the latter which are in the ascendant to a degree that vitiates the whole. In practice the theoretical statement which history is supposed to confirm is itself used to settle doubtful historical points and the alleged facts of the historical account are often directly dependent upon the accuracy of a theory that can be seen more correctly as arbitrary and conceived *a priori*. Still, this should not deter us from studying the significance of Gobineau's arguments. For, as we have been seeking previously to demonstrate, his essential concerns are with the present not the past. Therefore the following discussion of the *Essai* will not concentrate upon the curious and errant details of his historical argumentation. Rather, after summarizing the theoretical and historical expositions, it will examine Gobineau's description of the world of his day and proceed to consider more fully the implications of the *Essai*'s racist ideology for social and political thinking.

* For the structure of the *Essai*, as indicated by Gobineau's own headings, see the Appendix to the present volume.

2 The Racial Theory

On his thirty-fifth birthday Gobineau wrote of his projected *Essai* that it would be a work 'in which new ideas will not be lacking and whose theories will lead far'.[1] Both predictions were justified. The Dedication to the reactionary George v of Hanover is a striking introduction to the work. It is immediately and explicitly clear that Gobineau's historical interests are derived essentially from his contemporary concerns. He claims that he has been moved to his investigation by the recent prevalence of revolutions, wars and disorders and that his task is to reveal their fundamental causes. They are symptoms of the destruction of civilization and it is with the implications of this phenomenon for the present and the future that Gobineau is preoccupied. At the beginning of his very first chapter he remarks that,

> The fall of civilizations is the most striking, and, at the same time, the most obscure, of all the phenomena of history. It is a calamity that strikes fear into the soul, and yet has always something so mysterious and so vast in reserve, that the thinker is never weary of looking at it, of studying it, of groping for its secrets.[2]

In the Dedication he stresses that recent progress in historical, archaeological and philological methods has made the adequate investigation of this subject at last possible.

Thus Gobineau, like Gibbon amidst the ruins of the Capitol, starts with thoughts of decline and fall. Unlike Gibbon, there alone his thoughts were to remain. He begins by seeking the restoration of social order, but he will eventually conclude by admitting that such restoration is impossible. His consolation is his belief that he has succeeded at least in explaining the cause of decline: 'Passing from one induction to another, I was gradually penetrated by the conviction that the racial question overshadows all other problems of history, that it holds the key to them all, and that the inequality of the races from whose fusion a people is formed is enough to explain the whole course of its destiny.'[3] He claims that one other fundamental conclusion – relating to the Aryans – emerges from the study:

> Everything great, noble and fruitful in the works of man on this earth, in science, art and civilization, derives from a single starting-point, is the development of a single germ and the result of a single thought; it belongs to one family alone, the different branches of which have reigned in all the civilized countries of the universe.[4]

Of these findings Hannah Arendt has commented that, 'Nobody before Gobineau thought of finding one single reason, one single force according to which civilization always and everywhere rises and falls.'[5] This is an exaggerated assessment, which ignores for instance centuries of equally simple-minded assertion about divine dictation in history, but what Gobineau certainly does achieve with more claim to originality is a striking single-cause explanation in fundamentally secular terms.

Gobineau begins negatively, by rejecting certain conventionally alleged causes of social decay. Though he tends to choose only the most convenient examples, he marshals some quite reputable arguments to reveal the fallacious reasoning behind many then fashionable accounts asserting causal links between fanaticism, luxury, corrupt manners, irreligion and bad government, on one side, and such decay upon the other. He claims that societies have flourished despite these flaws. Aztec organization could have survived its excesses had not Cortés appeared; for the Phoenicians the corruption of morals was an essential part of their vitality; the Romans had as many honest men in the fifth century as in the golden age. Gobineau asserts that, since no nation has experienced discontinuity in some form of religious belief, irreligion should not be regarded as a cause of decline. The corruption of manners is 'a fleeting and unstable phenomenon . . . and so cannot be considered as necessarily causing the ruin of societies'.[6] He dismisses also the idea that the decline of societies – as opposed to that of states – is related to misgovernment: 'If nations invariably died of their sufferings, not one would survive the first years of its growth; for it is precisely in those years that they show the worst administration, the worst laws and the greatest disorder.'[7]

However agile Gobineau's dismissal of such arguments may be, his positive attempt to provide a universal explanation of social decay is subject to many of the same criticisms. His negative argument betrays already the presuppositions that there is indeed a single explanation to discover and that society can be treated as an organism in which one may always talk meaningfully of maladies, decay and degeneration. These features emerge as he comments on current reorientations in the study of such problems:

> It is being dimly seen that one ought not to have given such a preponderant importance to evils which were after all merely derivative, and that the true causes of the life and death of peoples should have been sought elsewhere . . . Men have begun to look at the inner constitution of a society, by itself, quite apart from all circumstances of health or disease. They have shown themselves ready to admit that no external cause could lay the hand of death on any society, so long as a certain destructive principle, inherent in it from the first, born from its womb and nourished on its entrails, had not reached its full maturity; on the other hand, as soon as this destructive principle had come into existence, the society was doomed to certain death, even though it had the best of all possible governments.[8]

The nearest Gobineau comes to a formal definition of society is as follows: 'An assemblage of men moved by similar ideas and the same instincts; their political unity may be more or less imperfect, but their social unity must be complete.'[9] Quite apart from the general inadequacy of the formulation, one immediately questions the degree of similarity required in ideas and the identity needed in instincts, and one wonders how the phrase 'social unity' can be meaningful until we have a quite independent definition of society.

Gobineau's organic metaphors are reified so that the degeneration of a people forming a society is related completely to physical phenomena: 'The word *degenerate*, when applied to a people, means . . . that this people has no longer the same intrinsic value as it had before, because it has no longer the same blood in its veins, continual adulterations having gradually affected the quality of the blood.'[10] A nation at its death has but a mediocre quantity of the blood of its founders. Gobineau compares the biological processes of organic renewal in which after a certain period the body retains few of its original elements. He thus claims that degeneration is caused by miscegenation between races and – remembering that we are discussing an age ignorant of modern genetical knowledge – his assessment of the worth of societies and civilizations becomes dependent upon a series of conveniently imprecise quasi-chemical analyses of their merged ethnic elements. Gobineau therefore faces this crucial question: 'Are there serious and ultimate differences of value between the human races, and can these differences be estimated?'[11] The *Essai* provides affirmative answers and a discussion of the social and political consequences of these inequalities. Miscegenation always implies betrayal of superior birth and Gobineau thus justifies the argument, fundamental to him both as racist and aristocrat, that, 'A constant characteristic of any social decomposition is that it starts from the negation of superiority of birth.'[12]

Because peoples exist prior to laws and constitutions and because he believes that the latter are but emanations from racial character, he denies that inequalities of race stem from any institutional factors. Nor does he allow that climate, which held an important place in the proto-sociology of Montesquieu for instance, or indeed any other environmental consideration may crucially influence ethnic development. The world has frequently seen savagery and civilization flourishing on the same soil at different periods. One notable example – which corrects the common assumption that the *Essai* embodies crude or simple antisemitism – is the achievement of the Jews. Gobineau suggests that, though Palestine was but a miserable corner of the earth, they became 'a people that succeeded in everything it undertook, a free, strong and intelligent people, and one which, before it lost, sword in hand, the name of an independent nation, had given as many learned men to the world as it had merchants'.[13] A nation derives nothing fundamental from its location; it is the people themselves, through their ethnic elements, who give the environment any value that it may have.

Gobineau's conception of the constitution and relationship of races is formed according to clearly dialectical principles. Just as Klemm had distinguished between active and passive races, so we have in Gobineau the idea, not uncommon among the romantics, of a constant interplay within and between races of a 'female-intellectual' current and a 'male-material' current. Every individual is alleged to partake of both in varying degree. The former has been most evident amongst the Hindus, the Egyptians and the

Assyrians; the latter amongst the Chinese, the ancient populations of Italy and the tribes of Germany. But such distinctions do not of themselves imply any direct value judgments as to the superiority or inferiority of either current.

A still more significant dialectical relationship is that connected with a double law of attraction and repulsion which is said to be involved in all racial intermixture. About this Gobineau remarks as follows:

> The human race in all its branches has a secret repulsion from the crossing of blood, a repulsion which in many branches is invincible, and in others is only conquered to a slight extent. Even those who most completely shake off the yoke of this idea cannot get rid of the few last traces of it; yet such peoples are the only members of our species who can be civilised at all . . . Mankind lives in obedience to two laws, one of repulsion, the other of attraction; these act with different force on different peoples. The first is fully respected only by those races which can never raise themselves above the elementary completeness of the tribal life, while the power of the second, on the contrary, is the more absolute, as the racial units on which it is exercised are more capable of development.[14]

Such a statement reveals the elements of tragedy and social nemesis at the heart of Gobineau's theory. Tribes that are incapable of overcoming their repugnance to blood-mixture remain in a comparative purity which is, however, stagnant and infertile and which gives no opportunity for participation in the work of civilization. On the other hand, the vital force of superior stocks, conquering even strong repugnance for their inferiors, drives them into the contact and communication which give to civilization the conditions for its efflorescence and its withering alike. The blood-mixture which is necessary for the development of society and for the very creation of civilization is also the cause of degeneration. Gobineau's literally organic view of history sees death in life itself and works with inexorable logic towards an utterly pessimistic conclusion.

He defines civilization as, 'A state of relative stability, where the mass of men try to satisfy their wants by peaceful means, and are refined in their conduct and intelligence'.[15] Underestimating the complexity of Guizot's views on the subject he rejected his contemporary's contention that civilization might be regarded as a 'fact' or 'event'. Gobineau asserted that it was rather, 'a *series*, a *chain* of events linked more or less logically together and brought about by the interaction of ideas which are often themselves very complex ... an assemblage of events and ideas, a *state* in which a human society subsists, an *environment* with which it has managed to surround itself, which is created by it, emanates from it, and in turn reacts on it'.[16] Gobineau does not conceive of 'civilization' primarily in the eighteenth-century sense of a phenomenon still in the process of creation, but envisages organic 'civilizations' in terms which Spengler and Toynbee have since made more familiar. When Gobineau wrote, 'civilization' was perhaps more frequently used to denote a progress towards the state of being civilized than to refer to particular societies in history. For him civilizations are 'complete societies',[17] independent of particular state boundaries or specific forms of government because based on elemental conditions prior to politics.

The discovery of a civilization is an exceptional event for Gobineau and it cannot be created through any merely random miscegenation. He asserts of history that, 'It shows us that all civilizations derive from the white race, that none can exist without its help, and that a society is great and brilliant only so far as it preserves the blood of the noble group that created it, provided that this group itself belongs to the most illustrious branch of our species.'[18] Gobineau's historical exposition is a description of the successive civilizations inspired by the white race, and principally by the 'illustrious branch' of Aryan stock. Historically it is the ability to create civilizations through favourable mixtures with lesser peoples, not any talent for isolated development, that Gobineau praises. He believes that when a people possesses the civilizing instinct sufficiently strongly to impose itself on great numbers of men, to satisfy their needs and feelings, a genuine 'culture' is formed. Miscegenation may contribute to the improvement of the lower races – as when we find that the greatest examples of artistic talent stem from a merging of white and negroid stocks – but the long-term result must be unfavourable to humanity as a whole, by virtue of the enervation of the noblest elements.

This account of the white race as bearers of culture and civilization implies a certain view of the ethnic divisions of humanity and a value judgment derived from those differences which relates to the superiority of some over others. Gobineau was forced to question whether such divisions had always existed. As one would expect from an enemy of egalitarianism, the trend of his argument was towards a number of separate human creations. His seeming rejection of the standard monogenist argument that racial differences resulted from environment might appear to make him an unequivocal supporter of the polygenist case. But religious orthodoxy reared its head and Gobineau felt obliged, as a nominal Catholic, to reconcile his argument with biblical monogenesis and he seized on the fertility of human hybrids as an indication of man's common origin. He boldly reintroduced the environmental argument – previously dismissed – in order to achieve this unconvincing reconciliation. He suggested that shortly after the creation climate and environment were forces dynamic enough to produce the racial divisions known by the time of the earliest historical accounts. He dated the creation at about 7000 BC and suggested that these changes occurred when the earth was 'still shaken by its recent catastrophes and without any defence against the fearful effects of their last death-throes'.[19] He believed that no later date could be reconciled with monogenist claims. He even suggested that the permanence of the subsequent racial types – except as it was affected by miscegenation – was itself the result of the vast amount of climatic energy then existing.

Having satisfied orthodoxy by these unconvincing intellectual convolutions, Gobineau transferred his emphasis to the importance of the later ethnic differences: 'Whatever side one may take in the controversy as to the unity or multiplicity of origin possessed by the human species, it is certain that the different families are today absolutely separate; for there is no external influence that could cause any resemblance between them or force them into a homogeneous mass.'[20] It is only the 'internal' influence of racial mixture that could produce such a drive towards homogeneity. Of primal Adamite man virtually nothing is known. But Gobineau suggested that he was almost certainly equally distinct from each of the new types formed in the great climatic cataclysm. In this manner the author of the Essai freed himself to elaborate the consequences of his real conviction that mankind is divided into races of unequal worth. History becomes the epic of racial relationships and, according to the logic of the racist theory, all social and political theorizing and observation must be related fundamentally to this ethnic separation. The latter is itself crude and arbitrary – a tripartite cleavage into White, Black and Yellow races: 'I understand by

white men the members of those races which are also called
Caucasian, Semitic or Japhetic. By black men I mean the Hamites;
by yellow the Altaic, Mongol, Finnish and Tartar branches.'[21]
Gobineau cautions the reader against regarding the criteria of
pigmentation as entirely satisfactory and he also suggests how
improbable it is that any of the three original types should ever
have existed in an absolutely simple and ideal form. These qualifications do not, however, substantially influence the arguments that
he subsequently pursued.

The black peoples are the lowest in his hierarchy. They are
marked by animality and severely limited intellect. They possess
great energy, desire and will-power, but are characterized also by
sensuality and instability of mood. The Black is careless of the
distinction between vice and virtue. He has little concern for the
preservation of his own life, or for that of others, and he shows an
horrific impassivity towards suffering. Gobineau stresses his leaning towards absolutism: 'The black character, fond of absolutes
and easily enslaved, will willingly enlist behind abstract ideas which
it wants not to understand but only to fear and to obey.'[22] He
refers to the race as a 'civilizational nullity'[23] but does allow that its
elements are indispensable in the creation of worthwhile art:
'Artistic genius, which is equally foreign to each of the three great
types, arose only after the intermarriage of White and Black.'[24]
Moreover, he conceded that, in terms of physical beauty as well,
this same mixture was supreme.

The Yellow is superior to the Negro and is his antithesis. He
tends towards apathy and lacks physical strength. He exhibits none
of the moral excesses of the Black because he has weak desires and
a will which is obstinate rather than extreme. Mediocrity and
material enjoyment characterize him and he loves utility, respects
law and can appreciate moderate liberty. The Yellows desire to live
comfortably and undisturbed: 'Every founder of a civilization
would wish the backbone of his society, his middle class, to consist
of such men. But no civilized society could be created by them;
they could not supply its nerve force, or set in motion the springs
of beauty and action.'[25]

The Whites are marked by 'reflective energy' or 'energetic
intelligence'.[26] They have a sense of utility less narrow and more
elevated than the Yellows. They persevere in the face of obstacles
and have great physical power. Their extraordinary instinct for

E

order is a result of desire not for repose but for self-preservation. Gobineau speaks of 'their preference for stability of organization and their natural tendency towards political regularity'.[27] The White is characterized by a singular love of life and liberty, but he values honour even more. Though less sensual than the other races the Whites have superior intelligence and have never, even in the earliest times, been worthy of description as barbarians. The most remarkable branch of the race is the Aryan whose members, having spread from the central Asian plateau, have contributed to the formation of the Hindu, Iranian, Hellenic, Celtic, Slavonic and Germanic peoples.

One of the chief weaknesses of the white stocks appears to be their great susceptibility to miscegenation and its consequences. As we have indicated, this failing is concomitant with their very vigour. Racial domination depends, in large measure, upon superiority of numbers. Although in their major role as catalytic agents the Whites have been less directly dependent than other races on sheer numerical supremacy, none the less they have been since earliest times at a significant disadvantage from this standpoint. Gobineau notes: 'In order to avoid disappearing in the midst of inferior varieties, the white family needed to add to the power of its genius and courage a certain guarantee of numbers, even if doubtless to a lesser extent than was required by its adversaries.'[28] Only too frequently for Gobineau this condition had been left unfulfilled.

In addition to the aesthetic results already noted, mixture with negroid stock has the following consequences for the Whites: 'It disarms their reason, weakens the power of their practical faculties and irreparably injures their physical activity and strength.'[29] In the political context this brand of miscegenation is an encouragement to despotic procedures. With the mingling of White and Yellow the emphasis is different, for there the calculated pursuit of material enjoyment through commerce and manufacture is predominant and utilitarian considerations are paramount. Summarizing the relationships between the three races Gobineau compared the past to an immense tapestry:

The two most inferior varieties of the human species, the black and yellow races, are the crude foundation, the cotton and wool, which the secondary families of the white race make supple by adding their silk;

while the Aryan group, circling its finer threads through the noble generations, designs on its surface a dazzling masterpiece of arabesques in silver and gold.[30]

Gobineau's universal history, to which we now turn, is a fabric woven from these materials. It is also the story of the disappearance of the silver and the gold.

3 The Historical Exposition

The bulk of the *Essai* discusses the rise and, still more particularly, the fall of ten great civilizations, all initiated by white peoples, which Gobineau discerns in history. The first was the Indian which he regarded as founded by a branch of the Aryans moving from their primitive home in central Asia. The second, the Egyptian, was initiated by Aryans moving from India to the Nile. With this development Gobineau associates also the Ethiopians and the Nubians. Thirdly there is Assyrian civilization, which relates also to the Jews, Phoenicians, Lydians and Carthaginians and which owes its rise to the Chamites and Semites, the white descendants of Noah's sons. Next is the civilization of the Greeks who came from the same basic stock as the Medes, Persians and Bactrians, but who differ from these in having strong semitic elements. Chinese civilization, like that of Egypt, was created by an Aryan colony from India. But on this occasion the mingling was not with clearly negroid peoples, rather with the comparatively pure mongoloid yellow races, as well as with the already much hybridized 'Malays' – the description that Gobineau reserves for the products of a certain degree of miscegenation between yellow and black stocks. It is claimed that the development of civilization in China was further assisted by other, but non-Hindu, Aryan elements coming from the north-west. Sixthly Gobineau describes ancient Roman civilization, allegedly produced from a mixture of Celts, Iberians, Aryans and Semites. There follows the civilization created by the Aryan-Germans who, in the fifth century, 'transformed the Western mind'.[1] The list is completed by the three civilizations of the American continent, termed the Alleghenian, the Mexican and the Peruvian, all resulting again from Aryan colonization. Whatever the value of all these civilizations, their creation inevitably must have promoted miscegenation and have led to the constant annihilation of families, tribes and nations previously pure: 'Omnipresent and everlasting racial intermixture – this is the clearest, most inevitable and lasting product of our great societies and powerful civilizations.'[2] Gobineau's first three civilizations, for instance, mark a gradually increasing element of negroid blood in a mixture still dominated by the white race.

He generalizes as follows from his universal racial history:

Of the first seven civilizations, which are those of the Old World, six belong, at least in part, to the Aryan race, and the seventh, that of Assyria, owes to this race the Iranian renaissance, which is, historically, its best title to fame. Almost the whole of the continent of Europe is inhabited at the present time by groups of which the basis is white, but in which the non-Aryan elements are the most numerous. There is no true civilization, among the European peoples, where the Aryan branch is not predominant.

In the ten civilizations no Negro race is seen as an initiator. Only when it is mixed with some other can it even be initiated into a civilization.

Similarly, no spontaneous civilization is to be found among the yellow races; and when the Aryan blood is exhausted stagnation supervenes.[3]

Here the eminence of Gobineau's Aryans is evident. They are descended from Japhet, son of Noah, and in the fundamental three-fold cleavage of the white race after the time of Noah it is these Japhetides who are regarded as being at first superior in blood purity to the Semites and Chamites. Within the Aryan family itself the colonizers of India (though in creating this civilization they were in some degree subjected to blood-mixture with Blacks) maintained greater ethnic worth than the Celts and Slavs who rapidly lost their Aryan character:

Already the Aryans were separated from the Celtic nations who were on their way towards the north-west and were going round the top of the Caspian sea. At the same time, the Slavs, very little different from this other vast mass of peoples, were taking a still more northerly route towards Europe.

Therefore the Aryans, long before arriving in India, already had nothing in common with the nations that were going to become European. Thus they formed an immense band altogether distinct from the rest of the white race.[4]

Henceforth the Aryans are considered to be the most noble, intelligent and vital branch of the white stocks. But their very vigour, love of migration and desire for conquest make them singularly susceptible to miscegenation.

Gobineau's greatest historical preoccupation in the *Essai* is to trace Aryan-German decline from the Teutonic invasions until modern times. Certain aspects of this development are particularly relevant to any discussion of his social and political thought. The most obvious point of historical comparison in Gobineau is between the decline of Rome and the decadence of modern civilization. The similarity is evident not least in relation to class rivalries:

> Does not the Forum offer us all the constituents of a modern social state? The populace, demanding bread and games, free doles and the right to enjoy them; the middle class, which succeeded in its aim of monopolizing the public services; the patriciate, always being transformed and giving ground, always losing its rights, until even its defenders agreed, as their one means of defence, to refuse all privilege and merely claim liberty for all. Have we not here an exact correspondence with our own time?[5]

Since both Greece and Rome declined, in Gobineau's analysis, because of 'semitization' we must clarify his view of this – particularly as it was misunderstood by many of the anti-Jewish vultures who subsequently plundered his work. It also encourages some investigation of his opinion of the Gauls, Celts and Slavs, all of whom are crucial to his racial assessment of modern Europe.

He means by semitization black admixture to a predominantly white base. In government such a combination generally results in unbounded despotism. He finds this ethnic situation prevalent through most of the imperial period of Roman history:

> I have used . . . the term 'Semitic'. We do not have to take this word as indicating a human variety identical with that which resulted from the ancient Chaldean and Hamite mixtures. I have only claimed to point out that, of the multitudes spread by the fortunes of Rome through all the countries subject to the Caesars, the majority were affected by some greater or lesser blending with black blood. Thus they represented in varying degrees, a mixing that was not equivalent but rather analogous to the semitic fusion.[6]

The Jews are but one branch of the semitic family. Thus they have an important white element by virtue of which it becomes impossible for Gobineau to treat them with the degree of contempt which Hitler reserved for his 'anti-race'. We have already observed that

Gobineau used the achievements of the Jews in arid Palestine to show that there was no necessary connection between environment and ethnic worth. He later returned to this theme, emphasizing how little the varied environments of the dispersed Jews had changed them physically. Being hostile to miscegenation he was impressed by the isolationism which distinguished the Jews from most other Semites. Abraham led a people 'destined for great trials and great glories'.[7] But naturally Gobineau wished to deny its pretensions towards being a civilizing force: 'This nation, like the Phoenicians, never possessed a civilization of its own. It was limited to following the examples that came from Mesopotamia, while adding just a little in the way of Egyptian manners.'[8] The real basis for any anti-Jewish prejudice which Gobineau later displayed is to be found in his belief that, despite their isolations and strivings, the Jews have become increasingly mixed with peoples tainted heavily with black elements. Such debasement through history is not of course limited to his account of the Jews; the contrast between Solomon and Shylock is in a sense parallel to that made later between the vigorous Aryan-Germans of the Dark Ages and their modern degenerate descendants. In his own account of their respective histories the anti-race and the master-race of Gobineau's spiritual heirs exhibit this same decline and they are both the subjects of similarly unflattering judgments. In the *Essai* Gobineau implies his criticisms of medieval anti-Jewish legislation and, in sum, does little there to justify his posthumous reputation as a notable contributor to the social theory of antisemitism, in its conventional sense.

Gobineau regards the Celts and Slavs as the first white peoples to settle in northern and western Europe. Like the Aryans they are descendants of Japhet, though much debased by contact with the Finns who were the very earliest inhabitants and were a branch of the yellow stock. The degree of mixture is such that Gobineau can scarcely distinguish Celts from Slavs, though he agrees that miscegenation is more advanced in the latter. For practical purposes he makes no distinction between Celts and Gauls. He had previously appealed to the latter in connection with provincial liberties on account of their alleged bravery and patriotism. Now, even as early as their contact with Rome, they are said to have been 'on the main road to decadence'.[9] It is crucial to Gobineau's view of Europe past, present and future that the Slavs are still more dangerous as purveyors of ethnic degeneration. With the Celts they form 'two amalgamating currents of influence'.[10] The Slavs are 'one of the most aged, worn, hybridized and degenerate families that exist'.[11] Their historical role is most conveniently summarized thus:

> Tenaciously wedded to the soil from which nothing can uproot them, the Slavs played in eastern Europe the same role, of an influence that was silent and latent yet irresistible, as had been fulfilled in Asia by the semitic masses. They formed, like the latter, a stagnant marsh in which, after brief triumphs, all the ethnically superior were swallowed up.[12]

Their geographical situation and their outstanding ability (independent of their own corruption) to transmit ethnic decay give the Slavs this key role, one which would bulk ever larger in Gobineau's thought.

He traces the history of Rome through four stages, characterized as Etruscan, Italiot, Semitic and Germanic. Of his treatment Janine Buenzod has aptly remarked: 'When Gobineau wrote these pages the polarization of the courageous barbarian with the decadent Roman was already a well established theme dear to historians and romantic writers. But rarely had Rome been put in the dock with such violence and such a welter of arguments – and not merely decadent Rome, but also Rome in the midst of its power and grandeur.'[13] By the eve of the Teutonic invasions Rome is allegedly the epitome of Semitic degeneration. Developing his earlier interpretation of the incursions Gobineau says of the Germanic essence then introduced:

> It animated the legions, captured the chief military offices and became a decisive force in the ruling councils. The Gallic race, which was moreover represented only by some northern groups that were already related to the Germanic stock, gave way to it completely. The spirit of its warrior chiefs laid hold upon the working of government.
> It was already justifiable to claim that Rome was germanized, since the semitic principle was sinking into the oceanic depths of society and was being visibly replaced on the surface by the new Aryan element.[14]

For Gobineau, as for Tacitus, the Aryan-Germans are heroic figures characterized by vigour, individualism and love of war and honour. They hold themselves in high esteem, eschew urban settlement and stress the dignity of woman. In sum, 'The Germanic race was endowed with all the vitality of the Aryan variety and needed it in order to fulfil the role to which it was destined.'[15]

Its reputation for brutality is played down and Gobineau pictures the so-called 'barbarian' in the following manner:

> A man with blond hair, of pale pink complexion, broad-shouldered and of good stature . . . This Leviathan had on every subject views that may have been true or false, but which were always reasoned, intelligent and worthy of a hearing. Through his nation he was reared upon the essence of a pure and severe religion, of wise politics, and of a glorious history.[16]

Gobineau stresses Aryan-German conservation of the traces of civilization left in the Roman world:

> Their task, from the middle of the third century until the fifth, was limited to preserving society, by one means or another, in the form under which it had been consigned to them . . . History has been falsified by those writers, modern as well as ancient, who have invariably and systematically depicted the final and complete arrival of the Teutonic nations at the heart of romanized society as a monstrous event and an unexpected cataclysm.[17]

But Teutonic influence moved beyond mere conservation to the creation of a new civilization and culture. Miscegenation with Celts, Slavs and Gallo-Romans enhanced their power to expand and thus helped spread the last of Gobineau's great civilizations.

To Gobineau the history of the Dark Ages and of medieval society is that of interaction between the elements of Aryan-Germanism and decadent 'romanity'. This period's fundamental social manifestation was feudalism. To some of Gobineau's commentators – Maurice Lange in particular – his *féodalisme* is always basic. Yet the account of the origins and development of feudalism in the *Essai*, at least, should lead us to qualify this. We must give due weight to Gobineau's estimate of the importance of the distinction between allodial and feudal tenure. The former alone is fully suited to the Aryan-German, for it combines uniquely 'the two ideas of nobility and possession, so intimately linked that we are puzzled to know whether a man was a landholder because he was a noble, or vice versa'.[18] It represents for Gobineau the social basis of a comparatively golden age of true Aryan liberty: 'The Aryan-German sitting by his hearth disposed of his allodial land and of all who lived upon it just as he pleased. Women, children, servants, slaves acknowledged none but him.'[19]

We may note that this situation suits perfectly the isolated individual or family but naturally it cannot be divorced from the necessity of living within a system of more complex social relationships. For instance, it is incompatible with a state of war or conquest, where success must be bought at the price of relinquishing complete independence, through submitting oneself to a leader: 'The free Aryan, the Aryan who was absolute master of his allod, abdicated for a specific time the exercise of most of his prerogatives. Thus, except as regards reciprocal pledges, he became the servant of his chief, and the authority of the latter could extend even so far as to dispose of his very life if he failed to fulfil his promised duties.'[20] As we shall realize increasingly, Gobineau's conception of isolation – implying also the maintenance of what blood purity still remains – leads us to the conclusion that any complex social life is anathema to him. Here we are confronted with the problem, which will recur, as to whether, in such a case, Gobineau can have a purposeful social philosophy at all. The contract with a leader, the formation of a feudal relationship, is a step towards the socialization of the comparatively independent Aryan. For this very reason it is a mark of further decline from Gobineau's utopia. Like Rousseau he has a pathological fear of the consequences of social dependence. Feudalism becomes for Gobineau, and for the best of the Aryan-Germans, the mark of an unfortunate reliance upon others: 'Military service in the pay of a chieftain was repugnant to many men, especially those of high birth. These proud spirits found it humiliating to receive gifts from the hands of equals, and sometimes even from those whom they considered inferior to themselves in purity of origin.'[21]

Commentators are not however entirely wrong in concerning themselves with Gobineau's more favourable remarks about feudalism, since he did regard it as a better form of social organization than anything known in contemporary Europe. It was, after all, the outcome of Aryan military vigour and it emphasized hierarchical organization. The ideal triple order of the feudal age is reminiscent of Gobineau's tripartite ethnic hierarchy. Although his radical conservatism really harks back to a primitive Aryan republic, he comes to praise feudalism for want of anything better in the recent past. But the limitations on his enthusiasm suggest qualification of his earlier and romantic view of the Middle Ages.

Gobineau depicts a triumph for romanity at the end of the fifteenth century when the lower elements in the ethnic mixture began to outweigh the more valuable parts. To Gobineau the fact that this movement should be generally known as the Renaissance is paticurlarly apt:

In this rebirth . . . this resurrection of the Roman essence, the political instincts of Europe became more flabby as it advanced amidst populations that were less attached to the Germanic instinct. It was among these that one found fewer distinctions in personal status, a greater concentration of governmental forces, more leisure for subjects, a more exclusive preoccupation with luxury and well-being, indeed more 'civilization' as conceived in the new manner.[22]

The Renaissance marks a rejection of Aryan-German cultural achievement. Whatever his previous – or indeed his future – remarks about this rebirth, here in the *Essai* Gobineau is hostile to it, describing its 'inexorable and violent crusade against the achievements of a milennium'.[23] He brings out its harmful tendency to remove social distinctions, opening the way to the hated age of equality. He cannot conceal that his main aim is to criticize France and to depict her as central to this movement. He therefore suggests that, since Italy, the birthplace of the Renaissance, rapidly became 'too romanized even to serve the Roman cause itself',[24] the leadership of European political and cultural decline fell to France: 'She pursued this task with a vivacity of which she alone was capable. It was she who chiefly directed and executed the absorption of the superior classes of society amidst a vast confusion of every ethnic element against which their incoherence and divisions left them defenceless.'[25] Gobineau's criticism is not that France has failed to be in the vanguard of modern European civilization. Instead it is the more striking reproach that it is from there that she has been leading its march to decadence. The undue governmental centralization, the materialism and the social levelling which he now castigates in the Renaissance are amongst the features that most perturbed him in modern France as well.

As early as 1843, in his article on Quinet, Gobineau had revealed a potential ambivalence in his attitude towards French claims to cultural hegemony. There he had written: 'Since the end of the seventeenth century France has marched at the head of the movement of civilization. That much is certain. But, while on one hand helping it, on the other she has also often hindered its progress.'[26] In the *Revue Provinciale* we noted his interpretation of recent centuries of French history as the tale of governmental assaults upon noble privilege. The *Essai* adds an ethnic commentary. Northern France lost its dominance and its ability to defend feudal and provincial rights at the very same time as the Gallo-Roman elements were strengthening themselves and increasingly showing their love of absolutes by minimizing these rights and maximizing central power:

> Paris, whose population is assuredly an epitomization of the most varied ethnic specimens, no longer had any motive for understanding, loving or respecting any tradition . . . This great capital, this tower of Babel, broke with the past . . . and drew France into myriad experimentations with doctrines that were most foreign to its ancient customs.[27]

The old hostility to Paris, its rootlessness and its concentration of the socially alienated is here provided with an ethnic gloss. It is the excessive miscegenation of the capital which explains its infamous role.

Here again we see that the racial theory and the historical judgments associated with its exposition are primarily reflections of certain of Gobineau's other and earlier social attitudes. The derivative nature of the former is now clearly shown as Gobineau shifts ground to depict the Enlightenment as an important contributor to decay. His generous attitude to socially progressive thinking in the eighteenth century, as manifested in his early debate with Tocqueville, could not be maintained after the adoption of the racial theory. The harsher attitude had begun to emerge in Gobineau's provincialist articles where, for instance, he had written of that age: 'At every point, in history, politics, philosophy and religion, men strove to break with the reality of the past.'[28] In the *Essai* antipathy to the Enlightenment is quite unambiguous. For example, Gobineau reversed completely his favourable view of Voltaire: 'The Voltairian way of preventing the ruin of society is to destroy religion, law, industry and commerce, under the pretext that religion is another name for fanaticism, law for despotism, industry and commerce for luxury and corruption.'[29]

With regard to the French Revolution there was neither need nor desire for any such shift of ground. But now its evils could be seen both within the context of these earlier developments and in relation to the new diagnosis of nineteenth-century decadence. Though Gobineau makes little explicit comment on the events of the Revolution in the work as published, it is evident from a letter to Caroline that in draft form the *Essai* was much more extensive in its treatment of them, as well as still harsher in its condemnation:

Having reached modern times, one of the great problems was to avoid running into agreements and disagreements on points of detail and to remain at the same level of detachment as when dealing with distinctly ancient periods. I had greatly insisted on the merits of the feudal era, and I had entered into too many considerations concerning the revolution of 1789. Even though dealing with all this from the ethnic point of view, I was leaving myself open to the accusation of having revelled in aspects that were not purely scientific.[30]

The Revolution embodied the results of ethnic decadence, manifested through the doctrine of equality and a debased conception of liberty. The latter negated provincial and aristocratic rights and Gobineau complains that, 'The innovating spirit considered the destruction of the old territorial subdivisions as a primary necessity.'[31] Gobineau's contention that he played down the Revolution in order to maintain objectivity suggests the need for some more general comments upon his methods as a historian. If, in addition, we remark that his opposition to the Revolution must stem partially from hostility to its attempt to introduce conscious purpose into affairs, instead of leaving them to uncontrollable natural laws, then we are also confronted with the problem of the significance of Gobineau's racial determinism. Before examining his treatment of the modern world we shall therefore assess the defects of his historical method and of this determinism.

4 The Method of Racial Determinism

Gobineau's alienation from his contemporary world encouraged him to believe that he saw it in a more objective fashion than could most of his fellows. His own view of his success in attaining this objectivity was substantiated by the references to scientific laws and by the adoption of that systematic and total exposition favoured by the positivists. But, whether or not he was aware of his failings, he cannot escape Ernst Nolte's charge that, 'The racial view of history consists in enumerating positive and negative qualities according to the social standing and personal preferences of the observer, and in claiming objectivity for this procedure by always reverting to the primitive fact of race.'[1] Gobineau certainly took pains to escape this kind of censure, stressing for instance the need for objectivity when dealing with unfamiliar civilizations, which were not to be dismissed as barbarous simply because they were different. In any case, it was at such points that Gobineau's weaknesses were least likely to matter. His primary concern is really with the contemporary scene and, despite his plea for objectivity in assessing this also, his greatest error is to misread it. Moreover, his misjudgments of earlier times are the direct result of this misreading. Jacques Barzun errs here in writing that Gobineau 'starts with a desire for truth about a great historical question and ends by finding a confirmation of his hypothesis in the contemporary scene'.[2] In reality, as should now be clear, the hypothesis is found in the contemporary world and is essentially social and political rather than narrowly racial. It is simply 'confirmed' by reference to a history distorted by racial determinism to meet the exigences of his assessment of modern times. Gobineau's truths do not need to be discovered, only demonstrated. One might add the observation of Melvin Richter that, in any case, his theory depends on a kind of history which requires from the past the sort of corroboration 'which could not be supplied by any records then existing or likely ever to be found'.[3]

The *Essai* is written with a dogmatism, as well as a turgidity, that betrays the speed and panic of its composition. The complexity of society must of necessity be reduced and processed by reference to the single explanation of race. A certain physique must be related to a certain mind, and these in turn must condition the production of a certain kind of society. This, together with its politics and institutions, is theoretically derivative and secondary. There should be no exceptions, for race must explain everything and, in every case, its explanation must be complete. Apparent exceptions must be denied or ignored more often than explained. For instance Gobineau comments thus upon the awkward fact of the Greek victories at Thermopylae and Marathon: 'These fine triumphs were only an accident, and the natural current of events – that is to say, the inevitable effects of the ethnic situation – was not changed in the least.'[4] It is such dogmatism which is dominant everywhere except in those passages where the author parades a set-piece of objectivity. It is dogmatism based, sometimes, on a complete lack of evidence and, on other occasions, upon the most tenuous arguments from fields such as philology and the then still primitive discipline of archaeology. His criticisms of other scholars are often unintentionally ironical. For example, he attacks Carus for turning symbols into physical realities – and no better accusation could be made against Gobineau himself. His appeals to natural science depend too frequently on the simple applicability of his organic metaphors to society. In the very last paragraph of the book, for instance, he writes: 'Science, while revealing our beginnings, has seemed to assure us that we must also reach an end.'[5] Though this may apply to organisms, Gobineau is not justified in making a projection into the lives of societies and civilizations and in regarding this procedure as 'scientific'. Once again, not unlike Carus, he is guilty of the reification of metaphor. It thus seems fair to describe his method as in part poetic, and his *Essai* as a vast prose-epic that carelessly utilizes poetic licence. Gobineau writes that, 'Epic poetry is the privilege of the Aryan family.'[6] With insight, he might well have regarded his four volumes as themselves proof of this point.

In his Dedication Gobineau suggested that, 'There is only one tribunal competent to decide rationally upon the general characteristics of man, and that is history – a severe judge, I confess, and one to whom we may well fear to appeal in an age so wretched as our own.'[7] The historical determinism necessitated by the racial theory was scarcely capable of reaching such judicious conclusions. Indeed, it was more suited to Gobineau's opinion, voiced in 1846, that history was 'a matter given over to the individual convictions, theories and caprices of a writer'[8] – a remark made in general criticism of modern historians, at a time when he himself was not of their number. His own brand of this caprice led him to suggest that, 'History is a science made up no differently from others. It presents itself as a compound of a thousand apparently heterogeneous elements which, beneath their complex interweaving, conceal or disguise a root that plunges down very deeply.'[9] Gobineau described the historian's interests as fourfold. He studies man in isolation (whatever that might mean); he examines the foundation of 'political centres'; he then goes on to investigate the reasons for the appearance of certain forms of social organization and concludes by tracing the relationships between societies. But all this must be seen strictly within the bounds imposed by the total racial explanation. For Gobineau history is didactic, instructing us through the confrontation of past and present. But his deterministic framework surely annihilates any practical usefulness that might be derived from such instruction – or indeed from education in general, except possibly in a limited context that we shall discuss later. Tocqueville's criticisms of the *Essai* centred on this very futility, and upon the practical ill-effects of such a thesis, right or wrong. He presented the unanswerable challenge that, if Gobineau's fatalism were justifiable, further practical concern with the social and political state of the modern world would be little short of pointless.

A further argument of Tocqueville was that the theory abolished free will and human liberty by reducing history to an impersonal and uncontrollable process. In the *Essai* Aryans, no less than others, are conditioned in their activity by ethnic laws and, within this context, the arguments for their freedom and vitalist vigour seem artificial. Since developments are controlled by natural laws, 'The destiny of civilizations is not a matter of chance.'[10] The working of these laws cannot be nullified. It is necessary to ask to

what degree Gobineau loosens these deterministic shackles by
allowing secondary factors such as environment and institutions to
slow the process of degeneration. This is the device by which he
escaped the complication of the inconvenient Greek victory at
Marathon. Again, the stable geographical position of the Slavs is
regarded as important to the processes of ethnic intermixture
amongst their neighbours, and their role in history would be much
more limited were it not for this geographical factor. Gobineau
best indicates his attempt to provide flexibility within inflexibiliy
by commenting: 'That a people is free or enslaved, at any given
moment, is a matter which often derives from a very long series of
historical considerations. But their having a natural predisposition
to one or other of these situations is always the outcome of racial
factors.'[11]

He was challenged on the status of non-racial considerations not
merely by Tocqueville but also by Professor Friedrich Pott of
Halle, who in 1856 was to publish there a hostile critique of the
Essai, under a title (*Die Ungleichheit menschlicher Rassen*) that
reflected Gobineau's own. In correspondence with Pott, Gobineau
sought to defend himself against the charge of determinism by
insisting that politics, morality and state organization, as such, had
not fallen within the scope of a purely scientific study. He had
limited himself, so he claimed, 'to finding at last a scientific basis
from which it would be impossible to escape and upon which one
could build with assurance'.[12] If Gobineau failed to understand
how such a rigid and exigent foundation must have more than
purely 'scientific' implications and how it could not fail to make
redundant any substantial discussion of non-ethnic factors, then
critics such as Tocqueville and Pott were more perceptive.

In outcome Gobineau himself always allowed the determinism
and the natural predisposition to prevail over the secondary factors. This is adequately indicated in the following typical passage
worthy of quotation at length:

The great events that I am describing . . . are not in any way the consequence of the direct and explicit wishes of the masses, or of any particular historical figures . . . I am not at all interested in retracing the
history of political bodies . . . Being entirely concerned with the constitution of races, I am assessing solely their organic resilience and the
predestined consequences resulting from it. I do not disdain the rest,
but I leave them to one side when they are incapable of explaining the

point under discussion. If I suggest approval or blame, it is in a sense that is comparative and, so to speak, metaphorical. There is really no moral merit in the oaks that thrust themselves majestically upwards over centuries . . . But I would no longer conceal the fact that the free action of organic laws . . . is often retarded by interference from other mechanisms foreign to them. We must pass unperturbed beyond these momentary disturbances which could not affect the essence of things. Whatever the by-ways into which such secondary factors may draw them, the ethnic consequences will always rediscover their true paths. They are led inexorably to them and they never fail to reach their destination.[13]

Here combined are the elements of fatalism, together with the relegation of political and social affairs to a subsidiary role and–most striking of all – the paralysis not only of the will but of moral judgment also.

The role of individuals in history thus conceived is necessarily limited. The allegedly great men of history are no more than emanations from their race. During periods of grossest miscegenation the achievement of greatness is handicapped by the marked tendency to universal mediocrity. In such a case, 'To be distinguished from the herd, it is necessary not that one should be constituted differently from it but, on the contrary, that, while resembling it, one should exceed it in everything.'[14] In an age which is ethnically purer, greatness is recognized 'because a man seizes upon a salient feature of the needs of the age, or even because he runs contrary to it'.[15] None the less, in the face of overweening natural laws, the scope for such men is still severely limited. One significant historical figure who attracts Gobineau's sympathy and who is allowed almost to escape from the bonds of the theory is Cornelius Sulla. The sympathy is for a patrician striving to preserve aristocratic influence:

There appeared upon one occasion in the history of peoples in decadence a figure manfully indignant at the degradation of his nation. Through the smokescreen of false prosperity he saw with penetrating vision the abyss towards which the general demoralization was leading the commonwealth and he was found determined to shrink from no expedient.[16]

Gobineau allows that his pitiless devotion to his ideals possibly earned the republic a few extra years of life and instilled some artificial vigour. But not even Sulla could avert for long the action of natural laws. The identity between Gobineau and Sulla is certainly not complete but it is hard to deny certain autobiographical implications in Gobineau's account of the dictator's failure:

At the end of a long career . . . being in despair for the future and sad, exhausted and discouraged, Sulla himself laid down the dictator's axe. Being resigned to living idly among a populace – whether patrician or plebeian – even the sight of which made him shudder, he at least proved that he was no vulgar self-seeker and that, having realized how futile were his hopes, he would not strive to keep a power which was sterile. For myself, I utter no panegyric on Sulla, But, to those who are not struck with respectful admiration at the spectacle of such a man failing in such an undertaking, to them I leave the task of reproaching him for his excesses.[17]

This is not simply a judgment upon the futility of Sulla's valiant efforts but also, like the implications of ethnic determinism, a statement suggesting the futility of Gobineau's own efforts, by pen rather than sword, to do any more than to slow the decay of his own world.

The liberal elements in Gobineau's emphasis upon Aryan individualism are attenuated in the light of these considerations. It is not surprising that Gobineau, given his racial determinism, should state that, 'I will not discuss the moral and intellectual worth of individuals taken one by one.'[18] Although the remark was intended merely to convey his belief that individual morality lay outside the scope of the *Essai*, it can stand as an accurate – if unconsciously ironic – condemnation of what he was doing. For, whatever his intention, the implications of his racist theory worked against even the possibility of a meaningfully individual morality. Men, taken singly or in groups, are in the relentless grip of the historical laws which not only determine the expression of individual and racial vigour but also cripple our ability to make moral judgments upon men as individuals independently of our own and their own ethnic situation. Not only are mind and matter closely bound together; morality is material too. Here are the foundations for a theory of moral justification by blood alone. It is physical being, rather than faith or works, which is important. Racial determinism results not only in a paralysis of true moral judgment but also in a paralysis of action. We have already noted Gobineau's potential hostility to society as the context in which miscegenation flourishes. The corollary of this would seem to be the negation of political life, not only because this presupposes social life but also because political activities are regarded as themselves impotent to avert social degeneration. Had Gobineau been able to escape the logic of racial determinism to a degree where he could allow that active men or healthy institutions might change the course of history its implications for action would have been less arid. But every theory with claims to total social explanation must brave all and concede as little as possible. To this rule Gobineau's racial determinism proves no exception.

5 The Theory and the Modern World

Towards the end of the *Essai*, having completed the historical exposition, Gobineau came to describe the contemporary world. He explained the importance of this final undertaking in a later letter: 'I am not much satisfied with the state of European society. But less than anyone else do I have the right to be surprised, for I wrote my *Races* in order to show how and why it certainly had to find itself in this position.'[1] The judgments of the *Essai* are harsher than those in previous writings and they are now associated with the racial theory. When Gobineau wishes to recognize virtues in modern civilization he still belittles it by attributing the major part of any credit to earlier ages and by arguing that there is little new under the sun. But when he discovers facets of modern life to which he is hostile he is more often willing to denounce them as unnatural innovations.

In France the Revolution has marked the country's spiritual annihilation. Again Gobineau attacks Paris as the seat of grossest corruption. He emphasizes her mass mediocrity and the degree to which the greater part of the French population is incapable of participating in civilized life: 'Out of the thirty-six million inhabitants, there are at least twenty million who take only a strained, passive, temporary role in the civilizational development of modern Europe.'[2] But, he adds: 'Except for Great Britain, which in consequence of its insular isolation is served by a greater unity of types, this sad proportion is still more considerable over the rest of the continent.'[3]

To Spain, despite its severely latinized elements, Gobineau is surprisingly sympathetic. She epitomizes a nation which, though weak in government, remains vigorous in other terms: 'It is perhaps in Spain, of all modern states, that the feeling of nationality is most intense.'[4] Certain Gothic infusions have aided the Spaniards, but Gobineau stresses still more the following curious argument: 'Spain, saturated with more directly semitic elements, enjoys a kind of relative racial unity which makes the present ethnic chaos less flagrant.'[5] Yet Gobineau's overall impression of Spain is pessimistic. Then, in the Italian peninsula his view of semitization is still sterner and there he describes the mass of the population as suffering from a decadence comparable to that from which the Teutonic invaders had once temporarily rescued them.

In his scorn for modern Europe Gobineau went so far as to suggest that modern Germans (*les Allemands*) had no significant connection with these invaders, being 'not of the Germanic essence'.[6] Many of his followers distorted his thesis at this point and refused to accept his argument that the Teutons were now much debased and that their most considerable remnants were to be found in modern England and Scandinavia rather than in Germany. His statement of the relative ethnic positions of contemporary Austria and Prussia indicates his increasingly favourable view of the former. The Habsburgs are regarded as consciously pursuing a policy of preserving the Germanic elements of their Empire in the face of the Slav peril. He concludes:

Prussia, with its present borders, has more Germanic resources than Austria, but is essentially inferior to the latter, where the highly aryanized Magyars sway the balance – not according to the standards of civilization, but according to those of vitality, with which (it cannot be emphasized too much) this book is specifically concerned.[7]

Still, this is no more than a comparative judgment and, overall, he brings out the sorry state of both. In some degree the leadership of Aryan-Germanism has passed to Scandinavia, but even there decline is evident: 'In our time, this productive peninsula, this hallowed land, is no longer inhabited by populations equal to those whom, for so long and in such profusion, it spread generously across the whole of Europe.'[8]

It is England (though not Britain as a whole) which emerges least scathed from Gobineau's general denunciation. There one finds the largest proportion of people still able to make a contribution to civilization and there too Gobineau emphasizes most strongly the link between polilical stability and relative ethnic purity: 'In England, where modifications of the stock have been slower and, up to now, less varied than in any other European country, we still see the institutions of the fourteenth and fifteenth centuries forming the base of the social structure.'[9] She has best preserved true Germanic usages and is 'the last centre of Germanic influence'.[10] He writes elsewhere: 'It has certainly not been the most brilliant, humane or noble of European states, but it is still the most vigorous.'[11] But again the compliment is simply comparative. Though England possessed in some remarkable degree the order and stability that Gobineau sought, he also noted her growing taste for democratic and egalitarian myths. To him order and egalitarianism were incompatible. Gobineau needed to assert that, whatever present appearances, England would soon experience the harmful consequences of 'progressive' political ideas:

The English legal system has lost its solidity. Reforms are imminent, and the Pandects are the reformers' ideal. The aristocracy is being challenged: democracy, hitherto unknown, is making claims which were not conceived on Anglo-Saxon soil. The innovations and ideas which find favour, and the reorganization of dissolving forces, all reveal an urge towards change which has been brought over from the continent. England is in the process of entering, in its turn, into the midst of romanity.[12]

The effects of Huguenot migrations, of Scottish Union, and of the recent Irish influx are essential to the harsher aspects of Gobineau's description. It would have been puzzling indeed had he exhibited unqualified approbation for a country which was in reality, from many points of view, the harbinger of all that he hated in society and politics.

Gobineau described as follows the area in which the last Aryan-German elements were to be traced:

The greatest abundance of life and strength is found today – fighting a losing battle against the inevitable triumph of Roman chaos – concentrated in the group of countries which fall inside a line which, drawn roughly, begins at Tornio in Finland and, after bringing in Denmark and Hanover, goes down the Rhine at a short distance from its right bank as far as Bâle, embraces Alsace and nothern Lorraine, closely follows the course of the Seine to its mouth, continues around Great Britain and takes in Iceland to the west.[13]

With comparative prudence Gobineau agrees that this should not be interpreted too rigidly. Even so, it reflects his indictment of the ethnic situation in the greater part of the German states. But even within the circle of Aryan influence the days of civilization are strictly numbered.

The observations farther afield are scarcely less critical. Africa, for instance, is dismissed as the seat of truly barbarous despotisms. Russia is the centre of the Slav menace and, as we noted previously, the combination of this predominant racial element and of her geography makes her an important contributor to the decline of Aryan-German civilization. He comments:

> The Russian Empire – a land of transition between the yellow races and the semitized and romanized nations from the south and from Germany – lacks essential homogeneity, has only been slightly and insufficiently influenced by the noble essence, and is capable of building up only imperfectly its multiple borrowings from Hellenic, Italian and French elements and from Germanic sources.[14]

This Slav peril is but the vanguard of the yellow menace beyond. In dealing with the Chinese Gobineau is ready to acknowledge the better features of their civilization, which stem from such qualities of the yellow peoples as their respect for law and their appreciation of moderate liberty. But he is equally aware of the fragility of this liberty, particularly in the face of the materialistic and utilitarian instincts of the Yellows. He claims that Chinese history shows these encouraging common ownership, as well as despotism from government and bureaucracy. Relating this to issues on his own continent, Gobineau suggests that, if socialist ideas triumph in Europe, then their application will create a form of society manifesting many similarities with that of China. Socialist doctrines are thus seen as materialistic in inspiration and bureaucratically despotic in outcome, and as especially the result of the old and insidious influences of the yellow race transmitted through Slavonic Russia. It was this connection in Gobineau's mind which led him to remark to Tocqueville that, 'Observing such a great desire to open up China and to become involved with all that part of the ancient continent, so voracious in its old age, I might be surprised that we do not examine more carefully the consequences of such camaraderie – that is, if I were still capable of being surprised by anything.'[15] This assessment of China and of her materialistic instincts produces the ironical result that her communist revolution fits more coherently into the thesis of Gobineau than into that of Marx. While her conversion to communism is difficult to accord with Marx's economic analysis of class conflict, it appears much more naturally within the logic of Gobineau's view of the intimations of her racial instincts.

Still, it is China's stability which most impresses him, and causes him to make frequent comparison with India whose society, based upon a caste system relating class to breeding, he naturally finds attractive:

The longevity of India is simply the beneficial result of a natural law which has only rarely been in a position to work for the better. Having a dominant race ever the same, this country has always maintained similar elements. On the other hand, everywhere else, groups mingling without restraint or choice have rapidly succeeded each other and have failed to bring life to their institutions, because these latter have themselves swiftly disappeared in the face of others derived from new instincts.[16]

It was such instincts which led Gobineau to prophesy the failure of British rule in India. Stressing the fundamental incompatibility between rulers and ruled he suggested that the time was near when India would again enjoy fully her indigenous laws and customs without foreign interference. Although he erred in underestimating the Sepoy disaffection which was the immediate cause of the forthcoming mutiny, much of his general picture of incompatibility was borne out by subsequent events. For Gobineau India past and present was an example of the need for, and the benefits of, racial purity and social segregation and isolation. He certainly did not use the example of India to justify any kind of European imperialism in terms of racial superiority.

The American continent receives little favour. Gobineau scorns the ethnic corruption of the Latin portion, concluding that, 'South America, corrupted by creole blood, has henceforth no means of halting the decline of its half-breeds of every class and variety. Their decadence has no remedy.'[17] His assessment of the North is more subtle but finally hardly less derogatory. Liberal contemporaries looked to the United States with optimism as the land of progress and freedom. Many of these shared with Gobineau a detestation of European society (though the reasons for revulsion normally differed) – but he and they clearly disagreed as to whether any improvement upon the old world could be found in the new. He wrote concerning them: 'The Western world is the vast stage on which they imagine the blossoming forth of nations which, through the inherited experience of past civilizations, will enrich our own and will accomplish things of which the world has yet only dreamt.'[18] It is allegedly in order to judge the wisdom of this view that Gobineau undertakes his examination of the United States.

The outcome is an extension of his earlier hostile view. Sympathy to the United States is only apparent when Gobineau faces again the problem of reconciling his hostility to democracy with his advocacy of participation in social and political activity – a difficulty already encountered in his provincialist writings. There he had referred to the Americans as 'our masters in administrative freedom'.[19] In the *Essai* he does not deny that the individualism associated with the white race has manifested itself in the United States, for he appreciates the real resemblance between what he calls the 'self-government' of contemporary New York and the autonomies claimed by the ancient Franks. Nor is he unaware of the possible racial echoes in the vitalist drive that spurs on the pioneers of the westward-moving frontier.

Yet he is altogether more insistent that mass immigration of debased stocks is swamping the Anglo-Saxon elements of North America. Of the majority of newcomers Gobineau comments:

They are a very mixed assortment of the most degenerate races of olden-day Europe. They are the human flotsam af all ages: Irish, cross-bred Germans and French, and Italians of even more doubtful stock. The intermixture of all these decadent ethnic varieties will inevitably give birth to further ethnic chaos. This chaos is in no way unexpected or new; it will produce no ethnic mixture which has not already been, or cannot be, realized on our continent. Absolutely nothing productive will result from it, and even when the ethnic combinations resulting from infinite unions between Germans, Irish, Italians, French and Anglo-Saxons join in the south with racial elements composed of Indian, Negro, Spanish and Portuguese essence, it is quite unimaginable that anything could result from such horrible confusion but an incoherent juxtaposition of the most decadent kinds of people.[20]

For Gobineau Crèvecoeur's 'new man' could exist only as a being virtually devoid of any ethnic worth. In expressing his disgust with the American present and future Gobineau provided one of the most vivid indictments of the great experiment. He had kept his discussion of the United States until towards the end of the *Essai*,

declaring that if hope could not be placed there then civilization
was indeed doomed. And he found no cause for hope:

Human society can be rejuvenated and a superior – or at least different – civilization . . . can be created only through the agency of a
relatively pure and young race. Such a race does not exist in America . . .
Though claiming to be a young nation, the Americans are in fact made
up of all the old peoples of Europe; they are less restrained because of
their more accommodating laws, but they are no more dynamic than
before. During the long, sad journey from Europe to the New World,
the Atlantic air does not change them. They arrive the same people as
when they left. A simple change in geographical location cannot regener-
ate races which are more than half exhausted.[21]

Such ethnic condemnation was in full accord with Gobineau's
need to denounce the political and social tendencies of the American experiment.

His stand on the slavery question is subtle. There was little
need for him to stress further the inferiority of the Negro. Instead
he used the issue to maintain his assault upon white America. He
castigated the inconsistency of those who advocated slaveholding
while proclaiming liberal and egalitarian doctrines in other spheres.
Of the enslavement of the Negro and the dispossession of the
Indians, Gobineau comments that the true Aryan invaders of old
were never so ruthless, since they did grant to the conquered some
part of the soil and, unlike white Americans, they did not exhibit
'the need to destroy everything around them which was not related
to their own thoughts'.[22] He adds: 'Our own civilization is the only
one which has ever possessed this homicidal instinct and at the
same time this murderous potentiality of inflicting death; it is the
only one which has constantly striven to wreak general destruction,
while advocating limitless gentleness rather than anger, and even
thinking itself excessively indulgent.'[23] Gobineau claims that he
does not find such inconsistencies reprehensible since the Whites
are acting according to ethnic laws in conformity with their debasement. But, in reality, we can observe an indictment of their
position:

They were not hypocritical in thinking themselves entitled to join in
the concert of protest which the eighteenth century directed against
every kind of political constraint, against Negro slavery in particular.
Sects and nations are just like women in that they enjoy the privilege of
being able to defy logic and be responsible for the most surprising

moral and intellectual incongruities, while still not lacking sincerity. Washington's fellow-citizens, while forcefully demanding the emancipation of the Negroes, did not think themselves obliged to set an example.[24]

In light of these arguments it is necessary to reject Hannah Arendt's firm pronouncement that, 'Gobineau tried in vain to get a wider audience by taking a side in the American slave issue and by conveniently building his whole system on the basic conflict of black and white.'[25] If he took a side at all, it was certainly (in form at least) not the one implied by her comment. Far from supporting Negro slavery in the *Essai*, Gobineau utilizes the issue to further his attack upon the principles and inconsistency of men such as Washington and Jefferson, and of their successors. Progressive political ideas he already regarded as misleading and chimerical; in the American case he now suggested also the insincerity of some of their most famous proponents.

In another context there is a further example of Gobineau's willingness to assume a benevolence towards the Negro in order all the better to assault the debasement of white men. Writing of the relative intellectual merits of different races, he had commented caustically that, 'I absolutely refuse to make use of the argument, "Every Negro is a fool." My main reason for avoiding it is that I should have to recognize, for the sake of balance, that every European is intelligent – and heaven keep me from such a paradox!'[26] Gobineau was fully aware that all these arguments and asides concerning the United States in general and the slavery question in particular could scarcely guarantee the *Essai* an unequivocally enthusiastic reception in any quarter across the Atlantic. None the less the preliminary theoretical exposition was speedily translated by Henry Hotz and published at Philadelphia in 1856 under the title, *The Moral and Intellectual Diversity of Races with Particular Reference to their Respective Influence in the Civil and Political History of Mankind*. The edition included a lengthy appendix on the theme of the plurality of human species by Josiah Nott, co-author of the *Types of Mankind*. At the head of the translation Hotz declared that, 'To the Statesmen of America this work, the first on the races of men contemplated from the point of view of the Statesman and Historian rather than the Naturalist, is respectfully dedicated'. Gobineau could scarcely share such sentiments. As pro-slavery publicists, Hotz and Nott made use of the parts of the *Essai* which implicitly supported their case, but they conveniently ignored Gobineau's strictures on American decay generally and upon slaveholding in particular. Gobineau resented this distortion of his views and wrote to Prokesch-Osten: 'Do you not wonder ... at my friends the Americans, who believe that I am encouraging them to bludgeon their Negroes, who praise me to the skies for that, but who are unwilling to translate the part of the work which concerns them?'[27] Thus, although a version of the *Essai* was soon used by the advocates of slavery, Gobineau disapproved of their text and in no way saw his work as commending either the slaveholders or those who believed in the myth of a great American future.

The reception of Gobineau's book in Europe was also unsatisfactory to him. But he could scarcely expect sympathy from the contemporary world which the work so pessimistically condemned. Most critics expressed polite dissent, but praised the author's boldness and originality. Their tepid response seemed to Gobineau further evidence of contemporary intellectual mediocrity and thereby confirmed his convictions. To Prokesch-Osten he commented:

I never thought that I could come and say to our present peoples 'You are in complete decadence, your civilization is a mire, your intelligence is merely a smoky lamp, you are already half-entombed', without getting some sharp retorts. I am therefore not much bothered by them. What I do observe is that I have struck at the very nerve of liberal ideas.[28]

Manfred Steinkühler concludes from his thorough, but as yet unpublished, study of the *Essai*'s reception beyond the Rhine that, 'The Gobinist racial doctrine did not have at that time any notable success at all in Germany.'[29] The harshest treatment came from professional scholars and the greatest degree of acceptance was naturally found among the dilettantes. Gobineau somewhat overestimated his success and claimed that, despite some German intellectual timidity, 'I have gained some valuable friendships there.'[30] Included among these must be that of Adelbert von Keller, who later wrote to Gobineau concerning the *Essai* that, 'It is the basis for all my historical and philosophical doctrines.'[31] Both Gobineau and Tocqueville felt that it might well be through success in Germany that the work would become accepted in France. The latter – no doubt in fear as well as in consolation –

wrote this to the author: 'Alone in Europe, the Germans possess the talent for getting impassioned about what they see as abstract truth, without any regard for the practical consequences – and it is they who could provide you with a really favourable audience whose opinions would sooner or later have repercussions in France.'[32] Although this prediction seemed irrelevant in the years immediately after publication, it was eventually to be justified in large degree.

The immediate French reaction was similar to the German, and it encouraged Gobineau to denounce his countrymen still more harshly: 'I should like to be seriously discussed in my own country. . . . But the French, who are always ready to set anything afire – materially speaking – and who respect nothing either in religion or politics, have always been the world's greatest cowards in matters of science.'[33] The disagreement of French intellectuals was, again, polite but firm. Most critics adopted the sort of formula epitomized in Armand de Quatrefages's comment: 'While not agreeing with M. de Gobineau, I none the less acknowledge what is interesting and useful in his work.'[34] Charles de Rémusat asserted that social explanation totally in terms of race was an exaggeration, but he allowed that, from the marriage of ethnology and history, 'a whole science is born' and that, 'in the future every historian must take account of it'.[35] Alfred Maury, secretary of the Institut de France, described the Essai as 'a singular mixture of the most serious learning, highly debatable ideas and hypotheses that are rash and very fanciful'.[36] Prosper Mérimée argued straight-forwardly against Gobineau that it was defective educational policies rather than any organic degeneration which occasioned intellectual mediocrity. Ernest Renan's reluctance to write a prompt review of the Essai disappointed Gobineau, but his re-action can be judged from private correspondence with its author. Again, equivocation is the most striking feature:

You have completed a most remarkable book, full of vigour and intel-lectual originality, but a work very ill-suited to being understood in France – or, rather, one entirely fitted to being badly understood there . . . At the beginning of things the racial factor is immensely important, but progressively it loses its significance . . . Civilisation . . . will doubt-less be inferior in nobility and distinction to that of aristocratic ages. But will it be inferior in any absolute manner? On that I myself hesitate to pronounce.[37]

But, whatever his reservations, Renan agreed that the publication of the work had been of some service.

It was however this last feature – the practical effects of the work – which particularly disturbed the most eminent of French commentators, Gobineau's friend Tocqueville. The latter had already suggested in his great work on America that racial explanations were simply the result of historians' laziness. Now he objected to the fatalism and materialism engendered by such arguments and stressed especially the inadvisability of airing these doctrines at such a moment. Tocqueville emphasized that, since racial determinism would limit, indeed abolish, free will and human liberty, the *Essai* could only weaken the already declining spirit of his contemporaries. Gobineau, convinced that the enfeeblement of mind was both irreparable and universal, felt absolved from considering any such effects. Parading as a pure scientist announcing social facts however unpleasant, he cleared himself of the moral responsibility with which Tocqueville tried to burden him. He contended that he was not acquitting or condemning mankind, but merely announcing neutrally that humanity was in its death-throes: 'I am no more a murderer than the doctor who announces that the end is at hand. If I am wrong, then of my four volumes nothing will remain. If I am right, then the facts will elude any desire to see them otherwise than as determined by the laws of nature.'[38] Tocqueville provided an extensive refutation of the medical analogy, suggesting that in such a case the remaining time might be used to prepare for eternity. Societies having no such eternity, Tocqueville believed that men would simply behave still worse after being informed of the imminent demise of the social body.

As a social pragmatist Tocqueville posed practical questions replete with future significance:

What advantage can there be in persuading base peoples living in barbarism, indolence or slavery that, such being their racial nature, they can do nothing to improve their situation or to change their habits and government? Do you not see inherent in your doctrine all the evils engendered by permanent inequality – pride, violence, scorn of fellow men, tyranny and abjection in all their forms?[39]

That final question contains implicitly the most devastating judgment upon Gobineau's work and upon the eventual historical fate of the Aryan myth. In his own time Gobineau denounced the modern world and, in return, the *Essai* met with little favourable response among contemporaries. He saw its rejection as supporting his case. The acceptance of his doctrine, in some form, was not found in the contemporary world which his work denounced so bitterly. Instead, a version of his theory was to be cultivated in a later age which then reaped the harvest of violence, scorn and tyranny that Tocqueville had prophesied.

6 The Question of Race, Religion and Morality

In the first confrontation with Tocqueville we distinguished between Gobineau's treatment of Christianity as a doctrine and foundation for morality and his account of the Catholic Church as a useful social institution. In the *Essai* the arguments are projected farther, but we also realize that his harshness towards Christianity has become a symptom of general hostility to all world-religions and to any ethical system which questions the ethnic determinants of morality. Though the thought is never explicitly stated, it is in reality dangerous to Gobineau's theory that God, however conceived, should stand in the central position which belongs to race alone. To the race-theorist the material body is of fundamental importance and he must regard suspiciously any ideas which dissociate the spirit of man from its corporeal framework and which make both in some manner dependent upon a transcendental spiritual power. World-religions are additionally dangerous because, with their bent towards proselytization, they promote the excessive racial mixture which Gobineau abhors.

Religion, particularly in its institutional manifestations, may be useful if kept in correct perspective. Gobineau allows that, 'Religion, even when imperfect or false . . . forbids men to give way at every opportunity to their destructive instincts'.[1] He concedes that it forms one of the principal features of every civilization. He emphasizes indeed the religious feelings of the aryanized Anglo-Saxons, though he is careful to add that they never accepted 'either the terrors or the despotism of the faith'.[2] But perhaps it was these very terrors which encouraged Gobineau to make a show of orthodoxy and talk of 'the recognition of the hand of God in the conduct of the world – a firm and ultimate principle to which we must adhere, accepting it in the full sense in which it is understood by the Catholic Church'.[3] This was an impressive opening to the work, but soon he was rejecting firmly any attempt to free religious beliefs from the trammels of racial laws: 'Like all other major social factors, the religion of a people is constituted according to their ethnic situation.'[4]

The theoretical section of the *Essai* contains not only the argument that irreligion does not necessarily bring about the fall of civilizations but also the assertion that, 'Christianity does not create and does not transform the aptitude for civilization.'[5] Gobineau argues that Christians are found in all climates and latitudes and does not openly deny that all mankind is able to recognize Christian truth. But this is not to say that all men can aspire to civilization through Christianity rather than by virtue of racial qualities. His point is that Christianity's chief concern is not with earthly existence, and he rejects its civilizing potential thus:

It uses all civilizations and is above all . . . No civilization whatever has excited its envy or contempt; and because of this rare impartiality, and the consequences that were to flow from it, the law could rightly call itself 'Catholic', or universal. It does not belong exclusively to any civilization. It did not come to bless any one form of earthly existence; it rejects none, and would purify all.[6]

Christian precepts have laudable social effects in so far as they condemn violence and encourage men to be more reflective and in manners more gentle. Christianity is seen as uplifting the spirit of man, but it can only do this to the degree that the racial make-up of the individual allows. The universalist appeal of Christianity presents Gobineau with dangers: 'The greatest novelty that Christianity has brought into the world is that of acting in a manner altogether contrary to preceding religions. While they had their own peoples, it had none. It had chosen no one. It addressed itself to everybody.'[7] However unwittingly, Gobineau was himself deeply indebted to the traditional idea of the Chosen People. The Christian adoption of a more egalitarian position could not fail to meet with his disapproval. In order to maintain publicly any kind of Christian position he was thus forced to ignore Christianity's contribution to civilization. The sole and inconvenient alternative would have been to suggest that it was indeed destructive of civilization. Having thus apparently removed

Christianity from any significant place in his social theory he was somewhat freer to pursue the inegalitarian implications of his own doctrines.

Other world-religions, even if regarded as less universalistic than Christianity, are seen as dependent upon racial explanations to the same degree. Gobineau writes, for instance, that, 'Mohammed discovered the religion that was most in conformity with the ideas of his people'[8] – ideas which are themselves ethnically determined. The ethical problems posed by a theory of racial determinism have already been touched upon, but they are best illustrated by reference to Gobineau's treatment of Buddhism. This he was able to criticize more freely than Christianity. Buddhism is regarded as a perversion of the one world-faith for which he shows any real sympathy – the hierarchical religion of the Hindu brahmins. Gobineau was naturally hostile to the Buddhist rejection of caste and he attacked vigorously the egalitarian implications which he had glossed over when discussing Christianity. Buddhism marks not only a denial of the need to organize the social hierarchy according to racial merit but also a refusal to base moral judgments upon ethnic considerations: 'Proceeding inversely from what we see in proper philosophies, instead of making morality stem from ontology, it is, on the contrary, ontology which is derived from the moral law.'[9] Gobineau might have made the same charge against Christianity had that not been inconvenient. He relishes his account of the decline of Buddhism into a religion of prayer-wheels and suggests that his examination shows 'what little a political or religious doctrine that prides itself at being founded solely upon morality and reason succeeds in producing for men and for societies'.[10]

If Buddhist prayer-wheels lead to this paralysis of action, it can scarcely be said that Gobineau's rejection of reason and conventional morality produces anything more conducive to moral activity. The ethical superiority of the white race is based on tautology and is implicit in its very definition. From this logic it is impossible to escape. Yet this does not prove the argument correct; it simply renders it immune from refutation within its own terms. In Gobineau's account man is unable to change the essence which controls the actions susceptible to moral judgment, and his theory implies the elimination of any notion of individual responsibility. This produces a paralysis of moral judgment and an inability to give significant political or social guidance. Within the terms of his own system Gobineau still had the power to describe society. But his logic annulled any right to make prescriptive – as distinct from predictive – statements about its future development. Gobineau never accepted the full consequences of this logic but the morally nihilistic results of his theory perhaps contributed to the absence of any adequate discussion of the fundamental questions of political and social rights and obligations. Within the framework of the racial theory such discussion would have been superfluous. In implication the theory is morally totalitarian and all other value systems must be annihilated or severely subordinated. Above all, traditional religious morality must be nullified. Gobineau develops instead an ethic of moral justification by blood alone which takes man beyond all conventional ideas of good and evil.

To a considerable degree Gobineau did accept the results of the prescriptive paralysis. He admitted not only that the decline of modern civilization was inevitable but also that it was already too advanced for men to retard appreciably the speed of decay. Thus the *Essai* is devoid of practical recommendations about politics and society. But the logic of the theory also calls into question the status of his descriptive statements about political and social ideas and institutions. The theory sees them as secondary and derivative. Yet we have noted that most of Gobineau's firmest social convictions antedate such a racial explanation. It is therefore realistic to regard these ideas and institutions, as depicted in the *Essai*, not as the secondary consequences of the racial theory but as representing the convictions which themselves originally justified the development of a racial explanation. In such an interpretation it is the theory of race which is itself secondary and the account of the political and social ideas and institutions which becomes primary. Gobineau readily admitted, indeed, that the *Essai* resulted from his meditation upon contemporary political disorders – 'the bloody wars, the revolutions and the breaking up of laws'.[11] He also proclaimed that, 'Deep down, this is my state of mind – a hatred of democracy and of its armed ally, Revolution. This hatred have I satisfied by showing revolution and democracy in their true light, and by stating from whence they spring and to where they lead.'[12] It is in the context of such statements and of our account of the evolution in Gobineau's thought that we conclude that the allegedly secondary political and social features must be given full emphasis and must be considered, to large degree, independently of the determinism imposed by the racial theory. Mindful of all this we shall examine firstly Gobineau's remarks on social order and then proceed to discuss his treatment of socially disruptive forces.

Gobineau's writings prior to 1850 indicated a search for social order. He was convinced that without the sense of hierarchy and stability which this implied there could be no meaningful freedom. The *Essai* continues the quest, but also forces the conclusion that it is now doomed to failure. Indeed by introducing his particular version of racial explanation Gobineau demonstrated a tragic weakness at the heart of society itself. Like civilization, society forms and grows through human communication, by war, conquest, commerce and migration. But it is by such means that miscegenation also is promoted. Thus social life seems to bring as many ills as benefits and carries tragically the seeds of its own destruction.

Gobineau denies any great social aptitude on the part of Yellows or Blacks. It is, ironically, the Whites who possess the strongest social instincts, as well as the greatest civilizing ability, and thereby hasten social decay. Among them the Aryans seem somewhat reserved, not because of any inability to promote social development but because they cherish their individual independence. Gobineau says of the Aryan-German 'The lofty conception of his individual worth and the love of isolation which followed therefrom completely dominated his thinking and inspired his institutions.'[1] This illuminates Gobineau's revulsion against his own society and his supposed desire to minimize his contacts with it. He alleges that European history marks a decline from a stage of equality among the Aryans themselves to a situation where feudalism introduced inequalities within their own ranks and where status in society as a whole was increasingly divorced from ethnic merit. He suggests that society is now moving on to a stage in which the equality and unity of mankind will indeed exist, but only as a wholly unpleasant fact and as the direct cause of continued miscegenation. In reality all this is simply a rationalization of Gobineau's social alienation and of his detestation for egalitarian ideas.

Although the Aryan is associated with liberty and though social order is cherished because of its contribution thereto, it is difficult to see what positive freedom Gobineau has in mind. The primitive Aryan is free in his isolation, guarding jealously his personal liberty, but this picture gives us no idea of freedom within more complex social situations. There is every sign that Gobineau conceives of it as freedom for a minority alone. If the derteminism is accepted then it is questionable, in addition, whether even Aryan freedom is meaningful. Gobineau's attitude towards modern ideas of liberty is harsh. For instance, even though so recently a journalist himself, he is extremely cautious concerning freedom of the press, writing that its independence seems 'scarcely compatible with any orderly government'.[2] Though he does not go so far as to deny this freedom he emphasizes more strongly its threat to social order than its contribution to the preservation of liberty. Similarly, while not condoning religious fanaticism (for instance, he reproaches the Aryan-Germans for the extreme hostility they showed at first to Christianity), he stresses that tolerance is often the mark of degeneration and undue apathy. He suggests, for example, that the growth of toleration in the later Roman Empire was the result of a 'theology in decay'.[3] His earlier sympathy for the Enlightenment's progress towards tolerance is absent. Again, in the *Revue Provinciale* Gobineau had repeatedly urged the link between local rights and political freedom. In the *Essai* this theme is discussed much less positively, appearing mainly – and by implication – in those passages where the author discusses Aryan isolationism and where he denounces the effects of urbanization and governmental growth. From all these various standpoints Gobineau's attachment to liberty seems far less firm than before.

His treatment of government and institutions takes on new significance if it is not seen merely as derivative from his racial exposition. Naturally in his previous, as in his subsequent, diplomatic writings he was compelled to give a more conventional institutional analysis than was possible in a thesis claiming that institutions were, in some sense, ethnically determined. The destiny of states he carefully separated from the fate of civilizations, and the *Essai* reveals a conception of the state embodying a form of the general-will idea:

A political centre, being the collective unifier of human wills, will have a volition of its very own . . . It has emotion and reason. Despite the multiplicity of minds from which it is constituted, it has a composite individuality, which results from the common pooling of all the notions, propensities and ideas suggested by the mass of men.[4]

Despite his hostility to centralized governemnt, Gobineau occasionally wandered into state-worship. In his search for order he approved the alleged Etruscan notion of the sacredness of the person representing the laws:

It was never believed that the agent of sovereign power could revert to being the equal of the herd. Because he had participated in the government of the populace, he stayed for ever above them. The recognition of such a principle placed the State in a sphere of everlasting admiration, gave an incomparable reward to those who served it, and suggested an example to be most nobly emulated.[5]

Thus, despite his concern for Aryan liberty, Gobineau is attracted to a more authoritarian position when confronted with the threat to social order presented by the claims of the masses.

Early in the *Essai* Gobineau indicated what constituted a bad government, while denying that it could of itself cause the decline of civilization. He suggested that government was bad, 'when it is set up by a foreign power, . . . when it is based on conquest pure and simple, . . . when the principle on which it rests becomes vitiated and ceases to operate in the healthy and vigorous way it did at first, . . . and when by the very nature of its institutions it gives colour to an antagonism between the supreme power and the mass of the people, or between different classes of society'.[6] So frequently did these conditions occur that good government was allegedly a historical rarity. With the primitive Aryans governmental control was naturally limited in order that as individuals they should have the greatest freedom compatible with a degree of social organization: 'The Aryans, divided into tribes or small nations concentrated in large villages, placed at their head leaders whose very limited authority had nothing in common with the absolute omnipotence exercised by sovereigns among black and yellow peoples.'[7] He adds that, 'a power deriving so completely from the general will could only be a fairly weak delegation'.[8] It was in order to maintain such control over the sovereign power that the Aryans refused to accept any single idea of patriarchal government. The emphasis on the general will seems similar to the apparent advocacy of political participation which was noted in the *Revue Provinciale*. Whereas there it implied, however briefly, some kind of support for democracy, it is evident that, in describing here participation in primitive Aryan government, Gobineau is referring to the activity of an élite alone. He defines a 'true spirit of government' as 'to know how to preserve the past while meeting the needs of the present'.[9] Having conceived of history as the tale of the élite's gradual annihilation and of the emergence of popular government, Gobineau tends to suggest that this need to reconcile past and present increasingly required sterner rule. The governmental freedom of the Aryan golden age is suited only to men of quality. For the modern world, assailed by mass mediocrity, the principle is surely to be inverted and strong rule provided instead. Still, advocacy of such firm government does not prevent Gobineau from denouncing the possible excesses of sovereign power – as seen, for example, in the despotisms of the black peoples and of those, such as the Semites, influenced by them.

Of governmental forms later than the golden age it is monarchy that Gobineau most favours. He describes it as the most rational manner of organizing government, and he explains his contention thus:

A people always needs a man who understands its will and epitomizes, explains and leads it where it needs to go. If he errs, the people resists and rises to follow him who will not go astray. This is clear evidence of the need for constant interplay between the collective will and the individual will. In order to get a positive result, it is necessary for the two wills to unite. Separated they are useless.[10]

Though there is nothing in this explanation which would prevent a republican president from fulfilling the same function, it is monarchy which is regarded as the co-ordinator. But it would be wrong to suppose that, despite references to the general will, the monarch is viewed as the mouthpiece for popular sovereignty. Gobineau's advocacy of monarchy is not unequivocal. He was already distrustful of contemporary French monarchists and had saddled the French kings with much of the responsibility for the destruction of feudal liberties. In addition, we have observed his contention that primitive Aryan government was a republic of equals within the élite. Monarchy, like feudalism, is not an ideal, but merely a comparatively satisfactory compromise with the realities of imperfect circumstances.

Although Gobineau emphasizes the personal rights of the Aryans he fails to undertake a more general discussion of the interaction of rights and obligations between the individual and society. In any case, strict adherence to ethnic determinism would have rendered such a question meaningless by paralyzing free judgment. Law, which in a less exotic political theory might have been regarded as a means of indicating and preserving these rights and obligations, is no more than the written manifestation of certain ethnic intimations. Though no general conception of political obligation emerges from the *Essai* there are indications of the rights and duties of the élite at least: 'For the Aryan peoples honour had been . . . a theory of duty which accorded well with the dignity of a free warrior.'[11] This embodied, above all else, 'the lofty obligation of preserving his personal prerogatives against the most powerful assaults'.[12] Gobineau mocks the French nobility for their own general failure to understand this conception of duty. They are accused of having exceeded their rightful obligations to the monarchy, of having mistakenly sacrificed their liberties, their goods and their lives to its insupportable demands. Writing of the well-born Frenchman of the pre-revolutionary era Gobineau remarks:

His ideal of noble behaviour consisted in an absolute devotion and, because he was noble, he felt that no royal aggression could relieve him, in strict conscience, of the need for this boundless abnegation. This doctrine, like all those which attain the absolute, was certainly not lacking in beauty and grandeur. It was embellished with the most splendid courage. But this was only a Germanic veneer over imperial ideas. Its real source . . . was not far removed from semitic influences and, in accepting it, the French nobility had ultimately to fall into habits verging on servility.[13]

While this does something to illustrate Gobineau's conception of the rights and duties of the aristocratic élite, it provides insufficient criteria for assessing those of others. On the one hand Gobineau strives to maximize the political participation of the true nobility of ethnic worth and to maintain their independence, while, on the other, he increasingly leans towards strong government in order to counteract the ill-effects of mass influence. It is implicit that Gobineau is prepared not only to defend the rights of the élite at the expense of these masses but also to maximize, to the point of servility, the obligations of the latter to the state. Conversely the élite itself must be preserved from undue state interference. In terms of the ethnic theory this is to advocate government by the racially superior for the increase of their own political freedom and for the annihilation of that of others. In so far as Gobineau has any conception of political rights and obligations it is not one which applies uniformly to all men by virtue of their common humanity. It favours an élite, in terms both of class and race.

The function of this élite is to preserve, as far as possible, not only itself but social order too, Since laws and institutions are allegedly emanations from racial foundations, Gobineau's denunciation of miscegenation normally amounts to a plea for political conservatism. Theories of racial superiority – as well as the actual practice of racial discrimination – are frequently the consequence of such conservative desires rather than their source. To suit this pre-existent political conviction Gobineau, when describing the Aryan-Germans, referred to 'the obstinate affection for conservation that is natural to them',[14] and he suggested that, in their spiritual conquest of the Roman world, they had progressed with 'the slowness that is the first precondition for any solid achievement'.[15]

Like most conservatives Gobineau cherished the institution of the family. Naturally he depicted respect for it as an outstanding trait of the Whites. It was ironical that the bourgeoisie he despised should have been proverbially associated with virtuous family life and it was especially unfortunate that both Gobineau and his father should have contracted marriages ending in separation. Despite these personal inconveniences, Gobineau's work stresses the respect paid to women by the Aryans: 'The influence of women in a society is one of the surest tokens of the persistence of Aryan elements. The more this influence is respected, the more one is justified in declaring that the race affected by it approaches the true instincts of the noble stock.'[16] Though there is never any doubt that the Aryan-German warrior-husband is still the dominant figure, Gobineau's stress upon the dignity of woman is an important adjunct to his conception of the family as a fundamental feature of society, and one to be preserved against those who advocate a rootless mode of social existence.

His stress on Aryan military vigour is symptomatic of his conservative attachment to the army as a bastion in society, and therefore as an institution comparable in function with the Church. Though he had shown little enthusiasm for the soldiery of democratic Switzerland, none the less it was his more usually prevalent belief in the military contribution to the preservation of order that had much eased his eventual acceptance of renewed Bonapartist rule in France. In the *Essai* such attitudes are clearest in Gobineau's account of the army as one of the redeeming features of semitized Rome: 'Unique circumstances . . . require that armies be organized according to a single principle, that of hierarchical ordering and obedience.'[17] It is such hierarchical organization together with a system of power and obedience according to this hierarchy that are central to Gobineau's search for social order and to his conservatism. The army, at least, may reveal such qualities. He comments again upon its fate in Rome:

> It was to remain isolated in the midst of the State . . . In time it would be the only active part of the nation . . . Its first duty was to contain and master not external enemies but rather the internal rebels, the masses . . . The army was thus not only the last refuge, the last support, the sole flame, the heart of society – in addition, it alone provided supreme guidance, and generally did this well. Due to the excellence of the principle upon which all military organization constantly rests – a principle which is moreover an imitation, however imperfect, of the admirable order deriving from racial unity – the army used its hierarchy and discipline in a way that remained beneficial, turning to general advantage the talent of its leading figures and restraining the activity of others.[18]

But yet again Gobineau notes regretfully that such an army can only delay, not avert, disaster. Indeed, despite its conservative contribution within the state, the existence of the army has a more dangerous aspect.

If it be granted that a civilization contains within itself the seeds of its own decay, then similarly armies – because they are concerned with war and conquest and are therefore also instruments of contact and miscegenation – contribute, despite their hierarchical organization, to the process of degeneration. As suggested earlier, conquest and its effects had been fundamental concerns of previous

French historians, particularly those interested in racial divisions. In their view also it had contributed to the organization of classes. Gobineau emphasized the contacts between conquerors and conquered as much as he did their separation, and he reiterated that rule based solely on victory in war was likely to produce bad government. But he saw no escape from war and struggle and from the assimilation which followed upon both domination and submission. He claimed that once a family or people became a nation it had but one of two future destinies: 'It will either conquer or be conquered.'[19] In whichever case, miscegenation and decline would lie beyond. Gobineau ridiculed the idea that war could be prevented: 'Even if the friends of universal peace succeeded in making Europe disgusted with the idea of war, they would still have to bring about a permanent change in the passions of mankind.'[20] He suggested that a world-wide confederation for peace would only be possible 'if all races were actually gifted, in the same degree, with the same powers'.[21] Of that he saw no likelihood for the moment; for the future he regarded the cure as no better than the disease itself. Gobineau had little faith in man's ability to conduct international relations peacefully – a peculiar disadvantage, perhaps, for a professional diplomat. His attitude to the Crimean War showed vitalist elements that relate more closely to his depiction of Aryan military vigour than to his warnings against its ethnic effects. In the spring of 1854 Gobineau showed enthusiasm for the prestige that France would derive from her declaration of war upon Russia. In the autumn he was writing thus to Caroline: 'After twenty years of a peace that has promoted only corruption and revolution, we find ourselves in a military atmosphere which, from its very beginnings, has encouraged many fine things . . . I consider war, despite its evils, as a blessing.'[22] Perhaps he saw his approval of this assertion of military vigour as a final gesture of defiance to a world sinking in corruption. Nevertheless, in general, war and conquest, like the imperialism associated with them and like peaceful migration also, represented the human mobility and communication against which Gobineau's theory worked in the modern world. Consequently his search for social order often approaches a plea for social stagnation, if not for the abolition of social life itself.

8 The Disruption of Society

Gobineau's quest for social order fails because he considers that the disruptive elements in society eventually prevail over the conservative forces. Before 1850 he was already aware that the primary symptom of the disruption of modern civilization was the assault upon his own class. In the *Essai* the concept of the aristocratic race was introduced in partial defence of that class and the work can be seen as an attempt, by reference to the ethnic hierarchy, to justify the separation of classes and to advocate their preservation as long as possible in something approaching their feudal form. The connection with the contemporaneous concerns of Marx is evident, though the implications of the theories are in many respects different: Marx aimed to abolish class distinctions, while Gobineau elaborated the ideal of a carefully structured class order. Among the most important passages in the *Essai* is the following observation upon the social structure of the earliest forms of European civilization:

> Every society was founded on three primitive classes, each representative of an ethnic variety: the nobility, whose form more or less resembled that of the victorious race; the bourgeoisie, made up of half-breeds strongly related to the better stock; the populace, enslaved, or at least severely oppressed, as belonging to an inferior human variety – negroid in the south, finnish in the north.[1]

Gobineau refers elsewhere to a perfect political order in which 'the governing classes, in proper hierarchy, are strictly distinct, ethnically speaking, from those of the masses'.[2] The problem of linking coherently the racial theory to his other political convictions is illustrated when he is confronted in history with a socially accepted 'nobility' that is in fact of poor stock. Further, he denied that bad government could cause the downfall of civilizations and therefore, since the growth of class antagonism was one of the symptoms of such government, he was forced – in logic at least – to ignore class conflict as a sign of civilizational decay. Yet there can be little doubt that, in reality, it was the denial of the status and virtues of nobility which gave rise to the *Essai* and its theory of the decline of civilizations.

Though feudalism embodied in some degree a class structure compatible with the racial divisions postulated by Gobineau, it is the theory of the Hindu caste system – despite all the imperfections of its actual implementation – that he regards most highly of all. Of caste he comments:

The genealogical arrangement of social functions is simply a direct consequence of the idea of racial inequality, and wherever there have been victors and vanquished – especially when these two opposites in the state have been visibly separated by physiological barriers – there has been born among the stronger the desire to preserve power for their descendants.[3]

We have seen already Gobineau's assessment of the stability which India derived from the system. It embodied not only his idea of order but also his stress upon rule by the élite. He concluded: 'No one can refuse approval to a social body organized in such a way that it is governed by reason and served by unintelligence.'[4] Gobineau naturally expressed his regret that Europeans, even in feudalism, had not mastered the practice of such a theory.

Gobineau's treatment of class rivalries is intimately linked to his detestation of bourgeois materialism and of the associated threat to social order caused by increasing urban growth and industrialization. In the ethnic theory the influence of the yellow peoples is constantly related to the bourgeois mediocrity and pursuit of material gain that he abhorred. It is they above all who embody the materialistic instinct. It was of course paradoxical that Gobineau should substantiate his assault on one brand of materialism with a theory which, by making virtue and vice questions of a mystical blood-chemistry, made even morality material in yet another sense. The hostility to democratic materialism, evident already in his judgments on Switzerland, is maintained in the *Essai* where, for example, he writes that, 'material well-being has never been more than an external adjunct of civilization'.[5] Gobineau saw nothing

inconsistent in combating bourgeois capitalism and industrialization while himself defending aristocratic landed property. He
associated the latter less with the pursuit of wealth and gain than
with its contribution to social order and family security. But he was
quick to denounce those who, lacking this security, having little to
lose, and being excessively attached to material utility, strove to
disturb the *status quo* through economic or political change of a
drastic kind.

With the growing utilitarianism and acquisitiveness that increasingly characterized the modern world Gobineau associated, as
a further instrument of miscegenation, the extension of commerce.
Although he could sometimes see vitalist redeeming features in
war, he could not agree with those who saw them equally evident
in the entrepreneurial struggles of trade and modern industrialization. He was loath to concur that a nation's businessmen might
be as important to its fundamental stability as the army he favoured.
He simply emphasized what he found to be the unpleasant effects
of commercial activity: 'In states where commerce promotes
wealth and where wealth brings influence, it is always difficult to
avoid racially mixed marriages. Yesterday's sailor is tomorrow's
wealthy wooer, and his daughters soon seep through, like golden
rain, to the heart of the proudest families.'[6] While stressing thus
the disruptive effects of commerce upon the legitimate ordering of
society, Gobineau completely neglected his previous – but fleeting
– insight into the potentially greater sense of social responsibility
which might stem from broader distribution of wealth.

Economic studies are vigorously attacked as attempting theoretical justification of these disruptive tendencies. The comparison
with Marx fails at the point where Gobineau denounces also any
predominantly economic interpretations of history. About these he
remarks: 'I do not believe that egoistical calculations are paramount in the politics of a whole class, nor that immense results
follow from tiny causes.'[7] Although Gobineau may have regarded
this as clarifying his thoughts on the socialist view of history, it
scarcely conceals the fact that similar calculations – not unconnected
with issues of class – were influencing him, even if the result was
couched in non-economic terms. In a remarkable passage he returns
to his attack on economic theories (and by no means only those of a
socialist tendency) and upon historical interpretations drawn
therefrom:

Nothing is more contemptible than the credit given to this so-called science which wishes to give dogmatic cohesion to some general observations, ones applied with common sense in every really Aryan age, and which seeks to produce from them the greatest and most dangerous practical absurdities. It monopolizes only too well the confidence of a public susceptible to its pratings and it is emerging to take on the baleful role of a veritable heresy that gives the impression of dominating, manhandling and adapting to its own views our religion, laws and customs. Basing the whole of human life, and indeed of the life of nations, upon 'production' and 'consumption' – terms that have become quite cabbalistic among its cliques – it debases the original sublime meaning of the word 'honourable' by applying it to something as merely natural and proper as manufacturing labour. It makes private economy the highest of virtues, and, by means of exalting the advantages of prudence for the individual and the benefits of peace for the state, its maxims have almost turned public devotion, loyalty, courage and intrepidity into vices. This is no science – for it has as its narrow foundation the negation of the truest and most sacred needs of man.[8]

Here we are far from Gobineau's early studies of economics undertaken at Tocqueville's behest. Bearing in mind his own deterministic methods in the *Essai*, this could scarcely be an attack on monolithic historical theories in general. Gobineau is combating here a single theory of this type, one which was not only determined by the kind of material values he despised but which was also an interpretation dangerously rivalling his own monolithic conception of historical laws.

The processes of urbanization and industrialization associated with material advancement are, as before, regarded as socially dangerous. They could not create or preserve civilization and, on the other hand, they were indeed able to hasten its decline. Regarding the progress of ethnic contamination in England, for example, Gobineau writes: 'The birth of heavy industry increased this tendency by attracting into the country workers from all non-Germanic races.'[9] Gobineau had consistently seen towns as the centres of greatest political disorder and this now receives a racial explanation, for he alleges that there miscegenation progresses most rapidly: 'In Paris, London, Cadiz and Constantinople, we find traits recalling every branch of mankind, and that without going outside the circle of the walls, or considering any but the so-called native population.'[10] It is in cities that the human flux – represented and caused also by war and conquest – concentrates and works towards social and political disruption. An almost Horatian Gobineau contrasts their inhabitants socially and racially with the noble elements surviving in the provinces, enjoying *la vie des champs* in comparative purity. In this the racial theory simply gives a new interpretation of the old rivalries between town and country, between complex modernity and superficially simpler tradition.

Within the strict logic of ethnic determinism it should scarcely have been necessary for Gobineau to trouble much about threatening economic and political ideas. Like institutions they should have been treated simply as secondary emanations from the racial foundations. But the concern he showed for demolishing new economic ideas and explanations is not less evident in his treatment of competing political theories. He even allowed an importance to political eloquence, which his own doctrine ought surely to have rendered irrelevant:

A political eloquence which is firm, simple, brief, which expounds only facts and reasons, assures the greatest honour to the nation that makes use of it. Among Aryans of every era . . . it is the instrument of freedom and wisdom. But a political eloquence which is ornate, verbose, cultivated as a special talent, elevated into a form of art – a political eloquence that becomes rhetoric – is altogether a different matter.[11]

Perhaps he considered that the former kind of exhortation might still make some small contribution to retarding decline. He certainly wrote as though the latter brand was capable of speeding the process of degeneration.

He saw the egalitarian idea as the most corrupting. It was the very negation of the presupposition contained in the title of his work. His was a study not merely of the self-evident differences between races but also of their inequalities, which, to him at least, were equally self-evident:

The idea of an original, clear-cut and permanent inequality among the different races is one of the oldest and most widely held opinions in the world . . . Except in quite modern times, this idea has been the basis of nearly all theories of government. Every people, great or small, has begun by making inequality its chief political motto. All systems of caste, nobility and aristocracy, in so far as they are founded on the prerogatives of birth, have no other origin than this.[12]

The idea of equality, and the present progress towards a situation in which men would be truly equal in their degeneration, were both products of miscegenation:

The more heterogeneous the elements of which a people is composed, the more complacently does it assert that the most different powers are, or can be, possessed in the same measure by every fraction of the human race, without exception. This theory is barely applicable to these hybrid philosophers themselves; but they extend it to cover all the generations which were, are and ever shall be on the earth. They end one day by summing up their views in the words which, like the bag of Aeolus, contain so many storms – 'All men are brothers'.[13]

Here, at least, Gobineau's hostility to Christian egalitarianism seems overt and clear. His is a theory of natural inequality – in strength, beauty, intellect and civilizational capacity. It was devised to justify his aristocratic stand against the encroachment of egalitarian ideas, which were not only racially but also socially unnatural. He had already declared roundly to Lesclide that, 'Equality really exists only under terrors and despotisms.'[14] We can perhaps sympathize with his impatience in so far as the supporters of egalitarianism often tried to found their case upon risky demonstrations of equality in particular capacities rather than upon a clear moral imperative urging that, despite natural differences, men ought to be treated according to the realization of the one fundamental equality – each man's inalienable membership in the whole body of humanity. Gobineau's arguments were therapeutically useful in revealing the weaknesses of his opponents, but it is clear that, on the more positive side, he was incapable of assembling a superior case. He too muddled the subtle relationship and interaction between social description and political prescription.

If we connect Gobineau's hostility to equality with the dual morality (reminiscent of Nietzsche on master and slave) implied by the materialist ethic, we might expect some degree of support for slavery as part of a mode of social organization. We have already noted his hostility to the hypocrisy of the American slaveholders, but it would be wrong to generalize from this. Gobineau elsewhere writes: 'At certain periods, slavery had some legitimacy and one would almost be justified in saying that it results as much from the consent of him who suffers it as from the moral and physical dominance of him who imposes it.'[15] Where there is a real gulf between the races then the vanquished, if existing in slavery, may even become 'sincerely convinced that in all fairness it is justifiable'.[16] But this cannot be maintained once the inevitable processes of miscegenation take hold. One may conclude that, despite Gobineau's attempt to indicate a voluntary element in submission, crude slavery would prevail in any ideal society which he conceived. The defence of slavery is not emphasized in the *Essai* only because such an ideal society is now far from attainable. Thus is reinforced our earlier point that his specific attitude to American slaveholding is less concerned with the arguments for and against slavery itself than with his immediate desire to attack the inconsistencies of politicians in the United States. Otherwise, Gobineau's anti-egalitarianism would have necessitated a somewhat more favourable view of the slaveholders.

His rejection of egalitarian doctrines naturally implied hostility to democracy. Still, he was more convinced than many democrats of the inevitability of their triumph. Democracy he associated with disorder, revolution, and the crushing of élitist individualism. The racial theory regarded it as an unnatural form of government which, in practice, inverted the proper correlation between power and breeding. In the *Essai*, discussing inequality, he referred to the work as containing 'proofs indestructible as diamonds and upon which the viperish teeth of demagogic ideas will be powerless to gnaw'.[17] Once again the indications are that the theory is subservient to the primary need for denouncing contemporary political and social ills. Socialism, which he associated with democracy, was also explicity combated. In his treatment of China we have observed the connections made between socialism and corrupt materialism. Gobineau went on to suggest that despotism was the indispensable precondition for applying socialist (as well as other generally egalitarian) ideas with efficiency. He reprimanded the followers of Fourier and Proudhon and sought to show the enormity of the deprivations implied by their doctrines:

> Sacrificing to the bread-bin, to the threshold of a comfortable home, to a place at primary school what science has of the transcendental, what poetry has of the sublime, what the arts have of grandeur; casting aside every feeling for human dignity; abdicating one's individuality in what is most precious, the right to learn and understand, and to communicate to others what is hitherto unknown – all this is to give away much too much to material appetite.[18]

He added, in a disarmingly optimistic manner superficially reminiscent of his earlier complacency towards socialism: 'I should be very fearful of seeing this brand of happiness threatening us and our descendants, were I not reassured by the conviction that our present generation is as yet incapable of yielding to such delights at the price of such sacrifices.'[19] But we have learned enough to appreciate that we need lay no considerable store by such apparent compliments to contemporaries. At best, this represents an isolated exhortation that they should become aware of the socialist danger.

Gobineau's antipathy towards all these progressive ideas is at one both with his social position and with his racial theory. But the hostility now expressed to one other great nineteenth-century political idea – nationalism – is, at first sight, less comprehensible. Still, as we suggested when tracing the evolution of his harsher attitudes even before the *Essai*, there can be fundamental incompatibilities between racism and nationalism that are capable of outweighing the similarities in their roots or manifestations. Gobineau himself came to see nationalism as a vulgar expression of mass arrogance. He was so attached to the idea of deducing inequalities from differences that he even castigated democrats for their inconsistency in believing simultaneously both in equality and in the existence of separate national characters. For Gobineau what is important is the race, and the individuals of the élite. The nation, implying too often an awkward loyalty to territory or to some other negligible factor, remains for him comparatively unhonoured. Indeed the *Essai* embodies a remarkable attack on patriotism as a tyrannical semitic device. Gobineau claims that the idea originated when the Greek world was in full decline, suffering from the effects of semitization and consequently tending towards the adoption of absolutist political ideas. The groups in this society were too heterogeneous to recognize a common monarch and, therefore, in order to create an object for absolute and unifying loyalty, the Patria was invented:

They thought . . . of creating a fictional entity, the *Patria*, and each citizen was ordered – by all that men could imagine most dread and sacred, by law, by precedent, by prestige of public opinion – to sacrifice to this abstraction his judgments, his ideas, his habits, even down to his most intimate dealings and his most natural affections; and this abnegation, from day to day, from instant to instant, was a trifle alongside that other obligation which consisted in yielding up – upon a single sign and without a murmur – one's dignity, fortune and very life as soon as this same Patria was thought to demand it.[20]

Under such tyranny men convinced themselves that they remained free because the domination was not exercized essentially by a visible person. But to Gobineau it was tyranny none the less and it incorporated everywhere 'a guarantee of hatred and contempt'.[21]

It was in connection with patriotism that Gobineau made his notable attack on political fictions – an attack which is so applicable to himself that, unwittingly, it provides the most consummate single judgment on his own myth of blood: 'Centuries of experience prove that the worst tyranny is that which favours fictions, for these are by their very nature unfeeling and pitiless, boundless in their impudence and their pretensions.'[22] He suggested that in Europe the feudal era had found better objects of loyalty than the Patria and that this form of political illusion only reappeared when semitized elements came again to the fore: 'It was with their triumph that patriotism once more became a virtue.'[23] Nationalism is seen as the modern term describing this vain and uncritical admiration for one's unworthy compatriots and for the attempts to transform this emotion into a guiding political principle. To Gobineau the aristocrat it was a denial of the primary significance of social differences within nations; to Gobineau the racist it was the negation of the value of a supra-national élite; to Gobineau the champion of social order it was the instrument of further chaos in society. Having thus dismissed patriotism as a harmful illusion the way was clear for his denigration of France in later works.

These ideas – materialism, egalitarianism, democracy, socialism and nationalism – were the forces working towards the further disruption of social order. The racial theory appears to link them all to the ill-effects of miscegenation and to suggest that they were simply its consequences. Our contention has been that the relationship was quite the reverse. In reality, the *Essai* sprang from the deep-felt need to provide an all-embracing explanation of the development of these harmful ideas. Its primary purpose was not to expound a racial theory, as such, but to manipulate such a theory for the sake of attacking the destructive 'progressive' doctrines of the nineteenth century. Although Gobineau believed that contemporaries should be instructed in the nature of the disaster overtaking their society and civilization, his unrelenting pessimism indicated that the march to disorder was inexorable.

9 The Pessimistic Conclusion

In the foregoing pages we have referred repeatedly to the pessimism of the *Essai* and here, by way of concluding our discussion of the work itself, it will be useful to make a few more explicit comments on that topic. We now need to question whether the pessimism is genuine or whether it is a subtle challenge made by Gobineau to his contemporaries in order that they might be provoked into discerning and even curing the evils of modern society. In the first part of this study we traced the emergence in Gobineau of a pessimism that was almost entirely independent of racial considerations. Examining the *Essai* we have seen ethnic explanations reinforcing, but not creating, that pessimism. What the racial theory added was an assertion of man's impotence to remedy the situation. Previously Gobineau had merely described such dangers as egalitarianism and democracy; the racial theory suggested reasons for the inevitability of their triumph. In doing so it annihilated the grounds for exhortation which Gobineau had striven to establish before 1850. In the *Essai* the gloom is unrelieved and there is no indication that it may be dispelled by action or exhortation. It implies not only moral and social paralysis but also the futility of political argument and activity. Gobineau, unlike Rousseau for instance, presents no analysis of possible institutional improvements that might help to remedy a condition of social corruption. The *Essai* provides no challenge and its pessimism is relentless. Indeed, the evolution of Gobineau's thought, which we have traced, indicates that the pessimism is more fundamental than the racial theory itself.

Gobineau naturally objected to the idea of progress in history. He suggested that modern man, though he may well have profited from and improved upon the discoveries of the ancients, had on balance lost important knowledge and abilities in such fields as art and architecture, poetry and philosophy. Certain forms of supposed advancement, such as the exploration of the globe, had simply hastened decline. The march towards democracy and the recognition of equality among men, which many others welcomed as truly progressive, Gobineau assailed as symptomatic of degeneration. He avoided the most obvious allegations of modern progress by a formula which he erected into a law fatal in its operation:

We have turned out minds to other inquiries and other ends than those pursued by the earlier civilized groups of mankind. But while tilling our new field, we have not been able to keep fertile the lands already cultivated. We have advanced on one flank, but have given ground on the other. It is a poor compensation; and far from proving our progress, it merely means that we have changed our position.[1]

Regarding the human intelligence Gobineau produced the unhelpful conclusion that, 'Held prisoner for ever within a circle whose bounds it may not overstep, it never manages to cultivate one part of its domain without leaving the others fallow. It is always at the same time superior and inferior to its forebears.'[2] He thus denied the infinite perfectibility of man and suggested that his contemporaries be told: 'Your autumn is undoubtedly more vigorous than the decrepitude of the rest of the world, but it is autumn none the less. Winter is coming and descendants have you none.'[3] To Tocqueville he declared: 'I am convinced that the present enfeeblement of mind is not only universal but also incurable.'[4] It was these elements, the universality and inexorability of decline, which the racial theory added to his previous pessimistic assessment of the contemporary world.

His rejection of human progress contributes to and depends on an unflattering view of human nature, which is fundamental to an understanding of the pessimism in the *Essai*. With religious orthodoxy still in mind, he is careful not to deny certain human qualities to any, however debased they may be. But his previous sympathy for Enlightenment humanitarianism is forgotten. The *Essai* emphasizes the differences between men. It is only for the future that he stresses the unity of mankind – a unity which, as the outcome of common degeneration, he deplores. As in all political thinking, there is a close relationship between such a view of human nature and a certain view of society. Just as the unflattering tenets of a Hobbes are intimately linked with his assessment of society, so, no less, may we seek such an interaction in the Gobineau who wrote that, 'Man is the most wretched animal of all.'[5] This association between Gobineau's view of man and his opinions upon society, as well as the relationship of both to his racial theory, must be clarified. When John Nef suggests that, 'the doctrines concerning race and civilization . . . lead legitimately to a cynicism and despair concerning human nature',[6] he is making the commonest error in studies of Gobineau. The racial theory is not a fundamental datum to which all else must be related. It is rather the product of an important evolution in Gobineau's thought and experience. On this question it is again Tocqueville who provides the most perceptive and acceptable suggestion. He writes to Gobineau: 'Whether naturally or in consequence of the painful struggles you courageously faced in youth, you are accustomed to being contemptuous of humanity in general, and of your own country in particular.'[7] Tocqueville thus grasped the essential probabilities: that the racial theory was the upshot of certain views of society and human nature, and that these views were inseparable from one another and were the result of the primarily non-racial experiences and observations traced in the first part of this study.

In a recent account of social thought in mid-nineteenth-century England, John Burrow has suggested that then, 'What was required from a philosophy of history was not that it should be an engine of radical reform, but that it should provide something more like cosmic reassurance.'[8] In general terms, this observation has a continental relevance as well. It is therefore all the more striking to note that Gobineau's work so totally failed to fulfil this requirement. The *Essai* is certainly cosmic, but least of all in its reassurance and most of all in its pessimism. It is, as Jean Gaulmier suggests, *'le roman noir de l'humanité'*.[9] In the nineteenth-century literature of alienation and cultural despair it must be granted an important place and its final pages contain some of the most striking passages in the literature of decadence.

There Gobineau describes the Aryan blood in the last stages of its absorption. A unity of degeneration is at hand and it will be marked by 'the greatest mediocrity in all fields: mediocrity of physical strength, mediocrity of beauty, mediocrity of intellectual capacities – we could almost say, nothingness'.[10] In this era of

unity he prophesies that, 'Nations, or rather human herds, oppressed beneath a mournful somnolence, will thenceforth live benumbed
in their nullity, like the buffalo grazing in the stagnant waters of the
Pontine marshes.'[11] During this process of degradation humanity
will suffer the effects of depopulation and eventually reach physical
as well as moral annihilation. As to the date of this disappearance,
Gobineau concludes, from the speed and nature of miscegenation
in the modern world, that we should assign to man's existence 'a
total of twelve to fourteen thousand years, divided into two periods:
the first, which has passed, will have seen and possessed the youth,
vigour and intellectual greatness of humanity; the other, which
has already begun, will see its waning and inevitable decline'.[12]
There is no statement of imminent cataclysm, but rather a lamentation of slow degeneration stretching through five or six milennia
devoid of any true civilization. In the final lines of the *Essai*
Gobineau adds: 'What is truly sad is not death itself but the
certainty of our meeting it as degraded beings. And perhaps even
that shame reserved for our descendants might leave us unmoved,
if we did not feel, and secretly fear, that the rapacious hands of
destiny are already upon us.'[13]

There is certainly a distinction to be made between these
oracular pronouncements and the more pedestrian formulation of
Gobineau's social and political ideas prior to the introduction of
the racial theory. But we must also grasp the connection between
them. In the foregoing we have sought to establish their relationship by tracing the evolution of Gobineau's thinking through time.
In doing so we have suggested that his theory of racial aristocracy
and the visionary statements accompanying it are dependent on and
derivative from his earlier and humbler meditations on politics
and society. The general conclusion, confirmed in most racist
thought, is that the theory is not to be taken at face value. Despite
its 'scientific' claims its appearance is, in Gobineau's case, the
direct result of other types of social and political experience and
attitudes. Where he diverges from most racists is in his refusal to
offer hope and to utilize the theory for political exhortation. His
intellectual descendants were, however, less reserved.

Because the race-theory was derivative in the manner described,
Gobineau may seem to have left himself open to criticism by
writing retrospectively in the foreword to the second edition of the
Essai that, 'It is the expression of instincts carried from birth.'[14]

This is certainly misleading if we are supposed to interpret these instincts as primarily racial. In the last manuscript draft of this passage more of the real conviction is revealed, for there he precedes the above-quoted sentence with the following: 'It is a natural consequence of my horror and disgust at equality and democracy.'[15] Once we have replaced in context that remark – deleted we know not why or by whom from the printed text of the posthumously published edition – then a more accurate impression emerges. It was that horror and disgust, rather than conscious racial instinct or experience of racial conflict, which were the original motive forces behind the development of Gobineau's social and political ideas. None the less, in discussing the future extension of his thinking beyond the *Essai*, we do need to take account of what Jacques Barzun has termed, 'the "quality of belief" that a fine intellect accords to myths of its own manufacture'.[16] For there is no doubt as to the sincerity with which Gobineau came to maintain his racist philosophy. Because of such a conviction on his part we must note the effect of the theory upon his subsequent thought.

Gobineau was not yet forty when he assumed the role of racial prophet, publishing the universal obituary described above. It was an early age at which to pronounce so dogmatically and finally upon the course of history and the fate of societies and civilizations. In the final part of this study we shall examine Gobineau's social and political thinking in the years after the appearance of the *Essai*. It is a story of enlarged experience and of confrontation with new realities. Our account will seek to explain how Gobineau related such experiences to his existing ideas and to assess how his thoughts were adapted, developed or confirmed.

PART THREE

The Triumph of Social Pessimism

I did very badly to enter
the world in an era when there
is nothing great for me to do.

GOBINEAU
to Dom Pedro II (1875)

You will not transform behaviour;
you will not halt the current
dragging the world into the mire.
But you will have done your duty
and made your mark upon the age.

PROKESCH-OSTEN
to Gobineau (1875)

1 Diplomatic Horizons: Persia

The *Essai* was a work which had only the most slender foundations in personal social observation. It predated Gobineau's experience of societies beyond France, Switzerland and Germany. In the twenty years or so following its publication his diplomatic service took him eastwards to Persia and Greece, westwards to Newfoundland, southwards to Brazil and northwards to Scandinavia. Gobineau used these opportunities of examining different societies and of developing his ideas. It is these ideas, rather than his official conduct as a diplomat or even the accuracy of his observations, which primarily concern us here. He claimed to have 'repudiated completely any idea, whether true or false, of superiority over the peoples I was studying'.[1] To a surprising degree this was true but, though he was assisted by his lack of purely nationalistic prejudice, it was rash to claim that he could escape the bulk of the conclusions now established by the *Essai*. His supposed dedication to fairness often became inverted prejudice, as when, for instance, in the best Enlightenment manner, he pursued his object of denigrating French or European society by giving inflated praise to certain aspects of those beyond. But, more normally, the conventional interpretation of the *Essai* remained dominant.

Gobineau has left us books and letters of travel, formal studies of the history and society of lands visited, and many somewhat neglected diplomatic reports. Naturally, in the last, limitations of protocol and convention precluded completely free expression, particularly of Gobineau's more extreme racial convictions. Yet the basic attitudes to society, as we have already depicted them, do reappear with some frequency. This fact probably contributed substantially to his professional failure. He seldom got on well with either his French or foreign colleagues. He frequently berated the mediocrity of both and never fully accommodated himself to his superiors' preference for facts over ideas. His whole career disproved Tocqueville's assertion that diplomacy was 'the stage upon which you are called by nature to most distinguish yourself'.[2] Financial exigencies alone kept Gobineau in the service and his career was a tale of diplomatic mishaps.

His missions to Persia and Greece took him to lands which had been prominent in his universal history and which had both been involved in his depiction of Aryan-Hellenic civilization. Now they were linked in Gobineau's thinking by their common interest in the relations between Europe and Asia, and especially by their shared concern with regard to Russian expansion. Gobineau arrived in Persia in July 1855 as part of a mission to re-establish commercial relations, report on Anglo-Russian rivalries and protect the rights of French nationals. The mission soon became a legation with Gobineau as First Secretary and in October 1856, upon his superior's departure, he became Chargé d'Affaires, holding this position until he left for Europe in January 1858. He returned to Teheran as Minister in January 1862, remaining until September 1863. During both his visits his dominant international concern was to contain Russian expansion: 'If the Persians ... unite with the western powers, they will march against the Russians in the morning, be defeated by them at noon and become their allies by evening. All the courses seem to me to have the same upshot.'[3] This obsession with the Slav menace remained to the end.

On Persian society itself Gobineau's writings provide much information. His visits gave an admirable opportunity of furthering his oriental interests. An excess of enthusiasm and a lack of modesty led him into the unwise composition of two pretentious but worthless works of supposed linguistic scholarship, the *Lecture des Textes Cunéiformes* (1858) and the *Traité des Écritures Cunéiformes* (2 vols, 1864). Rather better than these, and no more unreliable than the *Essai*, were a two-volume *Histoire des Perses* (1869) and a survey of *Religions et Philosophies dans l' Asie Centrale* (1865), the latter being a work of somewhat erratic scholarship but of abiding interest. The Persian experience also inspired a collection of short stories, the *Nouvelles Asiatiques*, published in 1876. Best of all, however, is the description of his first sojourn in Persia, as given in the illuminating travelogue *Trois Ans en Asie* (1859).

Here, in recording direct observations, Gobineau's orientalism was at its least fallible. Unlike many of the orientalist romantics he did at least see at first hand something of the eastern world. None the less, it must be admitted that he often rashly generalized about the whole of Asia from his still limited experience, and that the pre-suppositions now firmly implanted by the racial theory did seriously limit his capacity for accurate observation.

His love of the Orient is manifest in the fact that, however great his hatred towards the vain nationalism of individual European countries, he despised still more Europe's collective vanity in regard to Asia. He emphasized the magnitude of Europe's intellect-ual debt to her and, even while describing the present degradation of Persia and of Asia generally, he could none the less reveal his affection for many aspects of the oriental past. He sought to ridicule European vanity, not by showing the West as more corrupt than Persia, but by indicating that his own continent was simply at a less advanced stage of an identical and inexorable movement towards decomposition. He wrote of Asians generally: 'Their senility will probably lead us to reflect upon certain features at present emerging in Europe which do not fail to suggest analogies with this same decrepitude.'[4] His strictures on the Orient, when they occur, are thus closely connected with his prophecies of the Occident's own harsh future.

Of Persia's internal politics Gobineau once commented to Prokesch-Osten that, 'Nothing great, nothing tragic has happened here . . . since the time of Herodotus.'[5] But both the international position and the social condition of the country fascinated him. Regarding the former, he was convinced that in future Persia would exercise 'a decisive influence on world politics'.[6] The latter was interpreted as confirming the *Essai*'s contentions as to the consequences of miscegenation. He denied the existence of any-thing that might be called meaningfully 'the Persian race', remark-ing that it was simply 'a breed mixed from God knows what!'[7] These modern Persians were devoid of any feelings of racial super-iority and of any marked patriotism. With such excessive mixture democracy and egalitarianism were triumphant. The insight of Persians into their own social state was severely limited: 'They are an intelligent people, able to comprehend their own interests in the narrowest sense of the term, but they are also incurably decadent.'[8] Gobineau suggested that, although they did indeed show a certain affection for their country, they had no particular concern for the nature of its government and were largely indifferent as to whether it was in hands native or foreign, Muslim or Christian. They showed equal distrust of any government whatsoever, maintaining a large degree of apathy towards it and thereby hindering the positive development of the elements of social order dear to Gobineau. Their concepts of equality and democracy were applied less to the working of government than to the rationalization of their apathetic attitudes. Gobineau commented: 'In reality, the Persian state does not exist, and . . . the individual is everything.'[9] Despite his own distrust of state power and his attachment to the freedom of certain individuals at least, this situation was one which, within the Persian context at least, he did not favour. Though his theories often implied anarchical or asocial conclusions, he was here reluctant to forego a more pragmatic attitude towards the maintenance of social order. Persia had no means of preserving it. In a vicious circle, indifference encouraged instability, and instability promoted indifference. In partial mitigation Gobineau did however remark that in this democratic disorder, 'The Asiatic rabble has immense advantages over its European counterpart. However base it may be, it is never vulgar.'[10] Thus, without abating his censure of Persia, he strove again, in such obscure remarks, to fulfil his primary aim of denigrating Europe.

Further details in the pattern of degeneration traced in the *Essai* also appear. Gobineau depicted the masses as concerned solely with material well-being. Due not least to the requirements of his office, he was well aware of Persian commercial acumen and economic potential, which he saw as limited only by poor administration. Naturally Gobineau attributed this materialism primarily to the urban centres, and he repeated the association between materialism, urbanization, social movement and ethnic disorder. It was indeed in his *Histoire des Perses* that he gave his most vivid historical example of this syndrome. There ancient Babylon is described as uniting these features and as embodying also the tendencies to centralization and political disorder. This treatment connected with Gobineau's recent experience of all these social misfortunes in contemporary Persia, where he suggested, for example, that amidst general blood-mixture the last traces of purity and true nobility were to be found among the nomadic tribes:

The strictly aristocratic organization of the tribes, based on birth-right and illustrious genealogies, creates a hierarchy of men of gentle birth who are extremely proud of their origin but who derive hardly any real advantage therefrom in so far as they live in desert tents. As soon as they enter a town, there vanishes all the prestige with which they may be surrounded, and their family name matters only when courtesy allows, and no privilege is attached to it. On the contrary, the most absolutely democratic doctrines are there expressed and applied.[11]

Here again cities promoted disorder and negated the privileges to be properly associated with birth. But even the tribes with which Gobineau sympathized were open to criticism stemming from his antipathy to the physical movement in society which their nomadic habits implied. He complained generally in Asia of 'a really prodig-ious love of moving about',[12] and of 'its perpetual mobility, its constant agitation'.[13] Both speeded social decomposition and the disappearance of the ordered existence he sought.

He discerned decomposition which was moral as well as social. Persian politeness, he thought, scarcely concealed a passionate addiction to theft and deception of all kinds. Promotion was achieved not by merit but by corruption and the sale of offices. Gobineau also on occasion castigated Persian vanity and self-esteem. But, again, there is a mitigating element. Such failings are relieved somewhat by religious devotion: 'This whole country . . . is full of the idea of God. Decrepitude, old age, extreme corruption, in short, death is present everywhere in institutions, customs and characters; but this constant absorbing preoccupation with what is holy singularly ennobles all this ruin.'[14] But Gobineau testifies here less to the virtues of Islam than to what he considers to be its funda-mental moral impotence. Indeed, Persian religion revealed the syncretism which led to what he had denounced at the end of the Roman Empire as a theology of decadence – an accommodating and almost apathetically tolerant faith. One suspects that the religious toleration to which Gobineau always nominally subscribed was inconsistent with his racial theory. There, as here, it appears as a symptom of miscegenation and moral confusion. The extreme tolerance he stresses in Persia is closely linked to the 'hybrid ideas that bloom everyday from a soil that contains so much in a state of putrefaction'.[15]

Islam is simply another world-religion of which Gobineau must dispose – one which grew in towns and only slowly gained

acceptance in the ethnically healthier areas beyond. It coagulates
earlier ideas in a manner reminiscent of the Christianity depicted
in Gobineau's first letters to Tocqueville. The caution shown there
was less necessary in describing Persian religion. Thus Islam, like
Buddhism, was treated as a symptom of social decay. He even
sought to integrate deviant religious movements into this account
and, as Bernard Lewis has recently suggested, 'The first great
theory on the "real" significance of Muslim heresy was launched
by the Count de Gobineau. . . . For him, Shi'ism represented a
reaction of the Indo-European Persians against Arab domination –
against a constricting Semitism of Arab Islam.'[16] His assaults on
Islam were certainly not intended to give his fellow-Europeans
grounds for complacency. Gobineau strove to disabuse them of any
idea of a superior western morality. With his own continent very
much in mind he could assert of the Persians that, 'They are
rascals who are near enough our cousins. . . . This is what we shall
become tomorrow.'[17]

Gobineau discerned in the recently emergent Babist sect an
exception to the rule of tolerance, though not to the generalization
that all religion in Persia had to be related to the theme of decay.
In describing Babism he made his one really significant contribution to oriental studies. He saw the sect as political rather than
religious in its essential inspiration and he regarded its adherents
as 'veritable communists'[18] and as 'true and pure supporters of
socialism'.[19] He compared their reasoning and aims with those of
western economists striving to create tranquillity and material well-
being in a utopia where men would be at once productive, sociable
and contented. To Gobineau Babism exhibited the same valueless
utopianism that he had denounced among western socialists and,
in his substantive account within the pages of *Religions et Philosophies dans l'Asie Centrale*, he drew parallels between the economic
evangelism of the Babists and the preachings of Proudhon. Further,
his assessment of Babist prospects was also an implicit warning to
Europeans of the danger from socialism:

If I saw in Europe a sect of a nature analogous to Babism emerging
with the latter's advantages – that is, a blind faith, an extreme enthusiasm and courage, all deeply experienced, then a respect inspired
amongst the apathetic and a great terror produced amongst opponents,
and moreover . . . an incessant proselytization – if I saw . . . all that
existing in Europe, I should not hesitate to predict that, within a given

time, power and government would belong of necessity to those who possessed these great advantages.[20]

This was now certainly Gobineau's assessment of the nature of European socialism, and of its future prospects. Like Babism it was a symptom of race-mixture, materialism and the evils of urban democracy.

All these features of Persian society Gobineau undertook to explain historically in the two massive volumes of the *Histoire des Perses* published in 1869. Their primary importance relates to the development of his historical philosophy, into which we cannot enter fully here. We should however note his assertion that his history is 'less concerned with facts . . . than with the impression produced by these facts'.[21] He maintains this subjectivist and impressionistic attitude throughout his treatment of the myths and legends that make up a large part of his sources. He confirms his addiction to the poetical method by declaring that chronology is history's weakest aspect. These were tendencies which were already discernable in the *Essai*. But his treatment of Cyrus the Great, ruler of Persia in the sixth century BC, introduces a new element into his conception of the role of individiuals in history. Sulla had been impotent against the degeneration nurtured by ethnic decay. But here Cyrus, repulsing the Scythians and thereby pushing their migratory channels further westwards, is said to have produced a complete change in the subsequent history of Europe: 'Whatever we ourselves are, as Frenchmen, Englishmen, Germans, Europeans of the nineteenth century, it is to Cyrus that we owe it.'[22] Although the achievements of Alexander, and later those of Caesar and Charlemagne, would have been brought about by other hands in due course, it is not so with the deeds of Cyrus, whom he described to Caroline as 'the greatest of the great men in all human History'.[23] Gobineau explicitly regards the tale of his achievement as the climax of the work. Seemingly blind to the implications of the *Essai*, the author remarks that it is always historians of lowly origin who try to reduce the role of great men and he complains against those who have depicted Cyrus simply as 'a lifeless marionnette'.[24] This very charge must be made against Gobineau himself since generally he made men the puppets of the ethnic laws of history. We can explain his intention – without defending his inconsistency – by regarding the portrait of Cyrus as an early example of Gobineau's search for free individuals of the élite, for

those who might in some way overcome the stultifying laws he
had postulated. To this quest, and to its ultimate futility, we shall
return.

Gobineau relates the *Histoire des Perses* to his central social and
political concerns by remarking that, 'The history of Iran . . .
reveals . . . a picture of our own destinies.'[25] This fate was elaborated particularly in the concluding account, which deals with the
decline into centralizing semitization experienced by the Sassanids,
whose democratic misconception of the nature of order culminated
in despotism. Gobineau also reasserts in this work the influence of
race over environment, and much later he claimed that the history
had indeed been composed 'in order to show, from the example of
that Aryan nation which was the most isolated of its kind, just how
powerless are climatic and environmental differences, as well as
temporal circumstances, in transforming or curbing the genius of
race'.[26] The book also provides a detailed description of primitive
Aryan society, and of its progress from familial, to tribal and national
organization. He again emphasizes the limited nature of the sovereignty thus established. The most significant point is that the
allodial conception of landholding has vanished from the account.
Gobineau sees in ancient Persia a feudalism comparable to that of
the Aryan-Germans, but one which is not longer a mere decline
from allodial sovereignty and which is, from the outset, the most
satisfactory practical means of guarding liberty and social order.
Here he seems to be readily reconciled to this comparatively complex form of social existence, without any of the reservations expressed in the *Essai*. The *Histoire des Perses* is concerned with the
destruction, through semitization, of this principle of social organization and with emphasizing the parallels between the fate of
ancient Persia and that of contemporary Europe.

Gobineau not only saw Persia as the mirror of Europe's destiny –
he also regarded it, and Asia generally, as a breeding ground for
elements that would indeed speed Europe's decline. Fear of the
consequences of contact between Europe and Asia pervaded his
subsequent thinking. Persia itself was seductively susceptible to
conquest by a European power, yet nothing could prove more
disastrous to the aggressor. He remarked that, 'I am not inclined
to give favourable considerations to this extraordinary ardour
which is driving western nations towards Asia . . . Asia is a very
appetizing dish, but one which poisons those who consume it.'[27] He

denied that the remaining virtues of European civilization were communicable to the still more moribund Orient. In his view such attempts at communication would merely hasten the sorry end of both. Those who seek an imperialist doctrine in Gobineau's writings receive no support from his treatment of Persia which simply develops the *Essai*'s preferences for insularity. Although on his second visit Gobineau discerned signs of mild progress, of vitality even, and though, in terms of personal memories, he always looked back with some nostalgia to these oriental experiences, none the less he ultimately expressed himself relieved at leaving Persia and the decay that it embodied.

2 Diplomatic Horizons: Greece

For Gobineau the diplomat Greece was to be identified closely with the history of the Asian world. Like Persia it exhibited aspects of oriental decay, revealed the dangers of interference by the great European powers, and was threatened by the Russian menace. Moreover, like Russia itself, it stood between the civilizations of Asia and Europe, at once an index of their joint destinies and a means by which the advanced corruption of the former might be communicated to the latter.

Gobineau was Minister in Athens from November 1864 until September 1868. It was a posting he welcomed. He arrived only two years after the deposition of the Bavarian Otto and the enthronement of the young Dane, King George I. The French Minister's first impression was of a certain social stability even in the midst of chaos. Within a month of his arrival he was writing thus to Comte Adolphe de Circourt:

They are a fine people, the most monarchical in the world . . . During two years of real anarchy – when power (if there was any power) was in the hands of soldiers and junior officers who obeyed no one and whom no one else dared order about – there was no outrage against property, no affront to individuals even if they were political enemies, no theft, no violence![1]

At the end of his stay he could again write similarly to Circourt – though in terms which also showed his reluctance to consider Greece as essentially part of Europe: 'A European country would not survive six months of such disorder; but here this could last indefinitely.'[2] The chaos was political and ethnic alike. Gobineau wrote later that, 'The Greeks are the last remnant of the fusion and assimilation in ancient society which resulted in the Roman Empire.'[3] The Foreign Ministry duly received from him the opinion that, since common blood was lacking amongst this collection of Syrians, Arabs, Turks, Bulgars, Slavs, Albanians and others, it was pointless to expect any common commercial, industrial or administrative organization. Such elements would remain in constant antagonism and would promote a social chaos parallel to the ethnic disorder. Gobineau denied any significant connection between ancient and modern Greeks. This helped him to repudiate his youthful support for the Greek nationalist cause – a support that had been inspired, in part at least, by a belief in such a connection. In retrospect he was particularly critical of the manner in which Greek nationalism had been confused in the 1840s with extraneous political ideas, especially liberal and egalitarian ones. This had led to what he called, 'this charlatanesque exploitation of the miseries and troubles of a people in whom we claimed to show so much interest'.[4] He now renewed his praise of the earlier genius of Metternich, who had aimed to deny independence to a country so hopelessly devoid of common nationality. Indeed, Gobineau claimed to see little difference between the Greeks and the so-called Turks of the region. The latter were simply those who embraced Islam and accepted Ottoman sovereignty; but in racial terms they were regarded as virtually indistinguishable from the Greeks.

Decadence was perceived in the political and administrative sterility of Greece, as well as in what Gobineau termed its moral anarchy. Writing to Circourt he asserted that, 'Morally Greece is more devastated, more debased and much more surrendered over to anarchy in 1868 than she was in 1817.'[5] Although he believed that for this type of population decomposition was far from being equivalent to imminent destruction, he was reluctant to affirm with confidence that within the near future 'there might not come a time when this wretched edifice, undermined on all sides, would give up trying to stay erect'.[6] He suggested that in a more purely European state such disorder would be followed necessarily by revolution. But, because of her many Asiatic features, Greece might escape that at least – though he agreed that any firm prediction was impossible.

Criticisms concerning levity in the conduct of affairs, as well as accusations about national bankruptcy, military incapacity and lack of statesmanship, filled Gobineau's official dispatches. He regretted that Greece had no patience with aristocratic influence and that instead it was held in the grip of a few hundred demagogic agitators. His special hostility centred upon the attempted functioning of parliamentary government and here his Swiss observations were confirmed: 'Someone must be paying the Greeks to present the most accurate caricature ... of a representative régime.'[7] He suggested that every Greek election was tantamount to a civil war. The essence of Greek politics was intrigue, personal gain, distribution of spoils and financial chicanery. The resulting national bankruptcy prevented the establishment of an efficient administration and army, and also necessitated the invention of a fictional budget. Gobineau attacked the concomitant attempts to enlarge the budget of the state itself, and he warned against the moves towards centralization that these implied. The incompetence of the King and of his adviser Count Sponneck was also noted. The Greek chamber was regarded with no more confidence. Gobineau remarked in official correspondence that it was 'composed ... of people who are neither as wicked nor as corrupt as is sometimes claimed, but who are certainly very questionable statesmen, having not the faintest idea of political principles as these are understood in Europe'.[8] None the less, privately he did not feel that the adoption of such 'European' principles would necessarily be an improvement. Writing to Prokesch-Osten he exhibited a strong distrust of paper constitutions and of the theoretical constructions in which nineteenth-century Europe retailed these principles, and he again expressed his regret that Greece had lacked the conservative guidance of a Metternich. In sum, Greek politics were alleged to exhibit disorder and pettiness, together with a refusal to view affairs in terms other than those of immediate and selfish interest: 'Petty passions, petty interests, petty people, petty mischiefs, petty intrigues, everything petty, except the contempt which all this deserves.'[9]

As a diplomat he was confronted with one major political issue, the Cretan insurrection against the Turks. This he dismissed as 'the most perfect monument to lies, mischief and impudence that has been seen in thirty years'.[10] Being far from the Byronic aspirations of his youth, Gobineau now concluded that the revolt of the Cretans in favour of Greece might well bring the latter to final moral and financial ruin. Events directly connected with the troubles also contributed greatly to the ruin of the French Minister's own personal record in Athens. In the course of the insurrection Gobineau was gravely embarrassed by the activities of another Frenchman, Gustave Flourens (a future supporter of the Paris Commune), who considered himself the diplomatic representative of Crete at the Greek captial. From there Flourens infuriated the governments of France and Greece alike by making public certain information that Gobineau had foolishly let slip to him. This concerned the tactical unwillingness of both administrations to offend Turkey over the Cretan issue. In his demagogic fashion, Flourens was able to use the information to stigmatize the hypocrisy of the French and Greek governments. His activities culminated in his bursting into the royal palace to put his case. Gobineau then exceeded the terms of his own official instructions by agreeing to a Greek demand for the immediate and forcible transportation of Flourens back to France. The French Minister's altogether maladroit handling of the whole affair was an important factor in the decision to transfer him to another – and more remote – posting. We should however bear in mind as well the probable accuracy of Mérimée's broader comment that Gobineau was moved 'because he did not see the Greeks in the way that the Ministry wanted'.[11]

In addition the Ministry was probably uncomfortably aware of Gobineau's own perference for non-intervention by the great powers in the affairs of Greece. In the earlier case of Persia he had been keen to warn against interference. There the damage was scarcely begun, but in Greece the mutually unfortunate consequences of diplomatic embroilment were already very evident. Gobineau told Circourt that for over thirty years Greece had been 'the sad and living evidence of European ineptness and presumptiousness'.[12] The powers had mixed encouragement with vilification. Lord Aberdeen's attempt to give her constitutional rule had simply left her with 'the complete decay of a barbarous land'.[13] The English legacy of a parliamentary system incomprehensible to the Greeks is matched by the French error of trying to introduce liberal conceptions of 'the most inept Voltairianism'.[14] Europeans in general have mistakenly encouraged attempts at centralization, thereby working against the best interests of a population which could understand and utilize fully only the local institutions which the powers have been simultaneously destroying. As in the Persian case, Gobineau is at his most sympathetic to the temperament and tenacity of the Greeks at times when he is seeking to discredit the Europeans with whom they are contrasted. It is Europe that he blames most for the sorry state of the modern Greeks:

> She had decided . . . to make of them a representative, constitutional nation, a people in her own image . . . and she completely omitted to consider that, overnight, without transition, without further help, the Turkish subjects of one day would have to be gracious enough, upon the next, to think and act in all matters like citizens born in the realm of King Louis-Philippe.[15]

Gobineau not only opposed European attempts to transplant governmental forms; he also criticized the powers' refusal to accept the need for slow change and for the proper preservation of indigenous traditions. But, above all, he was hostile to the very brand of 'progressive' government and society the western theoreticians were endeavouring to force upon the Greeks.

His diplomatic experience in Persia and Greece reinforced Gobineau's awareness of the significance of the Eastern Question, upon which centred the relations between the powers of Europe and Asia. As he stated to Prokesch-Osten, the problem was at least as old as the reign of Alexander the Great. We now know that in Paris, around February 1861, Gobineau – doubtless drawing on the experience of his first Persian visit – prepared a memorandum for the Austrian Ambassador to France concerning the possibility of containing Russia's European designs by means of a Danubian federation under Habsburg leadership. It recommended *inter alia* the annexation of Epirus and Thessaly by Greece and the formation of a Slav state from Serbia, Bosnia and Herzegovina. This plan accorded with his support for Austrian conservatism but, since it also represented the current policy of Napoleon III and Thouvenel, his Foreign Minister, it is difficult to assess the degree of Gobineau's own commitment to the memorandum. Even the formation of one Slav state to hinder the expansion of another – Russia, more dangerous still – makes some sense within his system. The plan contains nothing contrary to his known views – except perhaps an element of optimism as to its fulfilment.

The Athens visit suggested to Gobineau that, even if the Greeks did perchance achieve their aim of replacing Turkish power in the Balkans with their own, there would be no overall improvement in the situation. As he said starkly to Prokesch-Osten, 'It is one rabble against another.'[16] The fundamental ethnic decay would remain unchanged. If Russia herself achieved dominance in near Asia then she would suffer the nemesis of imperialist expansion in the Orient and be affected by the more advanced degradation of the East. The Slav menace was but the harbinger of worse beyond. Gobineau's was increasingly a policy of isolation, most vividly expressed thus to Circourt in 1867:

The Greeks will not control the Orient, neither will the Armenians nor the Slavs nor any Christian population, and, at the same time, if others were to come – even the Russians, the most oriental of all – they could only submit to the harmful influences of this anarchic situation ... For me ... there is no Eastern Question and if I had the honour of being a great government I should concern myself no longer with developments in these areas.[17]

Upon departure he wrote to Prokesch-Osten that, 'I am leaving Greece in the most real and profound anarchy, without any possible element of government'.[18] But, in a certain degree, his subsequent remarks were more charitable – an attitude perhaps understandably most evident in his correspondence with two charming Athenian ladies, the sisters Zoé and Marika Dragoumis. While continuing to indicate features of social and political decay in Greece, Gobineau became ever readier to heap more of the blame upon the European powers. In doing this, he left himself freer to applaud any independent Greek achievement. It was, indeed, in an uncustomary spirit of optimism, albeit heavily qualified, that he published the articles of 1878 upon *Le Royaume des Hellènes*. He then remarked that, 'The transformation in ideas and practical behaviour which is taking place in that country gives me greater hope of seeing truth and a sense of practicality gaining a decisive triumph over error and vain chatter.'[19] Such tentative improvements were being accomplished despite the interference of Europeans. Gobineau was impressed by that time with Greek economic progress in general and, particularly, with her human fertility and rising population. He suggested that these augured well for the years ahead. He now argued that there were ethnic elements in Greece which, having conserved a certain energy even in the midst of degeneration, would assure her of a notable role for the future: 'This small people is neither dull nor inefficient and it has every reason to insist upon the honour of being counted for something in the world.'[20] Still, whatever the level of her vitality, Gobineau could by then scarcely deny Greece a place of significance. As a link between Europe and Asia the country was destined to loom ever larger in his mind as his thoughts turned increasingly in his last years to the confrontation of the two continents. The more sympathetic attitude to Greece is in no small way attributable to the fact that, for Gobineau, the threat from Slav and Mongol was by the late 1870s less a concern than an obsession. Within such a context the nation reviled a decade previously was now a bulwark – however temporary and imperfect – against the threatening forces beyond.

3 Diplomatic Horizons: The Americas

Gobineau's first Persian posting had come to an end early in 1858. For him it had proved an exciting experience but, quite understandably, his wife had adapted less well to the rigours involved. It was no doubt partly with her welfare – and that of two young daughters – in mind that in January 1859 he had declined an invitation to act as First Secretary to the French Legation in China. Thus he had lost an admirable opportunity of studying at first hand that yellow peril which was to bulk so largely in his later thoughts and writings. His refusal of the Chinese posting had not pleased his superiors and, until he returned unaccompanied to Teheran in 1862 for his second Persian mission, his diplomatic activities were limited. In the spring of 1859 he was appointed as a Commissioner for the investigation of Anglo-French fishing disputes in Newfoundland and in the following year he was made a member of the international commission supervising the cession of Savoy from Piedmont to France. The latter experience encouraged no writing, official or otherwise. But the Newfoundland visit was more fruitful. It inspired a novelette *La Chasse au Caribou* (which appeared in 1872 as one of the stories in Gobineau's *Souvenirs de Voyage*) and a notable travel book *Voyage à Terre-Neuve* (1861), and in addition it necessitated a series of diplomatic reports. Gobineau used the opportunity to pass comment upon North America as a whole. These impressions were subsequently enlarged when, in 1869–70, he was minister to Brazil. We consider here these two widely different American experiences, together with his further remarks upon the United States – which he was quite explicitly relieved to have been able to escape visiting.

Leaving France for Newfoundland in April 1859, Gobineau

spent the summer as joint French Commissioner considering the
hoary question of fishing rights on the Banks. Together with the
English commissioners he circumnavigated Newfoundland, coming
ashore to take evidence at a number of settlements en route, and
visited Cape Breton Island and Nova Scotia. Gobineau prepared a
bulky technical report but the problem remained unsolved. The
mission was but an episode in a much longer story and it added
nothing in the way of prestige to Gobineau himself.

His observations are none the less full of interest. He described
the population of Newfoundland as comprising a comparatively
small number of Anglo-Saxons, a few Germans, some French
remnants and odd Esquimo survivals, a larger number of Scottish
Highlanders and a great quantity of Irishmen. In discussing social
behaviour he was particularly interested in what he considered to
be the very singular attitude towards women taken up by the bulk
of the inhabitants. He alleged that in Newfoundland marriage was
principally a matter of commercial speculation. Yet, concurrently
with this, women enjoyed excessive social freedom, spurning
chaperones and indulging in a greater degree of dissipation than
was tolerated in Europe. Coquetry was the vogue and feminine
innocence was almost unknown. European horror at such behaviour
was the chief theme of *La Chasse au Caribou*. He concluded that
women received little respect from their menfolk. Remarking that
'this lack of esteem shown to women is not a good symptom in
society',[1] he indicated the extent to which life in Newfoundland
was removed from this aspect of his Aryan ideal.

Political life was closely bound up with religious loyalties.
Gobineau described the essentially religious basis of parties and he
emphasized especially the power of the Catholic hierarchy over its
flock. Regarding these Catholics in particular he wrote: 'Religion
has a great deal to do with the good attitude of this people and with
the extreme steadiness of their behaviour.'[2] Here Gobineau's
religious pragmatism and its conservative application are evident.
On the other hand, he also perceived that it was from the denomin-
ational divisions that there sprang the society's most dangerous
antagonisms. He even introduced an apparently environmental
argument to suggest that the intensity of such religious passion was
connected with the isolated existence led by the inhabitants. It was
his opinion that, since the surroundings allowed few other forms of
distraction, the people of Newfoundland were always ready to

devote themselves to the sport of religious sectarianism. He associated many of the non-conformists with a republican movement – though one sharing few of the libertarian excesses of European republicanism. He detected little fondness for egalitarianism and noted the keenness for distinctions and titles.

The isolation which encouraged religious passion was also, ironically, the foundation for some almost utopian reflections on Newfoundland. He admired the courage and vigour of the lonely fishermen of the Banks, to whom – in correspondence with Madame de Circourt – he referred as 'the best men that I have ever seen in the world'.[3] Their isolation and freedom from central interference encouraged the growth of the independent local spirit cherished by Gobineau. He compared the fullness and freedom of their life with the enervating and unchallenging existence suffered in towns. where 'there are policemen, judges, priests, administrators, every desirable guarantee; where no lives are risked from morn till night and men are worth just about the same as everywhere else'.[4] Gobineau's enthusiasm is directed towards the more isolated habitations where a harsh living is won in a daily struggle with the elements. In his travel volume he writes as follows concerning some of the coastal settlements:

I am not sorry to have seen once in my life a sort of Utopia . . . A savage and hateful climate, a forbidding countryside, the choice between poverty and hard dangerous labour, no amusements, no pleasures, on money, fortune and ambition being equally impossible – and still, for all this, a cheerful outlook, a kind of domestic well-being of the most primitive kind . . . But this is what best succeeds in enabling men to make use of complete liberty and to be tolerant of one another.[5]

He promptly agreed that this was far removed from any conventional utopian ideal and remarked: 'I do not know whether the followers of Fourier and Saint-Simon would want independence and virtue at this price.'[6] Unlike their laboured plans, his fleeting conception was marked with the vitalist Aryan ideals of challenge and struggle. But, perhaps still more significantly, it embodied Gobineau's striving for isolation and withdrawal from social communication. He commented that, 'He who loves solitude has many more chances of its realization here than in the midst of the European throng.'[7] This is a clear statement of the asocial implications of Gobineau's thinking. Perhaps migration to the New World was not, in itself, such an undesirable thing; perhaps it was defensible provided that it was an élite alone which migrated, in search of solitude. But Gobineau realized that this was a condition that could not be fulfilled. Throughout history the migrations of the élite had encouraged rather than prevented undesirable contact. This was the very price of their civilizing success – part of the nemesis of Gobineau's historical philosophy. In parts of New-foundland he was simply pleased to find a situation less removed than ordinarily from the ideal.

There is particular interest to be derived from Gobineau's assessment of the strategic future and development of the British North American colonies. He foresaw accurately their forthcoming confederation, but also appreciated rightly that Newfoundland's own participation would be long delayed. He denied that such a confederation would seriously rival the United States in military or economic terms. Regarding the strategic interests of France, he examined enthusiastically the implications of her possession of Saint Pierre and Miquelon. Here especially – both publically and in the more secretive diplomatic context – there is a patriotic and optimistic call for action. Regarding the strategic exploitation of these islands, he wrote in the *Voyage à Terre-Neuve*: 'It is to be wished that the Emperor's gaze may fall on this corner of the world. Great things might result.'[8] He also advocated the com-mercial development of these French holdings, even though this was scarcely compatible with his isolationist social philosophy. In fact, he even went so far as to declare that the economic and strategic developments would be worthless unless they could be administered in accordance with conventional American principles. Thus this administration should not conflict with 'the ideas that are accepted in this part of the world and to which all minds and imaginations are accustomed. It must approximate as closely as possible to – inded, must merge with – notions of "self-govern-ment".'[9] This surprising sentiment is expressed not within the privacy of a diplomatic document but publicly in the volume con-cerning his travels. It embodies most probably Gobineau's reluctant recognition that no political institution could be counten-anced anywhere on the North American continent if it were not already afflicted with a degree of debasement.

Gobineau was caught between his admiration for certain vitalist qualities surviving in Newfoundland and his general denunciation of the whole continent – north and south – dominated as it was by migrants of little ethnic worth. His equivocation is admirably captured in the following remark about the inhabitants of the British colonies: 'This is a population worthy not of admiration – for everywhere in the Americas "self-contentment" is taken to an excessive degree – but of much respect.'[10] On the whole, the tensions in his attitudes towards Newfoundland confirm the thesis of nemesis in the *Essai*. What he cherished on the island were the qualities preserved by comparative isolation – yet an isolation which itself rendered the inhabitants still less capable of any consummate achievement in terms of civilization.

It was ironic that Gobineau's second American posting should have been to Brazil, one of the most notorious centres of racial mixture. He regarded the appointment unenthusiastically and declared frankly to Zoé Dragoumis that, 'I have no intention at all of becoming a perfect minister in Rio.'[11] He was present at his post there only from March 1869 until April 1870. In his official capacity Gobineau was concerned primarily with the conclusion of the war between Brazil and Paraguay, with the subsequent pillaging of the French consulate in Asunción by Brazilian troops, with a Franco-Brazilian extradition treaty and with observing the developments towards slave emancipation. The issues of Negro slavery, European migration and advanced miscegenation, all of which bulked large in Brazilian life, were questions that had already attracted Gobineau's attention in other contexts. Although he derived stimulation from observing them here too, his greatest intellectual experience during the Brazilian visit was his encounter and friendship with the Emperor.

Dom Pedro II, of the House of Coburg Braganza, had succeeded to the throne under a regency in 1831 and had fully assumed his imperial powers in 1840. He was thus a monarch of long experience – though also one of more progressive a bent than normally appealed to Gobineau himself. For the Minister of France Pedro provided a cultural oasis in the midst of an intellectual desert. Gobineau valued the privilege of ready access to the ruler and the consequent opportunities for much informal conversation with him upon matters cultural as well as political. It was an easy familiarity which greatly annoyed the diplomatic representatives of other powers. The personal letters sent to the Emperor in the years that followed are a source of much illuminating information about Gobineau's thinking in the final decade of his life.

The French Minister naturally showed his abhorrence at Brazilian miscegenation. To Keller he remarked: 'Not a single Brazilian is of pure blood, but the combinations of marriages between Whites, natives and Negroes are so multiplied that there are innumerable variations in complexion and all this has produced, in higher and lower classes alike, the saddest form of degeneration.'[12] He suggested to Marika Dragoumis that the Brazilians were in many ways comparable to monkeys – but added that Europeans in Brazil were, from numerous points of view, more degraded still. His official reports were often scarcely less severe: 'He who speaks of a Brazilian speaks, with fairly few exceptions, of a coloured man. Without going into an assessment of the moral and physical qualities of these varieties, it is still impossible to fail to appreciate that they are neither hard-working, nor active, nor productive.'[13] There was, however, a continual tension between Gobineau's denunciation of such ethnic chaos and his appreciation of Pedro's efforts to improve the political condition of Brazil. It provides an excellent example of Gobineau's unwillingness to accept upon all occasions the full paralysis of political action implied in the racial theory. For instance, following a trip into the interior with the Emperor, he reported optimistically that, 'The sight of what I have just observed has left me with very favourable impressions as to the real situation and as to the future of the country.'[14] Though Gobineau was incapable of consistent optimism over her future, enthusiasm for the Emperor's efforts sometimes overrode the stultifying logic of ethnic determinism, as when he concluded: 'In a political environment as troubled as that of South America it is remarkable to find a place which does not share in the surrounding agitations and which is animated by truly conservative instincts.'[15] None the less his condemnations of Brazilian political life were commoner still. He had attacked her government in an article dating from as early as 1845 and, as recently as 1863, he had forecast to Circourt the social decomposition of the whole South American continent. Now he frequently remarked generally upon the aridity of Brazilian politics, scorning the obsessive preoccupation with commercial matters.

The issue of Brazilian slavery obviously related to important aspects of Gobineau's social thinking. We have noted already his attacks upon the hypocrisy of slaveholders in the United States. In full accord with this, we find him now denouncing slavery for its effects upon master as well as servant: 'In Brazil, as in the rest of America, slavery has done more harm to the slaveholders than to the slaves themselves.'[16] By the time of his visit emancipation was almost inevitable. The debates were over method and timing, and over the problem of absorbing its immediate economic consequences. In favouring cautious steps towards emancipation Gobineau dismissed the suggestion that Whites were incapable of undertaking much of the work then done by slaves. He appeared to have no qualms about advocating that the white man should now assist in such tasks – despite the improbability of reconciling this with the élitist arguments of his racist theorizing.

Gobineau's inconsistency went still further – and in an unexpected direction. Despite his hostility to trans-Atlantic migration and his lack of enthusiasm for Brazilian society in general, he subsequently advocated European immigration into that country. His attitude is partly explained by his affection for Dom Pedro who was keen, for economic reasons, to direct more of the New World migrations southwards. Gobineau began with certain qualms, but soon he was declaring that the existing German settlements in Brazil boded well for others. He reported as follows to Paris: 'Considered practically rather than theorectically ... it is obvious that this region is extremely suitable and favourable for the development of the German race.'[17] Though he was unimpressed by Brazilian political life, he felt able to recommend at least its comparative stability to migrants. By 1874, from his post in Sweden, he was commending Brazil to potential Scandinavian emigrants and communicating with the Emperor on this subject. In July of that year he published in *Le Correspondant* a study, under the title *L'Émigration au Brésil*, which suggested that the country was destined by its geography and natural resources to become an important centre of growth. In these pages he claimed that, 'Brazil seems to commend itself in a quite special way to the best of the migrants, to those who wish to attain the prosperity after which they aspire only through constant effort, good conduct and the calm and conscientious exercise of freedom.'[18] Gobineau was certainly consistent in maintaining that without further immigration the present Brazilian stock, so ethnically chaotic, was doomed to annihilation. In 1869 he had reported to Paris that the choice was between their rapid extinction and their absorption into a flood of newcomers from Europe. It is difficult to justify the

connection made again here between miscegenation and depopulation, since the world-history that Gobineau had traced was primarily a tale of blood-mixture without decline in numbers. In 1874
he was suggesting that the miscegenated Brazilians could not
survive more than another two centuries without European
infusion. To encourage their partial redemption he explained as
follows:

What it is right to point out is that the Brazilian administration,
enlightened by experience, is daily multiplying regulations and pre-
cautions favourable to the migrants, and that there is perhaps no
country which concerns itself in so consistent a fashion with the security
and prospects of the men upon whom, moreover, it has based so many
justifiable hopes for its prosperity.[19]

Still, whatever the laboured rationale, what was this but an exhortation for the still superior Europeans to sacrifice themselves to
debasement for the sake of preserving longer the worthless half-
castes of present Brazilian society?

This extraordinary inconsistency can be only partially explained.
In addition to Gobineau's desire to please the Emperor, it is
attributable to his determination to attack the United States –
which he could now exercise through striving to divert from her
the main currents of European migration. Although Gobineau
never visited the United States – and was indeed horrified at the
thought of any posting to Washington – he was keen to pass
judgment on the country. While in Rio he informed Zoé Dragoumis that he was planning a history of the Americas. Though this
was never undertaken, another article in *Le Correspondant*, dating
from 1872, entitled *L'Émigration Européenne dans les Deux
Amériques*, embracing the whole continent, dealt particularly with
the United States. The essay regarded much of the trans-Atlantic
migration as a direct expression of the suffering and decay of
Europe. To Gobineau it was part of a general historical law of
human migration from East to West, but as yet the extent of the
emigration had not been fatal to the old continent.

Migration to the United States he treated with particular
hostility – though (as in the *Essai*) he was compelled to admit that,
for a few, it evinced the best Aryan qualities of energy and adventure and might sometimes be interpreted as a quest for isolation in
the vastness of the Far West. He suggested that Germans and

Scandinavians especially were suspicious of American democracy and he emphasized the large numbers that were returning dis-illusioned:

Its political life no longer appears so constantly alluring in the sight of Germans and Scandinavians. They find hordes of rather savage Irishmen; it is true that these latter instil in them strong ideas of the power of democracy – but rather weaker ones as to the gentleness of its application, and still feebler ones as to its moderation.[20]

This migration was regarded as a spiritual failure. Those who viewed the United States as 'the temple of virtue and happiness'[21] were frequently disappointed to discover that it was merely the home of rapacity and violence. Naturally Gobineau questioned the disposition of those who found themselves able to adapt with sus-picious readiness to such an environment. These he described as, 'the displaced, those who leave their native home simply to shift their position, to escape responsibility for thier actions or to find troubled waters in which to fish for no matter what'.[22] His com-parisons between Newfoundland and the United States constantly worked to the detriment of the latter, which was suffering from an influx containing 'a heavy proportion of vagrants, who are much better equipped with European vices than with any sincere desire to prosper by honest means'.[23] To Gobineau the United States was the epitome of a violent, unstable society, devoted to ethnic eclecticism and the cultivation of a rootless population. He alleged that it was dominated by mob rule and deep-seated fears, and he wrote to Circourt of its 'longing for grandiose brigandage, which – it seems to me – can allow nobody any sleep'.[24] He was indeed surprised that the Union had survived the Civil War, for, during the conflict itself, he had prophesied eventual permanent division between northern and southern states. That struggle had only confirmed the pessimism of the *Essai*. After the war, as the bonds of Union began to strengthen again and as the slavery issue died, Gobineau's sympathies moved more clearly towards the southern states. The northern part of the union, as the seat of the greatest immigrant mixture and as the supporter of egalitarianism, was evidently in a more advanced stage of ethnic decline. It was in the light of all these assessments that he was prepared to advocate migration to Brazil.

In one of his final works, the unpublished essay *L'Europe et la*

Russie dating from about 1880, Gobineau repeated these denuncia-
tions of the United States. He undertook a comparison reminiscent
of Tocqueville's between the destinies of the United States and of
Russia. He emphasized in the former the political power of the
masses and contended that 'the unprecedented violence of the
"Struggle for Life" '[25] was now repelling prospective immigrants.
He repeated his attacks on the northern liberal hypocrisies in
regard to the Negro. He also combatted the general European misconception that the United States was ruled according to the
declared ideals of its founders rather than in accordance with the
exigencies of profit-making. Believing that it would still be divided
eventually into a number of separate sovereign bodies (whether
viable or not), he denied that the country was destined to enjoy
any predominant place in the world. The future – such as it was –
lay not with the Americas, which had for so long riveted the
attentions and aspirations of Europeans, but with Russia and the
lands beyond. Gobineau's vision of the future was concerned
primarily with the East. And it was devoid of the optimism of
those who looked to the West.

4 The State of France

Having returned from Rio on leave in May 1870 Gobineau was in
France during the war against Prussia and he experienced at first
hand the humiliating defeat and the chastening episode of the
Paris Commune. The chaos produced by these events prevented
him from having to return to Brazil and until his subsequent
posting, to Stockholm in May 1872, his time was spent in France
itself. Gobineau regarded the disasters that had befallen her in
1870-1 as further confirmation of the wisdom of his pessimism and
they left their mark upon all his future thinking. Even before 1870
he had many grounds on which to base criticisms of his native
country. Liberty he had construed differently from the bulk of his
compatriots; equality he had hated as unnatural; fraternity he had
seen ahead, but only as a symptom of mankind levelled into common mediocrity. The French intellectual world had treated his
Essai lightly and had since received his constant disparagement.
Disappointment was also his prime emotion when considering his
comparative failure as a diplomat. Generally he had come to
regard his colleagues as mediocrities and had interpreted the
modesty of his own promotions as the effect of their intrigues. It
had indeed been necessary for his friend Hercule de Serre to re-
assure the Foreign Minister of Gobineau's loyalty – by quoting
suitably patriotic extracts from his letters – at the point when the
author of the *Essai* had become the object of official suspicion.
Gobineau alleged that he was constantly betrayed in his attempts
at preferment and he had certainly regarded the posting to remote
Rio as the plot of a hostile coterie. On the eve of the Franco-
Prussian War he had written thus to Zoé Dragoumis about the
French diplomatic corps: 'There are . . . a thousand worthless and
untalented hacks who have a role to play and still the devil has it
that I should remain unused.'[1]

Official suspicion was understandable because Gobineau had a
spirit altogether too independent for the prudently conventional
conduct of diplomatic affairs. In addition, his approbation of the
French Emperor embodied a position only haltingly arrived at.
We have seen how he felt the need to explain to Keller that he was
the first member of the Gobineau family to begin coming to terms
with such novel political tendencies – and we may by now also
appreciate how little in fact that coming to terms had really signi-
fied. His sympathy for Napoleon III could be maintained only
upon condition that the Emperor sustained his authoritarian
attitudes. As he had written to Tocqueville in 1859, 'When we
come to the French people, I genuinely favour absolute power.'[2] It
is generally agreed today that the history of the Second Empire was
a tale of imperial vacillation, but with a gradually increasing stress
upon more liberal measures. As late as 1862 Gobineau could still
comment, to Prokesch-Osten, that, 'The Emperor shows much
prudence and good sense'.[3] But his attitude was to become more
critical in the years immediately following, and the fiasco of the
Mexican adventure in particular aroused his disgust. After the fall
of Napoleon III he emphasized that he had always had considerable
reservations about his rule – but he could add, no doubt with the
Emperor's old authoritarianism in mind, that, 'there is no need to
pursue and vilify him'.[4]

Gobineau's misgivings about French society and politics went
far deeper than doubts about any particular ruler or régime. He
once stated that, since under any régime France was afflicted with
an immoderate desire for state centralization, true freedom was
there impossible. He found himself defending Bonapartist authoritarianism as a means of combating democratic disorder and yet he
was loath to accept the increase of central control which this policy
necessitated. The inconsistency was never removed. He sustained
his hatred for Parisian corruption, for instance remarking to Zoé
Dragoumis that, 'I am very much a Frenchman . . . but a provincial
Frenchman, and that is something else.'[5] Since 1789 all political
life had been tainted by the French Revolution's acceleration of the
processes of centralization and aristrocratic debasement already
evident in the Ancien Régime. The original feature of the National
Assembly was that it so fully opened the way to violence and to the
atrocities of democracy: 'Few systems will have the honour of
being more repugnant to intelligence and morals than that which

reigned from 1791 to 1795.'[6] In 1869, in the final part of his narrative poem *Le Cartulaire de Saint-Avit* (part of his collection *Aphroëssa*), he unleashed another vigorous attack on the Revolution and the values of the modern world. As he explained to his sister, all political principle was now discarded:

Feudal spirits became royalists, who became moderate constitutionalists, who became conservatives, who became discreetly progressive imperialists, who are in the process of becoming – well, just what is it they are on the road to becoming, and just what remains of the original elements? As for myself, I am an excellent servant of my master and I limit myself to that.[7]

It was surely right for his superiors to doubt this excellence in one who showed such alienation from all contemporary political attitudes and whose loyalty lacked any truly firm foundation.

Gobineau warned that France should not err further into the parliamentary paths of the British, and he prophesied doom as the end-product of Gladstonian liberalism. Of British society after the Second Reform Act he commented to Circourt: 'It appears to suffer from exactly the same blindness as do our different classes of moderates who have always believed that the political machine, once released from a given commitment and shoved forward, would stop just at the point desired by their theories without rolling on further.'[8] The idea of any such control was illusory and he dismissed these human pretensions to influencing inexorable social developments whether by the application of theoretical constructions or by any other means.

As to foreign policy, he regarded the emergence of militant nationalism – particularly in Germany and France – as the most prominent feature of the international scene and he was opposed to the vanities thereby encouraged. During the Crimean War he had felt able to write: 'It would seem that there are going to be no more than three to speak of in Europe: France, England and Austria.'[9] Such a judgment was inapplicable to the 1860s not only because Gobineau was by then pondering even more upon the Russian menace but also because of the rapid progress of Prussia. Gobineau was disappointed by the Prussian victory over Austria in the war of 1866, and he bewailed the subsequent impossibility of achieving German unification under a leadership whose conservatism and nobility he could still in some degree respect. His fear of the consequences of Prussian dominance continued and, after the Austrian defeat, he wrote thus to his Prussian friend Keller: 'You have long desired unity. Now you are reaching it . . . Are you sure that there is in this trend nothing artificial and, consequently, liable to be revealed as empty and hollow in practice, and perhaps even painful?'[10] The vitalist view of warfare, expressed during the Crimean adventure, remained for a time but before 1870 fear of Prussia and her militarism had begun to cloud this attitude. After the Franco-Prussian War he could write simply: 'I consider war, in present conditions, as absurd, and devoid of what once made it heroic and productive'[11]; or, again, 'It is undeniable that war was once the most beautiful and noble thing in the world, but none the less at the present time it is the most foolish and degrading.'[12] The events of 1870 thus brought Gobineau to conclusions smacking more of pacifism than of Aryan vigour.

The war itself, which so profoundly affected every aspect of French life, strongly coloured the writings of Gobineau's last dozen years. He had forecast much earlier that if France were ever again engaged in a major war upon her own frontiers she would be greatly endangered by the moral consequences of her debilitating centralization. None the less, upon the actual outbreak of war he was sufficiently phlegmatic as to believe that the army would triumph over the Prussians and that thereafter it might even be able to take control internally and strike some palpable blows against French jacobinism. Two days before the capitulation he was still writing to a distinguished English correspondent – Robert Bulwer Lytton, shortly to become Viceroy of India – in confident terms regarding French morale and prospects. Though defeat had been implied by all his previous thinking, his immediate reactions to it were shock and disappointment. Only when the gunfire had ceased did he come to regard it again as an inevitable part of the inexorable process of French decline.

For most of the war he was at Trie, some fifteen miles southwest of Beauvais, in the small chateau that he had purchased for his family during his first mission to Persia. In 1859 he had been elected a Conseiller Municipal and four years later he had become Maire of Trie. Diplomatic activity had limited his local work but he took what opportunities he could of putting into practice his provincialist and decentralist beliefs. Gobineau in the guise of feudal lord loved to refer to Trie as his realm. Certainly during the war and occupation he was most able in guarding the interests of his village, even though he ceased to be Maire in November 1870. He was moreover instrumental in achieving a considerable reduction in the war indemnity laid upon the whole Département de l'Oise. In October 1871 he was re-elected, as a legitimist, to an office which he had first acquired just before the outbreak of war – that of Conseiller Général for his local canton of Chaumont-en-Vexin. In this position he was to share for eighteen months in the government of his Département.

From the records of the Conseil Général we can discover the chief spheres of Gobineau's activity. He clearly interested himself in regional railway development and in the conservation of local records. None the less his most vigorous activities related to the advocacy of compulsory and (where necessary) free primary education. This concern seems surprising upon the part of a race-theorist who had generally implied the impotence of all such social devices and institutions to affect significantly the moral or social worth of men whose capabilities were dictated primarily by the blood. He had explicitly cast doubt on the growing humanitarian faith in education as a cure for social ills and, after the publication of the *Essai*, he had dissented from Prosper Mérimée's strongly environmental and institutional argument that the mediocre development of the national intellect was primarily the result of a poor educational system. After 1870, in his polemics on contemporary France, Gobineau – while certainly prepared to castigate the weaknesses of this system – never suggested that these were fundamental to the degeneration.

None the less, whether or not Gobineau was fully aware of the fact, there is a certain sense in which his advocacy of educational improvement in the Oise can be made compatible with some of the *Essai*'s own arguments. We must recall his suggestion that only a minority of the French nation were still able to participate, even to the very smallest degree, in the development of Europe's remaining civilizational capacities. In that context he had written: 'The most elementary and accessible facts are sealed mysteries to most of our rural populations, who are absolutely indifferent to them; for usually they can neither read nor write, and have no wish to learn. They cannot see the use of such knowledge, nor the possibility of applying it.'[13] He suggested that this state of affairs prevailed even in spite of brave attempts at educational reform. Claiming that the rot went deeper still, he proceeded to comment:

> I could more easily approve of all the generous efforts that have been so fruitlessly made to educate our rural populations, if I were not convinced that the knowledge put before them is quite unsuitable, and that at the root of their apparent indifference there is a feeling of invincible hostility to our civilization.[14]

This hostility he firmly associated with ethnic decay. Yet, for our present purpose, it is essential to note the terms of his single qualification upon that decay:

> The only exception is to be found in the agricultural and even the industrial population of the north-west, where knowledge up to an elementary point is far more widespread than in any other part, and where it is not only retained after schooling, but is made to serve a good end. As these populations have much more affinity than others with the Germanic race, this result does not surprise me.[15]

It was in that very area that Beauvais and the Oise were situated. It was there that Gobineau had chosen to reside. And perhaps there alone his educational efforts of the early 1870s could be deemed compatible with the racist findings of the *Essai*.

Still, not surprisingly, his approbation for participation in local government became outweighed eventually by his dislike of popular elections and deliberate assemblies – as well as by his feelings about the futility of political effort in general. In 1864 he had commented to Charles de Rémusat that, 'I have not got what it takes to hold elective office.'[16] This remark was made after the failure of his first campaign for a seat upon the Conseil Général. Even before the election he had written to the Préfet de l'Oise exhibiting contempt for 'the petty miseries of universal suffrage';[17] after the polls he added the expression of his resentment at governmental intimidation of the electorate. When after the war of 1870 he did come to play an active part in the work of the Conseil he was swift to deride in private the activities of his colleagues. With his posting to Stockholm his personal participation soon ceased. Shortly after his final resignation in March 1873 he wrote thus to the sympathetic Prokesch-Osten: 'I am so little a part of my times that it seems to me that deliberative assemblies have but two possible faces: factious or inept. And as for spending hours talking of useless matters in the corridors, I realize that I am quite incapable of it.'[18]

Gobineau's general attitudes to France in the 1870s were ininfluenced not only by the war against Prussia but also by the especially painful episode of the Paris Commune. He had suggested long before, in the pages of the *Revue Provinciale*, that Paris was perfectly cabable of surrendering herself to the forces of socialism. His letters in the spring of 1871, written within the beleaguered capital itself, expressed profound sorrow, as he spoke for instance of 'this sad nation' and of 'this people in dissolution'.[19] The plea of the Communards for greater communal liberties all over France was far removed from Gobineau's own conception of provincialism and could not dispel his fundamental antipathy towards their activities. The government of Adolphe Thiers, rival to the Commune, was also unworthy of much approbation, since – as he declared very frankly to Dom Pedro – it seemed to follow the Empire in believing 'this uncommon maxim that the indispensable qualification for doing a job is to know nothing about it'.[20] In the very last days of the Commune he wrote to Zoé Dragoumis, expressing his gloom both at recent events and at what would follow:

Everything will become calm for a time. We are left with a people profoundly corrupted and shaking with anger who will before long make of the abominations they have committed a subject for pride, who will regard as evidence of their strength the tottering ruins of monuments that they have destroyed, who will lavish praise upon their dead as though these were martyrs, and who will be singularly encouraged in their wickedness by the platitudes, cowardice and idiocies of those whom we call conservatives – though why I never know, for they conserve nothing.[21]

The war and the Commune were both grist to the pessimist's mill. Almost immediately peace had been fully restored Gobineau undertook to explain these disasters within the general context of French and European corruption.

His polemical work *Ce qui est arrivé à la France en 1870* was begun at the end of that very year. It remained incomplete, however, and was not published during Gobineau's lifetime. In November 1870 he explained to Keller that, 'It is a summary of my consistent opinions and of the observations that twenty-one years' experience of affairs have allowed me to elaborate.'[22] It was regarded as a correction of the *Essai*'s underestimation of the speed at which France was decaying. Gobineau stated that the fundamental reasons for defeat were not military but moral – an inner degeneration. He wrote:

Evidently this situation could not have been brought about simply by the collaboration of a few able Prussians. For a country to disintegrate like this, the disease must wreak its work from within; the wounds inflicted by the foreign assailant produce cuts, but never this purulent liquefaction of the marrow and the blood. One thing is certain: France has arrived at its climacteric year. In 1870 it saw and underwent what it should never have experienced.[23]

The events of that year were themselves symptomatic of deeper problems, such as the encroachments of centralization and state power. But, more profoundly still, they were attributable to the great disjunction in modern France between racial merit and social status. The members of the ruling bourgeoisie ('descended . . . from Gallo-Roman slaves'[24]), no less than the monarchs who preceded them, had cultivated the now triumphant idea of state omnipotence. Gobineau attacked bureaucracy as the emanation of these centralizing tendencies and he criticized the administrators for their lack of loyalty to any particular government. He drew the dubious conclusion that the larger the bureaucracy the more likely was political disorder. Urbanization was seen yet again as a symptom and further cause of social turbulence. Gobineau ridiculed the aspirations of Napoleon III to make Paris the capital of Europe and asserted that, 'This city, pompously described as the capital of the universe, is in reality only the vast caravanserai for the idleness, greed and carousing of all Europe.'[25]

Such official glorification of Paris was also considered symptomatic of a national vanity that had further ramifications. The grand illusion of Louis XIV and the self-attributed intellectual predominance of France in the age of the Enlightenment were examples of contributions to this mode of misconception. The French had subsequently flattered themselves not only that the principles of 1789 were laudable but also that they were an invention of their genius alone. Similarly Gobineau ridiculed the manner in which French military prowess was hallowed by constant recollection of Jena and Austerlitz while defeats were ignored. France had been unable to forgive the Restoration and Orleanist régimes for their refusal to assert publicly this alleged pre-eminence. Now she was isolated from other European powers both by this vanity and by her continual political instability. It was such utterances which led Gobineau to be styled the Alceste of patriotism.

He expressed particular concern at the moral degeneration of the peasantry. Previously, though they had been illiterate, they had nevertheless benefited from the basic moral instruction emanating from the local curé. The rural communities had been highly conscious of their traditions and of their own organic nature as expressed in their common life. These values were now being lost due to the disruptive influence of urban values. Gobineau was especially concerned that the still more literate and disorderly working class was winning over the support of the peasantry by simplifying and distorting all issues. Though the imperial government had tried to cultivate this urban class it had failed to satisfy the growing lust of its members because it did not understand that, 'Envy is an essential malady of the Latin races'.[26] The government of the Second Empire, like its predecessors, failed to appreciate fully the necessary conditions of tradition without which loyalty and respect could not be obtained: 'Only the action of many succeeding years is sufficient to inspire awe, to tighten, cement and unify the bond in which rulers and ruled are joined ... This is the sole guarantee of permanence, of calm and normal living that political science has ever succeeded in discovering within a country.'[27] As the products and prophets of a rootless mode of existence hostile to Gobineau's conception of social order, the workers lacked this respect for tradition. Still worse than the enervation of peasants and workers was the inability of the superior classes to maintain their position. Recent French history had demonstrated, he thought, 'this absolute necessity for a nation to have ... superior classes who are morally and physically fitted to make it live under the conditions which its historical greatness, the size of its population and its wealth give it a duty to demand'.[28] He felt that the remnants of the French nobility were now self-evidently incapable of undertaking such a task.

All these failings contributed to the disastrous events of 1870–1. Gobineau also criticized the press for its chauvinistic optimism and emphasized the lack of honour with which the war had been conducted upon both sides. The French government was dishonest in suggesting that the war had been forced upon it by public opinion and it was clearly guilty of having made insufficient military preparations. Yet much of the purpose of Gobineau's polemic was to

stress that blame for the defeat could not be laid simply at the door
of the imperial government. The responsibility was truly national.
He described France in these terms:

It is a country where the nobility does not exist, where the bourgeoisie is no more preponderant as a political class, where the people's
wishes are in harmony with those of the administration, and where
religion is a purely administrative affair, like everything else – it is a
country where bureaucrats of every imaginable kind go on rapidly and
endlessly multiplying.[29]

The blame for the condition of France went deeper than the errors
of one régime. To Gobineau it seemed that France in 1870 was
reaping the errors of centuries.

In 1871 the political future remained gloomy. In February he
remarked that if the Government of National Defence succeeded
in establishing a republic it would soon be transformed into a
monarchy – but he added that the thought of the Orleanist Comte
de Paris as the triumphant claimant much disturbed him. He felt
that the divisions between Legitimists and Orleanists revealed the
incapacities of both. In correspondence with Dom Pedro he understandably assumed a more orthodox royalist position and warned
against the dangers of an interim republic. But, as monarchical
divisions continued, he wavered on this point. In an unpublished
fragment at the end of the manuscript of *France en 1870* we read
that,

Despite all the drawbacks, all the practical impossibilities of this form
of government, despite its constant failures and the general repugnance
that it inspires, we have to recognize that the Republic has immense
resourcefulness at its disposal. At certain moments this assures it of
superiority over all monarchical parties.[30]

Though he also denounced the régime as 'the republic of the un-
foreseen and the improbable',[31] he managed in the above not only
to rationalize his very real need to remain in official employment
for the sake of a salary but also to criticize the incompetence of both
royalist factions. This theme was repeatedly emphasized as the
monarchist offensives wilted. Gobineau suggested increasingly
that the republic had less to fear from the royalists than from an
imperial restoration or from some form of military dictatorship:

The vast jacobinism of Europe is continuing its revels and is making
more and more probable, possible, indispensable even, a chance

application of dictatorship. I confess that I can see nothing else in the future. I may be wrong . . . and I hope so with all my heart. But where there is revealed neither good sense nor wisdom of any kind – that is to say, as in all the French parties without exception – there is not much in the way of good to predict.[32]

These words were written to Dom Pedro, and it was natural that Gobineau, as a diplomat writing here (however informally) to a foreign head of state, should be cautious about pledging support to such a régime. But there is every indication that, as the monarchist alternatives vanished and as his hostility to the democratic republic grew, this solution – later championed by the supporters of General Boulanger – became ever more attractive.

Disillusionment with the state of France was accentuated by personal disappointment. The war had proved disastrous for Gobineau's own finances and, for this reason as well as for temperamental ones, his marriage became increasingly unsteady and during the 1870s it drifted into separation. At the end of 1871 his confident but presumptuous expectation of a seat in the Académie Française was confounded. This was interpreted as yet another republican plot, and when in 1878 he was given the Académie's Prix Bordin for his work *La Renaissance* he claimed to be accepting the award not as an honour but solely as a financial aid. There was yet more hollow honour in his having to represent the republic in a diplomatic capacity – this craft being difficult enough even for convinced republicans after the recent humiliations. He continued to despair at the inept appointments made by the régime, but he remained in the service for financial reasons while indeed seeking in desultory fashion another occupation. Though the Stockholm posting was comparatively congenial, his professional activities became increasingly subordinated to his writing, to his new pastime of sculpture and to the emotional demands of his probably platonic liasion with the Comtesse de La Tour, the wife of the chief of the Italian mission to Sweden. In 1876 the Emperor of Brazil visited Europe and Gobineau received permission to accompany him on his journeys to Russia, Greece and Asia Minor. In the event, Gobineau absented himself from Stockholm for an inordinate length of time and he was recalled to Paris in December to be informed that his retirement would be required early in 1877. Gobineau's reaction was predictable and he wrote as follows to Marika Dragoumis: 'The Republicans – or to be more accurate, the rogues under all the labels from beneath which this country is governed – are in need of jobs. They have got mine. To be surprised by it would be to confess that I had been wrong throughout my life in treating these people with the utmost scorn.'[33] In this he was less than fair to his superiors, who were confronted with the embarrassment of his growing contempt and inefficiency. But his virtual dismissal certainly fanned the flames of his hostility towards the régime.

It was in the following months that he composed his second polemic on the state of France, *La Troisième République Française et ce qu'elle vaut*. Again, it was left uncompleted and was published only posthumously. It was dedicated 'To the Provinces!' and it maintained a strongly decentralist flavour. He claimed that the republic purveyed a great chimera of Equality, which was not only an illusion but was known by most if its retailers to be so. Gobineau suggested – surely with his own enforced retirement in mind – that none were keener than they 'to plaster their hierarchy with gold braid and to allocate ranks'.[34] The socialization of property he regarded as the simple and more consistent extension of their egalitarian political beliefs. The socialist idea rested, he believed, upon two foundations:

the abolition of the idea of a personal God and of the different religions derived from the ancient forms of faith; and the uncompromising castration of all forms of learning, mutilated so that it must no longer investigate or produce anything but lessons which are positive and immediately applicable to a purely practical aim.[35]

The negation of private property involved the enhancement of state power and the weakening of the Church and religion. The Commune was the most notable monument to the errors of such egalitarian ideas. Gobineau repeated his now familiar assaults on centralization and disruptive urbanization. Democracy, representing 'an undigested conglomeration of undefined and essentially variable wills',[36] was castigated for its negation of the social coherence that could be achieved not by universal suffrage but only through respect for tradition. He further denounced democratic leaders for the mutual jealousies stemming necessarily from the instability of their support and the uncertainty of their authority.

He argued that no Frenchman should be misled by the republic's attempts at concealing such instability and uncertainty. He derided its endeavours to depict itself as the régime of moderation, compromise and good sense. These pretensions he criticized in a central passage that also underlined his own attitudes towards recent French history:

> To what degree of moral and intellectual abasement must a nation have fallen to allow itself to be called 'sensible' when, generally once every ten years, it finds itself piling curses upon itself for ever having elected and given massive support to the government which it has just overthrown! This government, previously so well loved, now dishonours, degrades and corrupts the people who elected it – and the people cry this out to the world! They began, however, by believing . . . that the Terror gave them liberty, the Directory rest, the Empire stability, the Restoration peace, the July dynasty order, the Second Empire tranquillity; and, to be fair, they still only ask of the present régime that it should terminate its office peacefully. But they now say that the Terror led to slavery, the Directory to theft, the Empire to servitude, the Restoration to inertia (by way of the sacristy), the July dynasty to the debasement of life through love of lucre, the Second Empire to the most deplorable corruption through the pursuit of pleasure; and the present régime has apparently lost all contact with reality and cannot even believe it is possible for it to leave office without causing an upheaval. And this is a nation whose distinctive quality is said repeatedly to be common sense! For sixty years its excesses have earned it a multitude of revolutions and three foreign invasions. There is still more to come, yet the people laugh and repeatedly and complacently invoke their so-called common sense![37]

It is unclear whether Gobineau has anything to offer as an immediate alternative to democratic republicanism. He certainly states forcibly the ideal role of French royalists: 'They are the tradition and the marrow of the French people. . . . These are hardy plants with roots in every part of French soil and the provinces produce them without any tillage.'[38] Remarking that they should be able to overcome the more divisive consequences of class differences, Gobineau is again advocating a feudal pattern in which these distinctions (while most certainly remaining) would not be allowed to disturb the coherence of society. Only the royalists could potentially provide it with the unity which would put into proper context its necessary differences. But Gobineau is also prompt to note that, in fact, the present royalists are incapable of fulfilling these designs. The elections of 1871 indicated, he thought, that the public had more faith in the royalists than these monarchists had in themselves. They cherish only the tarnished part of

French history – dating from the epoch of Louis XIV – and thereby ignore the more praiseworthy traditions of earlier periods. Thus the royalists are condemned to impotence and their divisions and failures in the 1870s are regarded as sufficient commentary upon their misconceptions.

With the royalists thus dismissed, Gobineau stressed again the possibility of military dictatorship. But he strongly doubted whether even that could survive long. He concluded that France was no longer capable of providing herself with any really durable régime. This fact was a symptom of decomposition and such a nation would soon be at the mercy of its neighbours. The decay was being daily encouraged from Paris and was being only partially disguised by a patriotism which was 'very loquacious, very verbose, very boastful and which has the advantage of making us ridiculous in the eyes of the whole world – after having isolated us from it'.[39] In his final pages Gobineau repeated his conviction that France must put aside a century of liberal-democratic phrasemongering and look again to the provinces, *la France véritable*. But his appeal now had a false ring. The exhortation of these pages was totally at variance with his prevalent view of inexorable French and European decline. Any traces of optimism discernable here did not survive in the views of France he recorded between the composition of this work and his death in October 1882. The *Troisième République* was not, as far as we know, offered to a publisher. The reason may have been that Gobineau realized that the ferocity of his attack on France would deny it much chance of acceptance. But it may also have been that, by the time that he was well advanced in its composition, he had recognized fully the futility of repeating the *cri aux provinces* of 1848.

A short uncompleted essay entitled *L'Instinct Révolutionnaire en France* brings out this despair. Although it too dated from about 1877, it remained unpublished until 1928. In it Gobineau argued that the paramount French need was for order and repose, but these were permanently denied because politicians had no clear idea as to what they themselves wished to achieve. The royalists could neither agree upon a choice of monarch nor decide upon a common conception of the very meaning of monarchical government. More generally there was disagreement about the whole structure of government, republican or otherwise. From a welter of political ideas there resulted merely disorder. Gobineau regarded the revolutionary instinct as comparatively sporadic elsewhere, but he suggested that in France at least,

Every political theory which does, or may, exist carries with it a germ of possible realization. It is more than probable that a political theory will be put into action, and for this reason every system practised is inherently bound to die and be destroyed. The essence of France's political sensibility is thus a revolutionary instinct. No party has this instinct to a greater extent than any other: they all have it. They are all revolutionary because they all want not to improve, modify or perfect, but to destroy everything and sweep the floor clean. Some say that they want to do this in order to put the clock back five, twenty-five or a hundred years; others say they want to create a completely new society. Whatever the motive or pretext, the instinct is always the same: total destruction.[40]

The revolutionary instinct was thus the only common denominator throughout these political confusions. The only faction which Gobineau regarded as in some degree immune from this contagion was that which supported a caesarist solution: 'It seems that the most reasonable and best placed part of the French population, from the standpoint of what it wants, is that which accommodates itself immediately and without quibbling to caesarism. The future dictator has but one programme to fulfil, that of dictating . . . That is neither doctrine nor theory – it is a material fact.'[41] One is tempted to suggest again that, with the royalists betrayed by their illusions and with provincialism increasingly irrelevant to the problem, Gobineau was now inclining towards this form of authoritarianism.

These works on the events of 1870–1 and on the Third Republic make only passing allusions to the ethnic theory. Indeed, as descriptions of political confusion they had little need for such reinforcement and they exhibit again the manner in which certain of Gobineau's political and social ideas can be seen as more fundamental than the racist tenets of the *Essai*. But the racial theory was certainly basic to the assumption that the decadence and disorder were irreversible. In the last two years of his life Gobineau worked on an uncompleted essay, entitled *L'Ethnographie de la France* (the original of which remains unpublished), and there we find indications that he wished to describe again more clearly and closely the relationship between the racial theory and his observations upon contemporary France. The work repeated many of the historical points of the *Essai* but, in its incomplete form, the manuscript does not reach as far as a full discussion of modern France. Its major point concerns her increasing latinization. And to this – as a vehicle of political and social degeneration within the more general context of western decline – we shall return in due course.

In addition to the thoughts that it provoked on France, the war against Prussia could not but affect Gobineau's attitude to Germany. Was the victory to be denounced as the result of crude Prussian militarism or was it indicative of inherent racial superiority? The Gobinist movement generally asserted that the latter was his interpretation. Having accepted this as an accurate description of Gobineau's view, Maurice Lange – in the 1920s – vitiated an otherwise praiseworthy study by constantly attacking him as an uncritical germanophile. In effect, Gobineau's firmly critical view of France by no means necessitated a sympathetic attitude to modern Germany, which in the *Essai* is depicted as equally afflicted by ethnic degeneration. We have seen that after his initial support for Prussian leadership in Germany he had grown increasingly hostile to her bid for supremacy over Austria. 1870 did nothing to change his new opinion. He regarded the German annexation of Alsace-Lorraine as a lamentable step which guaranteed permanent enmity and threats of renewed warfare. He noted with dismay the growing popularity of socialism in the new Reich and he was critical of Bismarck both for his precarious arrangements in foreign policy and, especially, for the hostility shown to the Catholic Church in the Kulturkampf. The militarism of the Second Reich was seen as far removed from the expression of Aryan vigour. To Dom Pedro he wrote in 1875: 'It is unfortunate that this great country ... is so completely ceasing to be intellectual in order to become especially military and is striving with all its strength to create a great industry in order to sustain its expenditure on war.'[42] After 1870 Gobineau regarded the Germans under Prussian leadership as a dangerous *Raubvolk* menacing all about them and he came to fear their Empire as he did that of the Russians.

This hostility to Germany was now all that could be considered conventionally patriotic in Gobineau's attitudes. The Patria he had already described as a semitic and despotic invention. In the imaginative works of his last years he continued to ridicule this patriotism. In the philosophical drama *La Renaissance* Machiavelli is made to remark, in words not inapplicable to the author, that, 'I

am a wretched official in the most wretched of states.'[43] Again, it is
surely Gobineau who speaks through the character of Casimir
Bullet in the novel *Les Pléiades*: 'I have . . . this great misfortune
of harbouring the most absolute comtempt and the most outspoken
hatred for that part of Europe where I was born. It does not suit
me to see a people once so great henceforth lying on the ground . . .
decomposing . . .'[44] In reviewing the *Nouvelles Asiatiques* Robert
Lytton wrote very perceptively: 'Monsieur Gobineau, when he
has occasion to introduce a European hero, never selects one of his
own countrymen . . . It may almost be said that with Gobineau
any reference to his native land is conspicuous by its absence.'[45]
Yet it was because Gobineau was imbued – by his very conviction
as to his origins – with a profound love of France that his subsequent disillusionment, disgust and even hatred, were all the more
tragic and painful. He could not share the wildly uncritical
patriotism of so many contemporaries. But, in his view, so serious
was the decay that even a critical love ceased almost to be love at all.
The Comtesse de La Tour was to write of him that, 'He loved his
poor country, he loved it with all the strength that was given to
him by his perfect understanding of its beauties and of its ills.'[46]
His strictures were not those of a traitor. They were those of an
émigré de l'intérieur, or even of Victor Hugo's *Châtiments – mais
sans Lux*.

The asperity stems less from clear hatred than from a conviction
of impotence. In 1874, writing to the Marquise de Forbin, he spoke
of 'national sterility' and remarked that, 'We revolve a little, this
way and that, as we move through the atmosphere like an exhausted
star that neither sheds light nor gives any impression of vitality'.[47]
In the political arena Gobineau was contemptuous of the party
divisions which rent France asunder while remaining in reality
meaningless in a situation where politicians shared a common
incompetence and rascality. After his retirement from the diplomatic service he continued to regard public offices as increasingly
the objects of their pillage, and he saw the conservatives as no less
guilty than others. His experience of participation in local government had only confirmed his hostility to democratic processes and
to the consultation of the masses in the direction of affairs.
Democracy was simply a form of despotism, but one lacking even
the pretensions to order made by open authoritarianism. He
exemplified thus its negation of freedom: 'From the moment that

a majority in a Chamber has discovered the means – through "the verification of credentials" – of transforming itself into unanimity by the complete expulsion of others, it is clear that there is no longer any possible division and ... the parliamentary régime arrives at the acme of its perfection.'[48] As a supporter of the Church as institution Gobineau resented republican anticlericalism and, as the brother of Mère Bénédicte of Solesmes, he showed a particular hostility to the attacks upon the religious orders. Such ill-conceived policies resulted from the human mediocrities in the seats of power and these he roundly condemned. In a fragment, which seems to be an obituary, we read his opinion that, 'Monsieur Thiers was from head to toe a ridiculous personage',[49] and similar attacks upon Gambetta and other dignitaries of the Third Republic were numerous.

Gobineau regarded ignorance and mediocrity as the outstanding features of modern politicians. He had long since rejected the idea of himself combating such men in the national arena. In 1875 he claimed to be resisting pressure from Legitimists, Orleanists and moderate Republicans in the Oise to enter the Senate. Four years earlier he had written, to the Dragoumis sisters, that, 'As for political ambition, I have less of it than ever. Is it possible during these times for anyone who is not a ruffian? It is impossible in France for ever. You are right to think that it is not I who dream of reconstruction, of regeneration.'[50] In these words he embodied all his despair at the state of France. They summarized his belief that both ideas and institutions were now incapable of redeeming her. He was inclined neither to enter her political life nor to dispense theoretical nostrums. He died in October 1882 at Turin while travelling through Italy, in voluntary exile.

5 The Viking Inheritance

In the whole of the modern world it was Scandinavia – perhaps together with the isolated settlements of Newfoundland – that appeared least remote from fulfilling the conditions of Gobineau's social ideal. It was therefore with more enthusiasm than usual that in May 1872 he took up the post of Minister to Sweden and Norway. Scarcely had he arrived than he was remarking on the admirable temperament and the intellectual vitality of the Swedes. As he exclaimed to Caroline, 'This is the pure race of the North – that of the masters.'[1] He was immediately tempted to embark upon a study of the achievements and present situation of 'the purest branch of the Germanic race'.[2] To the Brazilian Emperor he wrote: 'I notice more than ever that this essentially free and deeply reasonable people enjoy a considerable measure of vitality.'[3] This was manifest in their stress upon the value of the individual, in their predilection for the freedom of isolated habitation and in their hostility to foreign settlers – all marks of their Aryan origins and of their attempts to maintain a comparative purity of blood.

Early on he was impressed especially by the sense of social and political order and by the absence of class rivalries. In Scandinavia a large element of real personal liberty seemed still compatible with the maintenance of authority. Gobineau commented to Zoé Dragoumis that, 'There is no class hatred. The nobility lives on friendly terms with the middle class and with the people at large.'[4] He discerned few leanings towards republicanism and revolution. One of the most notable features of the society was therefore its immunity to socialist and communist doctrines, which had no great influence in a state of natural social harmony. To the wife of his orientalist friend Jules Mohl he wrote: 'Just imagine workers who agree with their employers without threatening strikes, and bosses who understand that their employees must eat and who increase wages without having to be begged – and both these parties lashing out at the International!'[5] Then to Caroline, 'The International has not a single adherent and deep calm exists here.'[6] This immunity from social disorder appeared a self-evident proof of the superior quality of Scandinavian blood, as opposed to that of the Slav, Latin or modern German stocks. Gobineau was impressed by the tranquil manner in which Oscar II succeeded to the throne in 1872: 'This country is unique . . . I have just seen one king die and another ascend the throne without anyone doubling the guard or alerting a soldier.'[7] The Swedish conduct of elections was no less orderly and worked strongly against demagogues. He explained to Dom Pedro that,

There is never any forced candidature. No one commends himself to the choice of the voters, no one makes any profession of faith. And hitherto it has been impossible to have as soap-box orators any but inconstant and discredited men to whom no one listens by virtue of the single fact that through putting themselves in evidence they are thought impudent.[8]

He contended moreover that the press had no disturbing influence and that its strong recommendation of a candidate did indeed reduce his chances of election. The Swedish Diet, in which the nobility was still represented, confined itself to practical issues and refused to be seduced by the false attractions of theorizers. Gobineau stressed that migration which in so many other parts of Europe was a negative response to political ills, was from Scandinavia a more vital and positive phenomenon. He was impressed also by the Aryan characteristic of devotion to historical tradition, especially as embodied in the sagas and great myths of the race. To Dom Pedro he declared that, 'The conservative feeling is amongst the most powerful in the national spirit and these people relinquish the past only step by step and with extreme caution.'[9]

Gobineau revealed a particular interest in Swedish education and he wrote an essay, *L'Instruction Primaire en Suède*, which appeared in *Le Correspondant* during February 1873. In Scandinavia, as in the case of north-western France, he doubtless considered that there was still some point in discussing educational issues. But here he was still more explicit in relating his account closely to the postulated ethnic situation. He alleged that the centuries of Scandinavian intellectual languor were due not to a lack of capability but to the diversion of spiritual vitality into other channels. Gobineau suggested that it had only been since the end of the reign of Gustavus Adolphus, slain in 1632, that the emphasis had been shifted. He felt that it was in praiseworthy accordance with the instincts of the race that military instruction should now be so well assimilated into the educational system. The pupil was thus coming to appreciate the value of discipline and legitimate subordination, and Gobineau noted with approval that, 'His whole school life is a constant application of the principle of order.'[10] He remarked that in few countries would he recommend the practice whereby the state had the right to withdraw children from parental control if their education were being neglected. But with regard to Sweden he exhibited no qualms at this potential infringement of family rights by the government since, such was the character of the people, the very threat was nearly always sufficient to ensure the intended and more acceptable result. Even so, this marked a notable exception from Gobineau's normal attitude to both state and family.

He was of course ultimately incapable of making his remarks on education compatible with his racial theory. The following arguments were seriously at variance with the latter:

The folk schools in Sweden have already made a considerable contribution to the nation's progress and have made possible and secure two current elements in the national character . . . the mildness of behaviour and the love of order . . . There seems no doubt that the habits derived from school have created this order and moderation . . . It is principally through education that one makes men and citizens.[11]

Though he denied that regardless of circumstances an educated nation was always worth more than an ignorant one, his enthusiasm for the instruction of all classes in Sweden not only gave an inconsistently generous role to the possibliity of social engineering but also appeared to be at variance with his fear of democratic encroachment. Towards the end of his life, however, this fear had succeeded in transforming his apparently liberal view of education. In 1879, in purely pessimistic vein, he wrote this to the Brazilian Emperor:

It will be difficult for the populations of America and Europe to attain the level of primary education existing in China, Persia and India, and I hardly see what use this diffusion of knowledge can be to the peoples who experience it, at least for their political life. As for their moral worth, it is enhanced in still smaller degree, and I believe that I shall die, as I have lived, in the firmest conviction that there is no greater absurdity in the world than a representative system of government – that is, one which consults and brings into the management of affairs the mass of the populace.[12]

The futility emphasized here was much more in accord both with the racial theory and his belief that the rule of the masses, educated or otherwise, was to be feared.

This harshening of attitude applied not merely to the particular subject of education but also to his opinion of Scandinavia more generally. This was especially explicable in terms of his inability to reconcile his racial and class views of its society. If the whole people were of comparatively pure stock then surely Gobineau should have criticized a class hierarchy with no proper racial correlation. On the other hand, if his earlier praise implied that there was indeed harmony between the racial and class structures, then Scandinavian society would be doomed eventually by the familiar triumph of the lower stock through miscegenation. Upon these points he is never sufficiently clear. As his attitude grew sterner he suggested, on the political front, that the Diet, though it lacked the hindering presence of disruptive theorizers, had come to be dominated by a majority that was greedy, parsimonious and aggressive. He ridiculed the timidity of King Oscar's treatment of them. By 1875 Gobineau had radically revised his earlier favourable view of Scandinavia. The written evidence suggests that he subsequently adapted his racial description to conform with these harsher social facts – and such a procedure, an inversion of the method he claimed to adopt in the *Essai*, should scarcely surprise us when we recall our assessment of the true status of his racial theory. On his journey of 1876 with Dom Pedro he wrote from Athens to the Comtesse de La Tour that, 'Sweden horrifies me'[13] and he commented on 'Swedish vulgarity and contemptibility'.[14] The country's materialism and worsening political conflicts had dispelled his earlier optimism, and so even Scandinavia was integrated into the picture of general European degeneration. The *Ethnographie de la France* completed the realignment of observation and theory. There he remarked, as in the *Essai*, that Scandinavia was ethnically less pure than England – a country which he proposed to visit at this time, only to be prevented by increasing ill-health. Still, by that stage, his assessment even of England was unflattering. To Dom Pedro he described her foreign policy as a series of wild adventures. The English, though embodying still the most truly Aryan-German remnants in Europe, were now under strong attack from Latin semitization, and the dominance of the vacuous liberal Gladstone and of the Jew Disraeli was indicative of this fact.

Despite this process of disillusionment with Scandinavia, Gobineau's Stockholm sojourn was of great importance in terms both of his literary productions (*Les Pléiades, Les Nouvelles Asiatiques, La Renaissance* and part of *Amadis*) and of the effect of mystical communion with the Viking-Aryan past. The impurities of modern Scandinavia could not dispel Gobineau's conception of its glorious history. This past inspired another narrative poem, *Olaf Trygvasson* (completed in 1874. but unpublished in his lifetime) and – still more significantly – it encouraged sustained work on a family history. Finally appearing in 1879, the *Histoire d'Ottar Jarl, Pirate Norvégien, Conquérant du Pays de Bray, en Normandie, et de sa Descendance* is a work whose title speaks eloquently. It is an attempt at genealogical history, in which boldness is matched in magnitude only by error and self-delusion. It is ironical that Gobineau was still to write in his *Ethnographie de la France* that, 'It is quite usual for a people to choose from among its ancestors a line which it finds particularly agreeable. They wish to see that alone and they pride themselves upon being descended exclusively from it.'[15] When however Keller made some similar – and justifiable – remarks on *Ottar Jarl* and suggested that it was primarily a genealogical romance in the tradition of *Dichtung und Wahrheit*, Gobineau dismissed such a judgement. Still, it was surely while enmeshed in these same romantic trammels that Gobineau piously supped mead by the royal tumuli at Old Uppsala and that, as his friend Philipp von Eulenburg later recalled, he stood upon the rocks at Djursholm and declared: 'This is the seat of Ottar Jarl. From hence I sprang – I can feel it!'[16]

Whatever the inaccuracies and the illusory foundations of *Ottar Jarl*, we must recognize the importance of Gobineau's sincere belief in a family ancestry reaching back to the Aryan-Scandinavian nobility of the ninth century. Even without delving here into genealogical details, we may quickly appreciate that the book is relevant both to the development of Gobineau's racial theory and to our assessment of his religious attitudes. He came to regard the

work as the completion of a trilogy whose earlier elements had
been the *Essai* and the Persian history – therefore as the final part
of what Jean Gaulmier has termed 'a poetic vision of the human
adventure'.[17] It is true that from youth he had borne in mind the
composition of a family history. But only with hindsight did he
suggest that it was this interest in the origins of his own family
which had prompted the writing of the *Essai*. There is no evidence
from the 1850s to support the idea that this concern was as important as he claimed a generation later when his Viking fantasies
were being developed. Still, by the time of *Ottar Jarl*'s completion,
he was ready to place it firmly in a context retrospectively construc-
ted. It was then seen as the culmination of a progression from a
universal history of all races (in the *Essai*) to an extensive treatment
of one of the great Aryan branches (in the *Histoire des Perses*) and
on to an attempt at tracing in detail the story of a single family.
The validity of this approach was questionable. Gobineau unwittingly damned *Ottar Jarl* by writing of it to Dom Pedro as follows:
'I have been wanting to show that the history of men – that is of
the families which are the whole man – would be a more realistic
base for knowledge than the vague collections of generalizations
that are presented as historical explanation.'[18] This desire to work
from the particular to the general was admirable – the only complication was that Gobineau was incapable of fulfilling it. In fact,
the final two works of the alleged trilogy are vitiated by the
normally uncritical acceptance of the highly generalized conclusions already produced in the nebulously cosmic *Essai*. In any case,
since the idea of the triadic relationship only seems to have occurred
to Gobineau after the completion of the two earlier works, it should
certainly not blind us to the fact that in many respects *Ottar Jarl* is
as closely related to other later works – particularly *Les Pléiades*
and *La Renaissance* – as to the *Essai* and the *Histoire des Perses*.

   In this Persian history Gobineau had strongly contrasted
original Aryan society with semitized societies marked by crude
materialism. In the most modern instances the latter had been
manifested in the dehumanizing processes of capitalistic industrialization. The Aryan race had a different and more vitalist conception
of labour: 'It has loved and praised work for its own sake, and
above all for the happy consequences that result from it in regard
to the inner man and to family ties. It has only envisaged the
question of profit in a secondary way.'[19] He reiterated that the

individualism of members of this race was expressed in the limitations placed upon the authority of the tribal leaders. Of the
Scandinavians during their invading activities he said: 'The state
did not exist. Heads of families were united and scarcely anything
more. The king was simply a military leader established for the
benefit of each, and he commanded only within quite restricted
limits.'[20] He suggested that the Aryans conceived of themselves as
masters of a universe created to benefit and serve them. Of
Christian universalism he remarked that, 'Nothing was more
opposed to the exclusive principles of the Aryan race.'[21] In *Ottar
Jarl* such thoughts were further developed. There he declared that,
'Aryans have a natural tendency to find god in themselves and to
believe that what is useful to them is in itself right and sacred.'[22]
It was because Christianity worked against this conception that it
was slow to attract Aryan support. Thus progressively Gobineau
faced the incompatibility between Christian and Aryan morality.
Although he still maintained that the twin foundations of the
European Middle Ages were Christianity and Aryan-Germanism,
there was increasing recognition of the tension between them.
Christianity was based upon a cosmopolitan ideal of unity and
equality; Aryanism was based upon inegalitarian ideas of racial
predestination.

Although after his arrival in Rio he had already written to
Caroline that, 'I have not brought a Bible . . . desiring to have done
with that whole phase of ideas',[23] his Scandinavian experience was
probably the crucial factor in evincing fully this realization. His
immediate intuitive sympathy with the paganism of the North
stimulated a more coherent attitude to religious questions. He
noted without regret the degree to which paganism had survived
and the extent to which Christianity was there a matter of merely
nominal faith and allegiance. To Caroline he suggested that, 'The
Scandinavians have never been either Catholics or Protestants,
except for administrative purposes. The fundamental ideas have
remained pagan.'[24] In the same correspondence his reference to
himself as 'a son of Odin'[25] intimates more than a mere jest. He
explained, again in the invaluable letters to his sister, that he found
no difficulty in accepting the existence of God or the immortality of
the soul but that he was reluctant to tie himself at all closely to the
beliefs of any particular religion. His relativism could scarcely
have been more accommodating, since he remarked thus of the

systems of belief linked to the names of Jupiter, Buddha, Christ
and Odin: 'These are types of ideas which I am inclined to think
fairly true or fairly false according to time and place.'[26] He agreed
that Scandinavian paganism was conducive to a certain degree of
laxity in morals, particularly in sexual matters – an assertion that
seemed to work against his conception of Aryan respect for women.
But he denied that it necessarily produced a morality worse than
that of less emphatically pagan societies. To Dom Pedro he commented: 'If the morality of the young has been greatly affected,
then undoubtedly the general life of the people has been much less
so than with us.'[27]

Nevertheless Gobineau managed (though without much plausibility) to maintain his support for the Catholic Church as a social
bastion. The leading Catholic powers had recently been defeated
at the hands of Protestant Prussia, and the Infallibility Decree of
1870 could be interpreted as a sign of weakness rather than strength,
as it emanated from a despairing Papacy deprived of temporal
realms. Gobineau was personally hostile to the idea of papal
infallibility, not merely to the expediency of its promulgation. He
explained reasonably to Caroline that, since he could not subscribe
fully to the Church's dogmas, he could not be wholly obedient to it,
however deep his sympathy with its social role. But he then added:
'I have never been included among free-thinkers and I never shall
be. On the contrary, I shall always be counted among the Catholics
and, if need be, I should take Communion with great ceremony at
the top of the towers of Notre-Dame so that people could see this
better. Do you know why? It is because I hate this age.'[28] That
final remark was scarcely satisfying theologically – but it forcefully
expressed the reasoning behind most of Gobineau's beliefs,
religious or otherwise. Similar comments in his last years – most
notably with regard to Bismarck's handling of the Kulturkampf –
demonstrate clearly that it was a certain social pragmatism (itself
somewhat rare in a philosophy rendered arid by racial determinism)
rather than faith, which was fundamental to his nominal Catholicism. That this pragmatism did not extend so far as to accept the
still greater emphasis upon papal power – which might seem to
accord well with Gobineau's authoritarian tendencies – was perhaps due to the fact that the Petrine see was practically an exclusively Italian perquisite. In fact, he never succeeded in solving the
general paradox that the northern Europe he tended to favour upon

ethnic grounds was mainly Protestant while the more miscegenated South was predominantly Catholic.

The Comtesse de La Tour, whose deep friendship was the greatest solace of Gobineau's last decade, remarked that, 'He wished to die like his forefathers, in the bosom of the Catholic Church.'[29] In a sense, this will had always been present, but Gobineau had lacked the faith to give it proper fulfilment. A recently discovered entry for January 1882 in the diary of his friend the Comte de Basterot confirms this judgment. Gobineau confided to him not only his fundamentally pagan convictions but also the fact that any thoughts of reconciliation with Christianity sprang merely from a nostalgic desire to die in the style of his Catholic ancestors. In the event, he ended his life in the manner of the still earlier pagan ancestors he had invented. There was no deathbed scene, no recantation or reconciliation that we know.

Without his peculiar form of agnosticism it is difficult to understand how two, at least, of the major aspects of his social and political thought could have been taken to their logical conclusions. On one hand, it allowed him to emphasize the moral dualism implicit in his élitist theory of ethnic determinism. On the other, this agnosticism contributed to confirming his view that Christianity's claims as a civilizing force were misconceived and that it was as impotent as any other system of ideas to save civilization. Thereby he was encouraged to develop further his pessimism as to universal decline. It is around this moral dualism and the triumph of this pessimism that we shall concentrate the final parts of our discussion.

6 The Élite and the Masses

Interpretations of the later thought of Gobineau have not infrequently placed heavy emphasis upon a certain doctrine of individualism. In these accounts it is alleged that he moved from the overt racial concerns of the *Essai* to concentrate on the vitalist élite figures of *Les Pléiades* and *La Renaissance* and on the heroes of *Ottar Jarl* and the epic *Amadis*. Here, however, we shall aim to show how the racial theory continues to influence these works in a manner which negates any liberating potential and which forces us to conclude that the moral dualism implied by the *Essai* is actually reinforced and made more explicit, to the detriment of any individualist strivings. The case for the maintenance of this individualism rests upon Gobineau's belief that, as ethnic differences are progressively removed through miscegenation, it is only certain figures who stand out as isolated instances of blood-worth. But we must note that praise for these necessitates condemnation of others. The more that Gobineau stresses their worth the further removed is he from a truly individualist position where all men, regardless of their racial origins, are granted certain qualities, freedoms and rights, in virtue of their common humanity. In *Ottar Jarl* Gobineau wrote: 'To appreciate properly the worth of a man taken in isolation, there is no doubt today that we must analyse his family.'[1] But the worth of the family itself is made dependent on race and thus we are brought back to all the implications of ethnic determinism and their necessary hostility to any truly individualistic social theory.

Gobineau did certainly strive to provide an individualistic gloss to racism in perhaps the most extraordinary of his works, a confusing pseudo-philosophical discourse entitled *Mémoire sur Diverses Manifestations de la Vie Individuelle*. First conceived soon after the appearance of the *Essai*, it was seriously taken up in 1866.

Gobineau completed a manuscript in opaque French, but subsequently, having found a publisher beyond the Rhine, he was himself largely responsible for a still denser German adaptation which then appeared publicly in 1868. Professor A. B. Duff, who over thirty years ago edited the parallel texts, referred to the work aptly as an 'amalgam of philosophy, natural sciences, linguistics and anthropology'.[2] Gobineau's highly unsatisfactory study embodied principally a complex, ingenious and ingenuous investigation into the relationship between race and language. But we are primarily concerned here with the value and status of his remarks upon *la vie individuelle* – 'life, in its proper sense'.[3] He suggests that, 'The greatest possible fullness of consciousness, the vivid sensation of being, of being individually, of being that is separate from all the rest of matter surrounding, of being for itself and in itself, all this alone can be assumed to bring the complete life.'[4] Such examples could be greatly multiplied. The limitation is that it is as ethnic uniformity grows through debasement that individual differences and their expression are put at a premium. As we shall see, the most notable individuality is dependent upon certain isolated instances of 'ethnic persistence' in the midst of miscegenation. These comprise the surviving ethnic élite, and they are placed in contrast to the masses.

Gobineau referred in the *Nouvelles Asiatiques*, within a human context, to 'the descending series of creatures',[5] and his introduction to the same work stressed again the differences and inequalities of mankind. In the *Ethnographie de la France* he explained that, once a superior race was brought into contact with lesser breeds, the resultant society could only remain stable so long as there existed 'some equilibrium or other between races in hierarchy'.[6] With such hierarchical presuppositions Gobineau had to regard the completeness of some lives as fundamentally more valuable than that of others. In the same work he states: 'There is a very great gulf between the worth of a man of pure race and one of mongrelized race, since the former is in quite entire possession of his moral and physical character.'[7] The individual must strive with all his energy to fulfil the promise of his essence; but the nature and limitations of that essence are preordained by the survival or nonsurvival of certain racial characteristics. In sum, Gobineau's individualism was for the élite alone.

This is brought out strongly in his novel *Les Pléiades*, to be regarded less as a single story than as a series of episodes centring on the activities of a small company of *esprits d'élite*. The book first appeared in 1874, but two years earlier Gobineau had explained to Prokesch-Osten that it was based on the idea 'that there are no longer classes, that there are no longer peoples, but only – in the whole of Europe – certain individuals who float like wreckage upon the flood.'[8] In his own life he had encountered such figures – Tocqueville and Mérimée, George V of Hanover and Pedro II of Brazil, Lytton and Prokesch-Osten himself. Those who try to make out a case of Gobineau as a defender of individualism maintain that in *Les Pléiades* the élite is simply constituted from certain individuals regardless of their origin. But Gobineau's point is more subtle. By now, having moved increasingly further from his simpler class-identification of the 1840s, he is striving to indicate the modern disjunction between social origins, on one hand, and racial ones upon the other. A member of the élite – *un fils de roi* – need have no connection with any modern king or any contemporary nobility. The proper ethnic and social hierarchy has been so disturbed that nobility of race is scarcely reflected still in social status. Gobineau indeed waxed eloquent in his last years about the meaningless of centuries of artificial ennoblement, particularly in France. As he was to suggest in the unpublished preface to the proposed second edition of *Ottar Jarl*, the creations of royalty could scarcely compete with those of divinity. True nobility was a matter of blood, not of occupation or royal decree. In *Les Pléiades*, commenting adversely on the aristocracy of his ruritanian state of Burbach, he wrote: 'It was religiously fulfilling the programme of all modern nobilities – carefully keeping itself in an intellectual and moral situation suited to rendering few services.'[9] In this and other ways the novel depicted the alleged irrelevance of modern interpretations of social hierarchy and status to the real issues of ethnic nobility.

Through the character of Wilfrid Nore Gobineau explains how *un fils de roi* would describe himself:

I have a temperament bold and generous, and am ignorant of the common motives of ordinary natures. My tastes are unfashionable. I feel for myself and my likes and dislikes are not dictated by the press. My independent spirit and the most complete freedom of my opinions are the unshakeable prerogatives of my noble origin. Heaven conferred them upon me in the cradle, just as the sons of France once received the blue riband of the Order of the Holy Ghost, and I shall keep them as long as I live. Finally, as a most logical consequence of these premises, I am not content with what satisfies the masses, and, among the gems which Heaven has placed within the grasp of men, I am looking for other jewels than those which excite the common people.[10]

It is through the German Conrad Lanze that Gobineau expresses the nature of the supremacy enjoyed by a member of the élite:

> What he is springs from an innate and mysterious mixture, a complete combination within himself of the noble or, if you like, the divine elements which his ancestors possessed of old in all their fullness, and which later generations by miscegenation in unworthy unions had for a time disguised, covered up, weakened, concealed, hidden, but which, never dying, suddenly reappear in the 'king's son' about whom we are talking.[11]

This passage exemplifies the mystical, intuitive and irrational aspects of racial belief, and also clarifies the meaning of Gobineau's assertion to Prokesch-Osten that the book was based upon the idea of the disappearance of classes and peoples. It is they which vanish as the processes of miscegenation and growing ethnic uniformity continue. All that remain distinct are certain isolated individuals, regardless of modern social prestige or alleged national boundaries.

The manner in which these isolated but powerful examples of 'ethnic persistence' appear is again discussed in *Ottar Jarl*, principally in a digression – three chapters long – extraneous to the text of the first draft. Here Gobineau claims that, although the Aryan branches are withering away, there are still individuals of ethnic worth whose superiority is manifested in forms both physical and moral. Environment, while remaining subordinate to the primary determinant of race, plays a more prominent role in this book than in the *Essai*. Its contribution, as in the case of Newfoundland, is primarily to create a situation in which the vitalist racial qualities are exercised in struggle against the elements. The interplay of challenge and response is exemplified in a passage such as this:

> Climatic influence in no way created, augmented or diminished the power of the Norwegian family, whether morally or physically, but it incessantly compelled that family to make use of its inner strength and, from the application of a natural law resulting from this tension, compelled it also to concentrate the most extensive part of its other abilities around its talents for attack and resistance.[12]

If life lacked this element of struggle it became sterile. It was during his Scandinavian visit that Gobineau realized fully the association between the spirit of blood and that of landscape and soil – an old romantic theme, with environmentalist implications, that became increasingly important in later racist thought.

The polarization of élite and mass is also illustrated in *La Renaissance : Scènes Historiques* (1877), which Gobineau termed a philosophical drama. The work is in five sections (headed with the names of Savonarola, Caesar Borgia, Julius ii, Leo x and Michaelangelo), each of which comprises an historical commentary followed by a dramatic dialogue – the latter alone being published in the edition that appeared in Gobineau's lifetime. It is in the Renaissance, to which fundamentally he is still hostile because of its association with latinization, that he chooses to depict more figures of the élite and to elaborate upon the moral implications of their superiority as 'golden flowers, great miracles of human vitality'.[13] Gobineau was relying increasingly upon a poetic and mystical method which overrode any great concern with historical accuracy or theatrical feasibility. To the Comtesse de La Tour he wrote: 'I am concerned much less with the drama than with the philosophy of the scenes.'[14] He explained to Zoé Dragoumis that, 'The theme of the work will be the popular passion for Italian unity, desired in various forms, its development, the efforts to attain it, the disaster, the impossibility of achieving it. The time-span will take in a period roughly from 1470 to 1560.'[15] It is an impressionistic depiction of heroes: Caesar Borgia dreaming of domination and Julius ii of freeing Italy from the foreigner; Michaelangelo and Raphael exhibiting the superiority of individual artistic genius in a period of political failure and corruption. It embodies a study of great men in the midst of decadence. For, despite his hatred against the resurgence of the Latin spirit, Gobineau could write that, 'It was the sixteenth century which saw the flower of the human spirit most vividly in bloom.'[16] He reiterates that the value of the Middle Ages had lain in the alliance between Germanism and Christianity. Medieval achievements had been at their height around the twelfth and thirteenth centuries, before entering into decline: 'Religion had begun by softening the Germanic spirit and providing it with reasons for sociability.'[17] And in this movement, away from the healthy isolationism of earlier Aryans towards a more enervating and miscegenated social existence, is embodied the downfall of the

Germanic spirit. The nemesis inherent in Gobineau's theory of the rise and fall of civilizations is maintained here: 'It is at the climax of things that we can ... see the appearance of the seed of their decadence.'[18] It is in the midst of this organic decay that, struggling against their environment, the great figures of the Renaissance emerge.

It is in such contrasts between isolated worth and mass mediocrity that the moral implications of Gobineau's ideas become clear. In the vast philosophical epic-poem *Amadis* they become clearest of all. The work stood in the tradition of *Manfredine*, and of a further long and turgid poem, *Le Paradis de Béowulf*, which dated from around 1870 and which remained unpublished until resurrected by Ludwig Schemann. The researches by Rahel Thenen into the history of the composition of *Amadis* have strongly reinforced the argument that, in these last years, Gobineau increasingly rejected doctrines of common humanity and emphasized ever more radically the racial and moral distinctions among men. The epic has three parts: the first was written in 1869, and published in 1876; the second was begun in 1876, and finished at the end of 1878; the third was composed during 1879–80. Under the scrutiny of the Comtesse de La Tour a posthumous edition, encompassing all three parts, was published in 1887. It nonetheless left certain evident gaps in the text of parts two and three, with the suggestion that the manuscript itself was incomplete. We now know, contrary to previous belief, that *Amadis* was indeed finished and that the lacunae in the 1887 edition resulted from the desire of the Comtesse de La Tour and of Caroline to remove passages which were offensive to their own conventional Christian susceptibilities and which they wished to regard as mere aberrations upon the part of the author. The restored text shows that, on the contrary, they were an essential part of Gobineau's progressively harsher distinction between the moral qualities of the élite and those of the masses.

The first part of *Amadis* was devoted to reproducing 'the ideal of medieval morals and activity'.[19] But it is the second and third Books, dealing respectively with 'the morals and deeds of the present era' and with their impending consequences in 'the ruin of the modern world',[20] which contain some of Gobineau's most mordant comments upon contemporary and future decadence. *Amadis II* reveals Europe plunged by ethnic debasement into materialism and worldly pleasure and ruled by the usurping bourgeois Théophraste. *Amadis III* depicts not only degeneration within but also further danger without. On one hand, there is the ruling demagogue Barrabas, man of the people; on the other, the external threat of yellow hordes preparing the final downfall of the West. In the subsequent battle the middle classes, who in their materialistic desires so resemble the invader, are the instruments of betrayal. The masses also are denounced, not least because they are allegedly devoid of soul:

> Une âme en eux? . . . Certes, très bien
> Ils savaient qu'ils n'en avaient rien.*[21]

Their mortality is put into contrast with the spiritual immortality of Amadis struggling manfully against the overwhelming forces within and without. The final canto, entitled 'The Twilight of the Gods' (suggesting strongly Gobineau's new friendship with Richard Wagner), shows the apotheosis of Amadis and his brethren of the élite.

Gobineau goes as far as to attack Christ (though without naming him) for trying to drag the poor from the mire to which their inherent weaknesses have condemned them. In the *Essai* he had compromised with religious orthodoxy to the point where he had at least allowed all men some limited rights and qualities by virtue of their common humanity. *Amadis* negates even that. It is an assertion of the ego, of aristocratic morality, of liberty, love and honour for the few alone. The élite is deified while the rest of humanity is denied a soul or after-life. Naturally, since we cannot be sure that Gobineau himself really believed in the existence of a supernatural paradise, we should not take too literally any associated remarks about the soul or immortality. The important point is not to question whether he believed the literal truth of his statements but rather to grasp the moral dualism based upon race which, literally or figuratively, they so strongly suggest. In such a context the triple ethnic division becomes superfluous and the only significant distinction is a dualistic one – between the racial élite and the masses.

While the Comtesse de La Tour was herself piously busy amending 'Gods' to 'God' throughout the text of the epic, she received from the puzzled Caroline a letter that included the following remarks:

* A soul for them? . . . To be sure, they knew very well that they had none.

According to the definition in *Amadis*, soul depends on blood purity and only the superior white race possesses this quality . . . This is the most utter materialism. Arthur certainly never had that conclusion in mind . . . It thus seems to me that we can only consider all this new theory – which is as unjustifiable religiously as it is scientifically – as an alteration to his system . . . I should be extremely happy were you to suppress these passages, because they harm the unity of the whole poem and they are moreover completely contradictory to what Arthur wrote in his better work.[22]

In reality the tragedy was that – whatever his intention – Gobineau's racial theory had always had this very materialism as its logical conclusion. The contradiction stressed by Caroline was more apparent than real. The alteration was not to the system itself; it simply affected Gobineau's degree of readiness, under the strain of increasing alienation from the modern world, to accept the full implications of the racist theory. Nor were such ideas purveyed only in epic bombast, which one might be tempted to discount as a reliable source if it had appeared alone. As we shall show, *Amadis* was simply a metaphysical manifestation of ideas which Gobineau was also enunciating in other forms.

The ethical dualism of *Amadis* accords with the master-morality developed through all the works we have mentioned in examining Gobineau's thoughts on the élite. Understandably he has been compared, in this respect at least, with Nietzsche. Such a morality of domination was implied in *Les Pléiades*, not only – as we noted – in the assertion of the elevated morality of the élite but also in the denial of a moral existence to the masses. There Nore is made to remark that, apart from the present élite (perhaps some three thousand or so in number), there remains only 'a world of insects . . . intent on bringing down morals, rights, laws and customs, all that I have loved and respected . . . I don't see that they have any soul – though that is scarcely their fault.'[23] Nore sees a mass of 'fools', 'scoundrels' and 'brutes', and he might well have said with Baudelaire that, 'From freedom cherished impiously is born a new tyranny, the tyranny of the beasts – zoocracy.'[24] It was such zoo-cracy that Gobineau denounced in the final part of *Amadis*. Around that time that *Les Pléiades* was published he made, in correspondence with Caroline, the following comparison to the detriment of Christianity: 'I find the primitive religions of the Aryan Vedas more straightforward and reasonable, as well as more simple. Every Aryan was saved and joined the ranks of the Gods by sole virtue of the purity of his race. Everyone else, black and yellow, came to naught for the same sort of reason.'[25] Here the justification by blood alone, which was implicit in the *Essai*, becomes explicit. It reveals one of the roots of the moral nihilism eventually embodied in the racist-totalitarian movements of the twentieth century.

In 1868 Gobineau had written to Zoé Dragoumis: 'You know that deep down my sole political belief is that any man of real blood is created and put into the world in order to take charge of lesser people.'[26] He felt it his personal tragedy that, born out of his time, he was too late to exercise his inherent mastership. Others, less modest, who followed would use these same moral presuppositions to justify in practice the rule of the ethnic master over the slave belonging to the anti-race. They would act in accordance with what he had written of the Aryan race in *Ottar Jarl*: 'It accepts none but itself in the world, and it seeks as much dominance as possible, because the sole guarantee that it can envisage to ensure its perpetuation (that is, its life) would be to exist alone surrounded by a void.'[27] In other hands this could be twisted into a plea not so much for glorious isolation as for the extermination of the anti-races – into a justification for genocide. It is a reflection of the moral nihilism expressed in one of the central scenes of *La Renaissance*. Pope Alexander VI's words to Lucretia Borgia epitomize the racist's ethical imperative:

Know from henceforth that, for the kind of person whom destiny calls to dominate others, the ordinary rules of life are reversed and duty becomes quite different. Good and evil are transferred to another and higher plane. Then the virtues which might be applauded in an ordinary woman would in you become vices, simply because they would only be the source of obstacles and ruin. Now the great law of the world is not to do this or that, to avoid one thing or pursue another, It is to live, to enlarge and develop our most active and sublime qualities, in such a way that from any sphere we can always strive to reach one that is wider, more airy, more elevated. Do not forget that. Go straight ahead. Simply do as you please, in so far as it serves your interest. Leave weakness and scruples to the petty minds and to the rabble of underlings. There is only one consideration worthy of you – the elevation and greatness of the House of Borgia, the elevation and greatness of yourself.[28]

Predestination by blood must of necessity take us, in Nietzsche's phrase, *jenseits von Gut und Böse* – beyond Good and Evil, in any conventional sense. The only question remaining is whether or not it can allow the élite to attain the goal of its own freedom.

Not even here are Gobineau's ideas liberated from the shackles of nemesis. In the final version of the foreword to the second edition of the *Essai* we find him ridiculing his contemporaries for failing to admit that, once one allows that man's intrinsic worth depends upon his racial qualities, one must then disclaim any belief in equality. But it is most illuminating to note that, in the first draft, Gobineau stressed rather the need to accept the suppression of belief in *free will*. Though he omitted this from the final manuscript version, it constitutes a minor – but very instructive – example of the manner in which ethnic determinism is self-defeating. It works against both equality and free will – even though Gobineau was understandably reluctant to accept openly the consequences in regard to the latter. He thus wilfully ignored the limitations placed by racial determinism upon the moral freedom of the élite itself. We must conclude that, in the last resort, such a theory necessitates the stultification of everything that depends upon the notions of free will and free moral activity, including the most basic of political choices. This is as applicable to the élite as to the masses. Although such a theory may grant the former a title to domination, the philosophy is prevented by the shackles of its own determinism from being a doctrine of freedom in any meaningful sense – even for the master-race itself.

The Triumph of Social
Pessimism

We saw in the first part of this study that Gobineau's earliest
political and social concerns were not primarily racial. In the
second we investigated the connections between the ethnic theory
and these concerns, and in this final part we have attempted to
trace the later development of this relationship. Here we have
noted that Gobineau strove in his final writings to integrate his
works on 1870 and the Third Republic into the racial theory by
undertaking the uncompleted *Ethnographie de la France*, while on
the imaginative plane *Amadis* re-emphasized, in a more explicitly
racial direction, the theories of the élite and the masses contained in
Les Pléiades and *La Renaissance*. The result of the ethnic theory
was that his pessimism became irreversible. Without the ideas
elaborated in the *Essai* Gobineau might have been able to regard
the social confusion around him as symptomatic of the decay of
states rather than of a whole civilization. Without these same ideas
he might have been encouraged to devise a strategy of piecemeal
social engineering and repair. It is the ethnic theory which represents the paralysis of political action and exhortation and which
imposes a philosophy of resignation not regeneration. It is this
theory which, negating the Christian optimism and the more purely
secular humanitarianism of those about him, leaves him immersed
in profound pessimism. It reinforces an attitude to human nature
which, as it progressively emphasizes the bestiality of the masses,
exonerates him still further from attempting to produce a theory
giving hope to society as a whole. These are the functions, these
the implications, of Gobineau's racist theory.

The sporadic traces of optimism are neither sustained nor integrated into the rest of his social thinking. In his last years he

simply noted that the processes of degeneration already depicted were accelerating and that the last of the great civilizations was ending. His pagan Valhalla gave him but passing consolation and these years were marked by ill-health, failing sight, loneliness and disappointment at lack of recognition. He became ever more alienated from the world about him. In 1873 he had already written to Prokesch-Osten that, 'In all of Europe, I like only that which is no more, and what there is seems to me a sad preface, with sadder chapters to follow.'[1] Though he persisted as the prophet of decline, he could also declare in *La Renaissance*: 'Man rarely predicts with accuracy. His reason is only unreason constantly upset by the course of events over which it has no power.'[2] Yet he never seemed to recognize the application of this fallibility to himself.

The validity of his predictions was supposed to depend upon the accuracy of his historical assessments, and there too he was no less muddled. In the mid-1870s Gobineau composed an essay, again left uncompleted and unpublished in his lifetime, entitled *Vues sur l'Histoire Générale*. It aimed to illuminate his conception of the nature of history but, in its incomplete state, this object was scarcely achieved. He does however make a plea for the scientific history which he considers possible in the light of all the new material then becoming available. There is surprising criticism of the political uses made of history through the ages and a particularly startling assault on Boulainvillier for distorting the record in the interests of the French nobility, as conventionally conceived. These are attacks equally applicable to Gobineau himself. The very progress in historical knowledge, which he claimed to applaud, increasingly discredited his own offerings and he was singularly ill-equipped – by temperament rather than talent – to purvey 'scientific' history. In 1873 he had written to his sister that, 'Men of broad genius are pleasant amateurs who produce nothing at all.'[3] He neglected to see how self-condemnatory that remark was. His historical relativism and mysticism were embodied in his additional comment that, 'All is true, all is false. Each man's point of view has some good in it and every point of view is incomplete.'[4]

Pessimism concerning the modern world is highlighted by a progressively more utopian vision of the Middle Ages. The reservations about the period made in the *Essai* are no longer brought out. For instance, in his fragment *L'Histoire des Mérovingiens* (1882) he contrasts the chivalrous medieval élite with 'the present world, dying, suffering, exhausted, groaning . . . battered and thrashing, butchered and near to death'.[5] As it began to take shape this essay dealt less with the Merovingian dynasty than with the contemporary world. The latter is compared with Rome in its decadence:

> The present situation, like the Roman, . . . has reached the stage of reducing to money all ideal, moral and fundamental authority. This results in the same catastrophe. The nineteenth century stands beside the fifth . . . Just as its predecessor might have been, it is stripped of all the qualities innate in a people which is of good race, which reasons like a race, which wants what its race wants and which, having the opinions of its race, can never depart from them.[6]

The study was intended originally to reveal 'a complete history of the Merovingians in which I shall show amidst just what rabble they had the misfortune to live – that is, among the Gallo-Romans who at this very moment are turning to Monsieur Grévy and Monsieur Gambetta.'[7] He praised the Germanic Middle Ages for establishing and maintaining personal rights against the encroachments of state and monarch. This was an achievement which previously he would have been inclined to attribute only to a much earlier Aryan society. Similarly his more sympathetic and positive view of feudalism was sustained. Truly could he at the end of his life declare to Dom Pedro that, 'I am a man of the middle Ages – and remain so.'[8]

A proposed second edition of the *Essai* seemed to provide Gobineau with an admirable opportunity for revision in the light of the progress of historical studies and in consequence of the evolution of his own thinking. There is no doubt that he felt some corrections and elaborations were necessary. In 1874 he had commented that, 'It requires a very long introduction and much revision in the text.'[9] The tone of the intended revisions can probably be discerned from his remark to Caroline that, while writing the first edition, 'I was rather more timid than I am today.'[10] He reported that he was studying Darwin with a view to considering his ideas within the context of the new edition: 'I am sure to smash what has to be destroyed in Darwin's system and to do it in a manner that will please me, while keeping what needs to be kept.'[11] He referred to this as the most important of the revisions, but regarded the whole recension as 'a long and important business'.[12] He thought that the second edition might require an extra volume or even more. In 1877 we find him correcting the Conclusion – 'the object of my work'[13]. Yet by the following year, when he was encountering difficulty in finding a publisher for the revised work, he had resigned himself to changing nothing.

Eventually a second edition, in two volumes unabridged, appeared posthumously in 1884 under the imprint of Firmin Didot, the original publishers of the book. Its republication was probably aided by a subvention from the Wagner circle at Bayreuth. It included a brief biographical sketch by the Comte de Basterot, but the substantive text of the *Essai* was left unaltered. The edition did however contain a new foreword by the author himself. He reported completing one such introductory piece in 1877 – and this is probably the earlier of the two versions conserved in manuscript at Strasbourg. The later – published – version was completed almost certainly early in 1882, for in her typewritten acount *Les Dernières Années du Comte de Gobineau* the Comtesse de La Tour states clearly that Gobineau finished preparing such a foreword during his last winter in Rome. In this short prefatory essay he writes thus of the new edition's relationship to the first: 'The present edition has not altered a single line of the original book. In the interval much research has indeed illuminated many matters of detail, but nothing has shaken any of the essential truths which I set forth, and I have thought it necessary to maintain the truth such as I found it.'[14] But, from the foregoing, we may realize that, if energy and publishers had allowed, the second edition would have shown considerable changes. The only surviving notes for the preparation of the second edition are a set of jottings on cards – mainly concerning anthropological works. The discovery of the emendations upon which Gobineau worked in the 1870s would be highly illuminating. Still, one suspects, from what indirect evidence there is, that the emendations would have been principally in the direction of making still more dogmatic statements and elaborations of points already made.

The various interpretations being placed upon the work of Darwin were obviously topics of significance for any revision. Gobineau would surely have been hostile to the liberal evolutionist school of Herbert Spencer, but we know from various of Gobineau's remarks that he found confirmation of his own views on ethnic conflict and on vitalism in that part at least of social darwinism which emphasized life as a struggle and as a process implying death as well as survival. For Gobineau the outward-looking vitalist urge, which had once been utilized so fruitfully to fertilize and spread civilization, was now in fact a liability in a world of mediocrity. Now the activism of the élite could remain of value only so long as it was turned inward upon itself, as the remnants of the great race searched for an isolation to delay their own inevitable absorption. The laws of survival, so he thought, were now working in favour of the mediocrities – those best adapted and attuned to life in the contemporary world. In contexts such as these Gobineau went so far as to suggest that Darwin – and indeed Thomas Buckle – had borrowed and abused certain of his own ideas. On the popular debating point regarding descent from the apes Gobineau was careful to insure himself against charges of religious heterodoxy. But what he called in the *Ethnographie de la France* his 'complete self-abandonment to the theological solution'[15] was scarcely ever noticeable, except occasionally at this level of unsubstantiated piety. It was certainly contrary to the predominant tenor of his later thought. He was certainly keen to leave open the possibility that certain groups of men might have some form of ape-ancestry. And he used this to confirm his new emphasis upon dehumanization among the masses and upon the void separating them from the élite. To Caroline he explained:

I am convinced that Darwin's system – which does not say, as it is generally made to say, that man is descended from the ape – has some truth in it, in the sense that some of our present mongrelized races are indeed descended from certain beings intermediate between man and the monkey, as a consequence of intermixture between these types and man.[16]

Here again, in an arbitrarily selective application of Darwin, the assertions of common humanity in the *Essai* are forgotten.

Gobineau's hostility extended beyond Darwin, Buckle and Ernst Haeckel to the ever more fashionable *préhistorains*. He attacked findings which argued for an enlargement of the chronological extent of prehistory and which thereby made his own ideas more vulnerable to environmentalist rebuffs. The Englishmen Lubbock and Evans and the German excavator of Troy, Heinrich Schliemann, were the particular objects of his charge that prehistorical studies sadly lacked the scientific status which their practitioners increasingly claimed. Though Gobineau sought such a status for the *Essai* we have noted that, in reality, his racial theory was less a body of learning than a political idea, an example of the quality of belief rather than of the power of knowledge, an essay in myth and symbolism rather than in realism. This made it in large degree immune to the influences of new discoveries. Thus, despite his attempts of the 1870s to assimilate these into his work, there was a sense in which his final inability or refusal to make significant corrections was much more fitting. In his new foreword to the *Essai* he declared:

I have changed absolutely nothing. This is the exposition of a system, the expression of a truth which is as clear and certain to me now as it was when I first propounded it. Developments in the study of history have in no way made me change or modify my opinions. My convictions have remained totally unchanged from the beginning. Nor has the increase in factual knowledge done anything to weaken them – I am quite happy that more factual details have come to light, for they have done nothing to change my initial observations. The testimony of experience has, to my mind, even further demonstrated the reality of racial inequality.[17]

The self-delusions of the racist and the ability of his ideas to re-emerge unharmed and phoenix-like from the ashes produced by empirical objections are both illustrated here.

In Gobineau's opinion the *Essai* stood fundamentally unscathed – its only significant failing being its underestimation of the pace of decadence. As he observed Europe over a quarter of a century after the first exposition of his racial ideas, his social pessimism was confirmed and aggravated. The danger was manifest both within and without. In Europe itself degeneration was evident in the incessant movement and increasing disorder he witnessed: 'The present age is a time of general disquiet . . . No one is at ease. Assuredly neither political stability, nor institutional vitality, nor morality will gain from this morbid disposition.'[18] Not only migration but also the growth of cities was promoting miscegenation apace. Industrialization was both a cause and a symptom of this urban malaise. The dependence which it necessitated was part of the negation of Gobineau's concept of freedom. The division of labour and the alleged diminution of craftsmanship were working to the detriment of *la vie complète*. Industrialization was a symptom of mediocrity and materialism, as well as a means of dehumanizing those of worth who remained. Gobineau had remarked in *France en 1870*, within the immediate context of war but with more general considerations in mind, that, 'The greatest part of what we today call science is striving to find new means of destruction.'[19] Knowledge was increasingly being used to improve the techniques of physical destruction in war, but it was now also – intentionally or otherwise – the instrument of a far subtler process of social decay, operating through the speed and complexity of a society in which contact and communication were ever more easy and where healthy isolation was ever more difficult.

The chief racial responsibility for this he settled upon the semitized Latins – the chief enemies from within. In the *Ethnographie de la France* he explained that attempts to use the term 'Latin' in a properly scientific sense made 'a complete abstraction of any idea of race, since there does not exist and has never existed a Latin race.'[20] One of the traits of the motley and miscegenated so-called Latins is that 'of regarding themselves as the epitome of all civilization, when on the contrary it would be fair to consider them as being its negation'.[21] Here, at least, Gobineau appears to make explicit a certain idea of anti-race. Though this is semitized, it is important to remember that in the present context it is not specifically Jewish. On the other hand, this kind of assertion by Gobineau left his theory dangerously open to such an interpretation from others.

The triumph of pessimism was completed by his view of the danger to Europe from without – the perils emanating from Slav and Mongol. These constituted one wing of the assault upon the vestiges of white Aryan civilization, and their action was complementary to that of the negroid-tainted forces of latinization. With regard to the danger from Mongol and Slav, Gobineau implied in the *Essai* and made explicit in his last years the belief that there was a law of historical movement revealing that, 'Without any desire or awareness, and by virtue of a kind of gravitational driving force, alert and active humanity moves from East to West, absolutely like the magnetism of the earth.'[22] Here are the foundations for the *Götterdämmerung* of *Amadis*, stated not in wild epic verse but in the considered judgment of his *Vues sur l'Histoire Générale*. Both as diplomat and writer Gobineau had become progressively more concerned with the Eastern Question and had intensified his nostalgia for the wise policies of Metternich. In 1876 he remarked to Zoé Dragoumis that, 'The Slavs, Serbs, Montenegrins and others

are in the process of irritating the nerves of the whole world.'[23]
But his greatest fears related to what lay beyond the Balkans and
for him the Eastern Question became essentially 'the question of
the Empire of Asia'.[24] He castigated the West for continuing its
petty parliamentary squabbles oblivious to this great danger. A
little before the Congress of Berlin in 1878 he wrote: 'It is the end
of the West'[25]; and of the conference itself he exclaimed: 'The
world has never been served with such a brew of ignorance, frivolity,
stupidity and senile infatuation.'[26]

The comparative vigour of the Russian Slavs represented the
first stage of his fears. He had been particularly impressed by his
stay in Moscow with Dom Pedro in 1876. From there he had
written to the Comtesse de La Tour that, 'It is undeniable that
this country is well on the way to power and aggrandizement.'[27]
Early in 1879 he commented to Charles d'Héricault that Russia was
about to present 'the spectacle of the creation of the greatest
Empire that the Universe will ever have seen'.[28] It was around this
time that Gobineau was working on the essay *L'Europe et la Russie*,
which aimed to illustrate the prospective development of Russian
power into Asia and the eventual implications for Europe. The
work is unfinished, breaking off at a point where it appears that the
recent Russo-Turkish War is about to be discussed. Its central
theme, which the *Essai* had earlier indicated, is the importance and
danger of the Slavs as ethnic agents between Europe and Asia,
positioned as they are 'at the chief cross-roads of the world'.[29] His
claim is that, since the end of Tartar domination, Russia's prime
historical function has been that of an intermediary making Europe
gradually more vulnerable to Asiatic influences.

It was the Yellow Peril itself which activated the second stage of
Gobineau's fears. In an article of 1880–1, entitled *Ce qui se fait en
Asie* and first published in German in Wagner's house-organ the
Bayreuther Blätter, he integrated these fears not only into his view
of Russia but also into his horror at the threat from latinization
within Europe itself. Thus the piece represented, as he told
Caroline, 'the sequel and present condition of the *Essai*'.[30] In the
article he wrote that, 'The modern world, even more than the
Roman world . . . , was born with a superabundance of heterogeneous and Latin elements. This formed the basis of a particularly
striking weakness.'[31] The debility is manifested in Europe's susceptibility to revolution and it is this which, in turn, renders the

continent almost powerless in the face of the yellow danger. In 1879 he had commented to Dom Pedro in the following terms:

What the Russians will have done within ten years will be to have opened towards the West the flood-gates to the vast human horde that we find so ill at ease in China; and it is an avalanche of Chinese and Slavs, mottled with Tartars and Baltic Germans, that will put an end to the stupidities and indeed to the civilization of Europe. The United States, which fears a yellow invasion from the direction of California, will gain little from all this. Europe will lose everything.[32]

This prophecy, subsequently given epic form at the end of *Amadis*, was elaborated in his article, in which the Chinese are regarded as objects of horror because of their numbers, their perseverance and their debasement.

It is claimed that through miscegenation their influence will pass rapidly from Russia into the West:

Whether we care to recall the most ancient migratory movements – of Slavs, Celts, Germans or Huns – or simply restrict our attention to the Hungarians, Turks, Mongols or Tartars of Tamburlaine, it is evident that the route history has taken is being reopened. It is again opened in and around China, where we can already see the masses on the move. We may well tremble at the danger which threatens us.[33]

Gobineau regards these developments as a confirmation of the *Essai*, in everything except its assessment of their pace:

I am struck by the amazing speed with which these dangers grow and develop. I think it quite possible that within ten years the face of the world will be on the point of changing. When I see so much rapid movement and upheaval in the East, I do not consider any less strange the rapid decline and spreading torpor in the whole Western World. I foresaw and predicted these strange phenomena a number of years ago in my book, *The Inequality of the Human Races*. But I must admit that I did not then expect these things to come about so quickly. I can thus only revise my opinion and admit that the world is more mutable than I thought and that the advanced state of the intermixture of races should have made me suspect the speed with which it would push the present perils to their logical conclusion. This is what we are now going to see happen – with all the violence, upheaval and misery that this will inevitably entail.[34]

None of these developments were to be seen as in any way reminiscent of the kind of calculating international conspiracy Gobineau had once depicted in Switzerland. The tragedy was that the triumph of the yellow race was a natural, inexorable and involuntary process which was, in essence, neither the result of intentional endeavours nor susceptible to prevention by human effort. Even if Gobineau could have conceived of a Western policy aimed at Slav or Mongol extermination he would have regarded that too as doomed ultimately to failure. Finally, due to his determinist philosophy and its necessary annihilation of moral responsibility, there is not even much point in blaming the Yellows for their destructiveness.

This critique of the triumph of Gobineau's pessimism suggests two major points upon which he has been frequently misinterpreted. We may now realize, firstly, that his is not a philosophy of colonial imperialism. If it is imperialist in the sense that certain races are superior and have been fated to follow a master-morality and to dominate for a time by virtue of it, nonetheless it is far from being imperialist in the sense of actually advocating that this dominance should be pursued any longer by purposeful expansion. Indeed, such expansion must be avoided if the better stocks are to maximize the period of their survival. The fear of the results of contact within society is here projected on to a broader plane where the isolation of societies from each other is also recommended. Gobineau had much earlier noted, for example, the unwisdom of continued British domination in India and of attempts to open up Asia to the West. Regarding the latter activity he had commented in 1859:

> I understand . . . that Europe cannot reason against the force which is thrusting it beyond itself and against the activity which is driving it afar, and, indeed, that societies do what they must do, even though their deeds often work completely inversely to their true interests. I therefore limit myself to stating this fact – that Asia is a most alluring dish, but one which poisons those who eat it.[35]

Civilization was a rare and perishable commodity not easily transportable and Gobineau severely criticized the common European and Christian conception that it could be purveyed anywhere. Whatever his other failings, he was at least never guilty of cultivating the nineteenth century's most insidious breeding-ground for tacit racism and uncritical imperialism – the complacent and unquestioning acceptance of Europe's civilizing destiny in the modern world. This Gobineau regarded as a misconception – and one that was literally fatal. Twenty years after his Persian travels his convictions in this anti-imperialist direction were stronger still and they contributed fundamentally to his assessment of the Slav and Mongol peril. It was especially Russia's expansion eastwards that was opening the western world to Asiatic influences, and these would filter through from the Slav intermediaries.

The second misconception relates to Gobineau's idea of the Jews. It is the Slavs and Mongols, and the Latins in general (rather than the Jews in particular), upon whom he centres his analysis of doom. Certainly as part of the semitic and semitized enemy within the Jews play their role in the twilight of the Aryans, but they are far from being the protagonists in the drama and are certainly not the prominent anti-race of so many subsequent theories. Gobineau was indeed particularly impressed by their isolationist tendencies. In the *Histoire des Perses* he suggested that, in terms of ideas, the original Hebrews had more in common with the Aryans than with other Semites, and that, from the point of view of familial and tribal organization, they could well be compared with the Germans. His attitude to the modern Jews, well on the road to greater debasement, was less generous. But since some such debasement applied to all peoples discussed by Gobineau in the contemporary world, we need lay no particular store by this change of attitude in itself. It is however true that Gobineau, through his own lifetime, became more critical of contemporary Jews. For instance, in 1878 he characterized Disraeli's manoeuvres for the acquisition of Cyprus as a typical example of 'semitic politics'[36]; in 1880 he complained of Karlsbad that, 'There are too many Jews'[37]; and in the following year he described to his sister how they were consuming Swiss and German society. Still, it would be rash to make much of these and similar cursory remarks, which probably express no more than conventional anti-Jewish sentiments.

The idea of the Jews as an anti-race scarcely emerges at all. In so far as it does, its form is very imperfect. Any such tendency here towards polarization picks out the Jews not because of base failings but rather on account of the very qualities of persistence and isolationism which they share with the Aryans themselves and which are elicited most powerfully in contexts of competition with that race. Gobineau's most interesting account of this is found in

the *Ethnographie de la France*. There he remarks on Jewish persistence being maximized in conditions of mutual antipathy and rivalry
and he stresses that, 'This is a powerful race, which merits all the
respect that we owe to strength.'[38] Moreover, the Jews are alleged
to possess a sufficiently vitalist element to make them welcome a
challenging situation in which they stand out in ethnic contrast.
Gobineau suggests that it is for this reason that in France, for
instance, the most active of this people had been found in the comparatively Germanic atmosphere of Alsace. In printing extracts
from the *Ethnographie* Ludwig Schemann conveniently omitted a
passage which not only brings home this particular point but also
illustrates generally the complexity of Gobineau's attitudes towards the Jews. Concerning them, he writes.:

> For France the loss of Alsace and part of Lorraine has taken on the
> significance of a misfortune of the highest order, not because she is seen
> stripped of some territory or other and of a few hundred thousand
> souls. It is because she no longer has the means of utilizing in her
> domestic affairs a population which is not Latin, a population of excel-
> lent worth, irreplaceable in her banks, her workshops and her army.[39]

For straightforward Gobinist anti-semites such as Schemann such
an argument was uncomfortably complex. Yet it is essential to
understand that Gobineau, while certainly regarding the Jews as
an element in the harmful semitization of Europe (and in the
movement to modern complexity and social, economic and ethnic
corruption associated with this), nonetheless reserved for them a
respectful awe, even admiration, which is totally lacking in his
treatment of Slav and Mongol. He never contemplated the extermination of the latter; it is still less likely that he would have
approved of genocide applied against the Jews. Indeed, one of the
results of the paralysis of political action inherent in Gobineau's
racial theory was his refusal to concentrate Aryan hostility against
a particular race. Because the end was deemed inevitable this
would have been a futile endeavour.

Gobineau's followers made less use of their hero's attempted
qualifications than of his defective methods and reasoning. In their
minds degeneration and paralysis of action were replaced by optimistic doctrines of regeneration through the expansion and perse-
cutions that Gobineau had refused to advocate. Both the Gobinist
movement and the distortion of that pessimism we have traced

throughout his thinking were a result of Gobineau's association with Richard and Cosima Wagner and with the Bayreuth circle after 1876. Their first encounter took place in that year and Gobineau was an honoured guest at Wahnfried for a month both in 1881 and in 1882 – visits which, in the final volume of Ernest Newman's great life of the Master, are admirably sketched and placed in the context of the composer's own last days. Wagner presented an edition of his collected writings to Gobineau and inscribed this verse in dedication:

> Das wäre ein Bund
> Normann und Sachse
> Was da noch gesund
> Dass das bleibe und wachse!*

In the early 1880s the *Bayreuther Blätter* published a number of essays on Gobineau and reprinted some of his own pieces specially translated into German. The later tendencies towards misinterpretation were already exemplified in Wagner's own article of September 1881, *Heldentum und Christentum*. There, while praising the *Essai* and accepting Gobineau's contention that racial mixture could lead to degeneration, he denied that the decay was irreversible. The evident mutual admiration of the two men could not conceal their divergencies with regard to Christianity, regeneration and optimism. Their differences were crystallized in the context of Wagner's final opera, *Parsifal*, with its strongly Christian and regenerational themes. Gobineau also distrusted Wagner's democratic leanings and the Master was in turn unimpressed by the Frenchman's arguments in favour of a necessary negroid contribution to all artistic creation!

After the death of both within a few months of each other, it was through the support and enthusiasm of the Bayreuth circle that Ludwig Schemann, already a prominent Pan-Germanist, was able to promote the cult which led to the formation of the Gobineau Vereinigung in 1894. Its membership (drawn principally from Germany but also in some small degree from France) was until the Society's dissolution in 1919 small but influential. Schemann himself was not untypical of the assortment of writers and academics who were the principal supporters of its activities. Apart from

---

* May there survive and flourish all that is still wholesome in the bond between Norman and Saxon!

his own writings on Gobineau, Schemann brought out, in four volumes between 1897 and 1900, a German edition of the *Essai* that ran to a thousand copies. This went into second and third impressions in 1902 and 1903. Though it requires a study other than the present one to tease out the threads of the particular contributions made by the Society and its publications to the web of European racist thinking already woven by 1914, we can discern at once the direct links between Gobinism and the most significant racist treatise to emerge in these years: Houston Stewart Chamberlain's *Grundlagen des Neunzehnten Jahrhunderts* ('Foundations of the Nineteenth Century'), which appeared in two volumes in 1899.

Chamberlain, who was eventually to marry Wagner's daughter, was an Englishman who had fallen completely beneath the enchanting spell of Bayreuth. Though he was reluctant to acknowledge the extent of his debt to Gobineau's ideas and though he indeed roundly criticized aspects of his predecessor's work, the *Grundlagen* are closely akin to the *Essai* in scope and method. From his own vast collection of sources Chamberlain endeavoured to substantiate two basic racist arguments already central to Gobineau's own work: first, that the races of man are not merely different from one another, but are also arranged according to a hierarchy of talent and value, wherein the Aryan peoples are supreme; second, that the interplay of these unequal races is the fundamental key to explaining social and political phenomena in all their complexity. Where he differed principally from Gobineau was in his evocation of modern Teutonic-German potential, in his explicit polarization between its virtue and Jewish vice, and in the fact that he claimed to provide not merely a racial diagnosis of the ills of civilization but also an actively racist cure. Urging the Teutons to greater effort, the *Grundlagen* are marked by messianic and dynamic elements. Evading the contentious issue of whether there had ever been a pure Aryan race in the distant past, Chamberlain emphasized that the really important point was its creation for the years ahead: 'Though it be proved that there never was an Aryan race in the past, yet we desire that in the future there be one. That is the decisive standpoint for men of action.'[40] For the achievement of this desirable racial creation it was necessary that one should begin with a nation composed of ethnic elements that had in the past suffered only limited blood-mixture and that subsequently the strain should be improved by rigid programmes of inbreeding and artificial selection. This emphasis upon future fulfilment is that which Hitler himself was to adopt in the later stages of the evolution of Nazi racial doctrine, when the Führer stressed that the Germans were not yet properly a race and that they could only become one by devoting themselves totally to his messianic programme of racial redemption.

From Gobineau and Wagner, via such figures as Schemann, Nietzsche, Chamberlain, Oswald Spengler and Alfred Rosenberg, on to the author of *Mein Kampf* there is a chain of intellectual and personal links. A fourth German printing of the *Essai* had appeared in 1920 and, under the Third Reich itself, a fifth was produced in 1939–40. As Manfred Steinkühler has shown, during the 1930s extracts appeared in popular anthologies about the racial question and portions of the *Essai* were even used in prescribed school-readers. In all of these publications Gobineau's more charitable references to the Jews were sedulously suppressed. As with any question of influence in the history of ideas, the assessment of the role of Gobineau and his work in the context of Nazi racist thinking is a complex matter. Its investigation can only be attempted within the setting of a more general account of the history of racist ideology than the present study has set out to provide. Nevertheless we can immediately appreciate, at the climax of that story in the pages of *Mein Kampf*, the direct echoes of the *Essai* written seventy years before. Though it is unlikely that Hitler had ever given any sustained attention to Gobineau's complex book, it is impossible not to hear the text of its opening Dedication reverberating in these lines written by the prisoner of Landsberg:

History shows, with a startling clarity, that whenever Aryans have mingled their blood with that of an inferior race the result has been the downfall of the people who were the standard-bearers of a higher culture . . . All that we admire in the world today, its science and its art, its technical developments and discoveries, are the products of the creative activities of a few peoples, and it may be true that their first beginnings must be attributed to one race . . . Every manifestation of human culture, every product of art, science and technical skill, which we see before our eyes today, is almost exclusively the product of the Aryan creative power. This very fact fully justifies the conclusion that it was the Aryan alone who founded a superior type of humanity; therefore he represents the architype of what we understand by the term: MAN. He is the Prometheus of mankind, from whose shining brow the divine spark of genius has at all times flashed forth, always kindling anew that fire which, in the form of knowledge, illuminated the dark night by drawing aside the veil of mystery and thus showing man how to rise and become master over all the other beings on the earth. Should he be forced to disappear, a profound darkness will descend on the earth; within a few thousand years human culture will vanish and the world will become a desert.[41]

Such words could almost be Gobineau's own. But, like Wagner and Chamberlain and yet unlike Gobineau, Hitler trusted in regeneration and erupted into world politics to achieve it. Never was hope more harmful. From much the same 'facts' about race Gobineau and Hitler drew very different conclusions. But, then, the facts were comparatively unimportant – it was the symbol that that was the same.

Whereas the Führer had pledged himself to racial redemption, Gobineau had despaired of the world and had withdrawn from it, overcome by its degeneration and by the triumph of his own pessimism. His philosophy of impotence led him towards a form of stoicism. Of the latter Casimir Bullet in *Les Pléiades* had been made to remark: 'Times such as the present have always produced its severe authority.'[42] Still earlier Gobineau had commented to Dom Pedro that, 'At a certain point in the breakdown of societies all who have preserved something human flee into the desert and become monks.'[43] Perhaps it was truly one of the monkish virtues and privileges to have no further concern with politics either in practice or as a subject for potentially ameliorative speculations. The final implication of Gobineau's social pessimism was that political institutions and theories alike were almost completely impotent in the face of imminent ethnic and social disaster. Even before 1870 he had written to Keller: 'We have seen sad things . . . We shall see worse . . . and . . . our children will see worse than worse.'[44] There was little point in attempting to provide remedial theoretical constructions: 'A decidedly baleful preoccupation is that of applying learning to public affairs . . . Unfortunately the present century is imbued with the dangerous craze for putting on its doctoral bonnet whenever it is a question of political interests.'[45] Within the pages of *Les Pléiades* Gobineau had derided the social tamperings of his well-minded Monsieur de Gennevilliers. In the same novel Louis de Laudon's case for social engineering is dismissed by Nore and the philosopher-prince, John Theodore of Burbach. The latter advocates a set of purely introspective attitudes for the isolated figures of the élite:

> I think that a decent man, a man who feels that he has some soul, has now, more than ever, the strict duty of falling back upon himself and, since he can't save others, of striving for his own betterment. That is the essential task in times like ours . . . We have to work upon ourselves, improving the good we have within us and spurning the evil, stifling our worst parts, or at least restraining them. From now on that is our duty – and it is the only duty of value.[46]

Convinced of the inexorability of degeneration, Nore sees the applicability of human effort limited to the fabrication of 'make-shifts which will provide a few more or less brief moments of peace and quiet for the sick body of Europe'.[47] Gobineau makes him continue: 'Statesmen will be merely the suppliers of rather in-effectual plasters, and distillers of opium, morphia, chloral and other soporific cure-alls, and, after a few months or a few years, they will see their patient lapsing into convulsions. The very name of the illness is evidence that it is incurable – it is none other than senility.'[48] The tension in Gobineau between faintly positive exhortation and starkly pessimistic description is only present in the same degree as such expedients have a marginal relevance to the pace of future change. And it is that relevance which Gobineau progressively reduces.

His assertions of impotence had worried Tocqueville and they certainly left Gobineau open to the charge of being, in Jean Gaulmier's words, 'a true master of anarchy'.[49] His racist ideology, though rooted in social and political concerns and though claiming to explain the nature of society itself, could not on his own terms effect any transformation. But Gobineau unfortunately failed to realize the degree to which such a theory – whatever his own view of its impotence – might be capable of use and adaptation by others to affect society and history. His work would in time be plundered by racists with an interest in preaching explicitly reformatory doctrines. At the very end Gobineau himself was further than ever from such optimistic beliefs and in one of his last letters to Caroline he wrote: 'We are at the end of European society . . . Its present state truly represents its death agony.'[50] This pessimism was only partially the result of his conception of the magnitude of the dangers within and without – from Latin, Slav and Mongol. It was even more the consequence of his conviction that no ideas, of his own or of others, were capable of averting any danger whatsoever. Hope might have stemmed from the possibility of meaningful political action. But this, no less than moral activity, had been ultimately nullified by the laws of ethnic determinism. Thus we witness in Gobineau the victory not only of despair but also of political and moral nihilism, the triumph not merely of pessimism but also of political and social irresponsibility.

Conclusion

And the old nobleman, dispossessed and uprooted, went away to maintain his family where he could. Being no longer at the head of civil society he suffered the oscillations forced upon it by others, just as a passenger on board ship must accept the consequences of bad steering from a blundering helmsman. We can well see how the superior racial qualities possessed by such fallen families no longer usefully served the state, and how only with difficulty they served the interests of those who, though they had them, were without any opportunity for making the most of them.

GOBINEAU
Ottar Jarl (1879)

Conclusion

In any critical analysis of the racist ideology of Count Gobineau it is hard to convey the genuine personal charm and cultivation perceived in him by so many contemporaries. It was suggested, for instance, by Albert Sorel, himself a great commentator on eight-eenth-century France, that here was a man of grace and charm worthy of a court of the Ancien Régime. However manifest and numerous his failings, Gobineau's racism is never crudely vulgar. Nonetheless his errors of method, his tautologies, his determinism and his uncritical over-simplifications left many hostages to fortune. Because of them he can have little right to complain at the perversions which his ideas suffered at the hands of later, and much more truly vulgar, racist theorists who wished to use them in pursuit of programmes of ethnic and eugenic regeneration. With the premise of common human rights and dignities once denied, with that of the social and political inequality of races once em-braced, no amount of charm, cultivation or benevolence can exorcise the danger of headlong descent into the depths of an uncompromising confrontation between man and man. Once there, we find ourselves far beneath the realms of genuinely political questioning and speculation, being faced simply with the single problem as to who shall be killer and who victim.

Even if Gobineau is deemed to escape the charge of being a mere gutter-theorist, the first part of this study was nonetheless devoted to explaining how the emergence of his ideology – like that of the related doctrines which followed from others – was closely related to a self-interested defence of social status and economic interest. His exposition of Aryanism was antedated by an association with the aspirations of certain sections of the French nobility. Of this Hannah Arendt has properly remarked: 'Step by step, he identi-fied the fall of his caste with the fall of France, then of Western civilization, and then of the whole of mankind.'[1] Still, it is wise to bear in mind the degree to which even this universalist projection embodies a limitation of vision. For Gobineau's treatment can never conceal that his central concerns are always with France and Europe. As he emphasizes in his last writings the increasing speed of degeneration, it is not so much the span of world-history as the life-expectancy of European civilization that is shortened. When he discusses the Yellow Peril, for example, it is solely as a threat to the peoples of Europe, since he neglects to examine the turmoil of the Mongols for its own sake. He would have shared Pareto's view of history as the cemetery of aristocracies – but it is above all the European graveyard that he tends.

In common with many extremist thinkers, Gobineau reveals the symptoms of alienation and cultural despair frequently encountered among those whose status is devalued by social and economic change and who experience significant disjunction between desire and gratification, between the conditions of their present existence and their assessment of the previous situation of their class or family. In him these symptoms were aggravated by the further humiliation he suffered from inadequate recognition of his talents. He experienced a form of bastardization complex – combining both pride in himself in defiance of accepted values and the desire for conventional legitimation and recognition. Such a complex is especially relevant to a justification in terms of race, since this is necessarily connected with denouncing blood-mixture, regarded literally or figuratively, as the outcome of illicit or undesirable union. His unhappy family experiences, first with his mother and then later with his own wife, doubtless reinforced these feelings. Although he could never formulate his position in this way, Gobineau strove, in a society that progressively refused recognition to himself and his caste, for self-legitimation by stressing that it was not he but the bulk of his contemporaries who were debased.

Having firstly surveyed the development of his social consciousness and his class identification, we described in the second part of the book how these came to be expressed in racial terms and, in the third, we investigated how the racist conclusions eventually came to condition all aspects of Gobineau's later thinking. The subject matter itself has seemed to fall most naturally beneath such tripartite treatment. Perhaps it is more than coincidental that triadic forms also appealed to Gobineau himself. Much of his thought is expressed according to such a pattern. His triple categorization of races is, from this standpoint, comparable with his view of the triple order of feudal society. Further, in their history races appear to undergo a quasi-Hegelian process, moving from the thesis of purity into the antithesis of miscegenation and then on to the synthesis of decadence which Gobineau fears. As we have also seen, eventually and retrospectively Gobineau came to see the *Essai*, the Persian history and *Ottar Jarl* as a trilogy, describing progressively more detailed aspects of the Aryans. But, despite all this, we have been compelled to note that, by the end, the triple distinction among races culminates in a simpler dualism. In this the remnants of racial nobility, of true aristocracy, are placed in stark and uncompromising contrast with all others. Increasingly the latter are denied a moral existence, through arguments that gear conveniently both into a deepening conviction of pessimism and into the disappearance of a conception of common humanity. The ethical dualism is associated with a gradually more insistent distinction between true men and those who are virtually half-human or even sub-human. The implications of depersonalization and dehumanization, eventually actualized in the concentration and extermination camps, are already present here.

Gobineau himself was no advocate of extermination. The brand with which he was concerned – as an object of lamentation not encouragement – was the extermination of his racial élite and, with it, of civilization itself. The obsequies he chants are arid in an almost unique way. Unlike most social philosophers, and certainly unlike the vast majority of racist theorists, he shows no substantial interest in using his talents to change reality. In other racists, exhorting ethnic regeneration through struggle, such reserve was absent, and in their influence and success the disjunction between descriptive accuracy and political persuasiveness would be amply shown. Gobineau is more typical of a considerable number of them in illustrating strikingly the degree to which the racist may evolve his doctrine independent of any significantly intimate experience of inter-racial relationships. It may seem surprising that the *Essai* should have emanated from a man who before the 1850s possessed no such personal experience and who wrote in an age when the relations between races were seldom a primary concern for that vast majority of Europeans who remained within their own continent.

But, in preparing it, Gobineau exemplified how easily other social preoccupations and frustrations could be made susceptible to a racist gloss. We have tried to show that it is these, rather than race itself, which were at the centre of Gobineau's earliest interests and which prompted the speculations of the *Essai*. We have also sought to indicate more generally that, for social and political purposes, what is important is not the accuracy of ideas regarding race but rather their plausibility, their degree of acceptance and their social significance as sincere beliefs.

It is perhaps tempting to suggest unequivocally that Gobineau, far from intellectualizing any pre-existent racial prejudice of his own, simply concocted a racist theory as a convenient instrument by which to explain (if not to solve) certain political and social problems. But this would imply our acceptance of an over-simplified and distorted view of the complex inter-relationship between the post-rationalization of 'genuine' racial feeling and the more cynical concoction of a doctrine solely for political convenience. The matter is really not one of complete contrast but of emphasis. What is clear is that Gobineau falls into the category neither of a Hitler, whose racial prejudices clearly precede his theoretical exposition, nor of a Mussolini, who stands towards the more cynical and calculating end of the spectrum. Any latent racial feeling in Gobineau emerges but slowly, under stimuli which have little direct connection with race, and, having appeared, it is used as an instrument of social explanation, but certainly not in a cynical manner, nor to implement political desires, nor to fulfil future political purposes. In him, at least, the racist theory works pessimistically towards the annihilation of such will and purpose.

This tendency also complicates the generalization that racist thinking – as well as prejudice and discrimination – may be associated particularly with political and social crisis, embodying at once a response and a solution. Though Gobineau's theory is certainly a response to crisis, we have stressed his originality in declining to provide any solution. From our own standpoint we can see that ethnic determinism must necessitate a paralysis of will and moral judgment – an upshot which Gobineau could not bring himself to accept without equivocation. But he certainly admits more freely that his own version of race-thinking amounts to the negation of meaningful political action. In William Morris's

Earthly Paradise (an ironic title in our context) we find lines most suitable to Gobineau's predicament:

> Dreamer of dreams, born out of my true time,
> Why should I strive to set the crooked straight?

Although we have noted that Gobineau did not always accept with complete consistency the abolition of political exhortation which his theory imposed, we have also seen that he did become increasingly more resigned to this impotence. One might quote against him his own early criticism of Christianity's irresponsibility, in so far as it was alleged to debase men's temporal social duties and utility. Not only was Gobineau's theory devoid of usefulness; it could also be positively harmful when adapted by others. Eventually he agreed that the worship by contemporaries of pragmatism could well be regarded as itself a mark of degeneration. Bertrand Russell has an apt comment for this context: 'Modern definitions of truth ... which are practical rather than contemplative, are inspired by industrialism as opposed to aristocracy.'[2] While Gobineau never formulated the distinction in that manner, this opinion of pragmatism was implicit in his attitudes and was essentially related to his aversion from modern society.

Gobineau's particular response to this alienation was thus associated with a paralysis of political action, which he accepted, and a paralysis of moral action which, despite his attempted denials, is also implicit in his arguments. We have suggested in our treatment that his theory is ultimately asocial and conducive only to stagnation. Note, for example, this passage in the manuscript of his *Vues sur l'Histoire Générale*:

> Contacts with the surrounding world, conquest, the influence of the strong upon the weak, of the eager race upon the idle one, of the intelligent upon the violent, of the intolerant with their determined beliefs upon the dreamers of vague ideas, all this produced fusions that were more or less thorough or, at least, penetration between peoples, and the circulation of some in the midst of others.[3]

The influences and relationships enumerated here are the very stuff of social life. But in Gobineau they are regarded primarily as the means to hated ethnic fusion. His response is a plea that now social isolation, for the vestiges of the élite at least, should be maintained as long as possible. That is the extent of his political programme. Enchained by that historical determinism which – in Isaiah Berlin's words – 'represents the universe as a prison'[4], Gobineau can produce only this arid conclusion. It brings us back directly to his original alienation from a society marked by increasing complexity, mobility and disorder, as manifested in urbanization, industrialization and materialism and in the associated ideas of equality, democracy and socialism which he hated.

The rejection of such ideas is part of his hostility to what Oswald Spengler came to call 'Megalopolis', the devouring world-city. This embodies the destruction of classes and states – indeed of all conventional social barriers. But what to Marx was an ideal was to Gobineau a prospect of unmitigated disaster. For Marx such destruction was the necessary precondition of true social harmony. But Gobineau, throughout his search for social order and the true freedom which a racial élite alone could appreciate, maintained, like Shakespeare's Ulysses and like those who adhered to the idea of a Great Chain of Being, that such harmony was possible only through the preservation of degree and hierarchy. The caste system of the Brahmins, not the classless society of Marx, was to him harmonious. It was only in Gobineau's ideal of hierarchical concord that freedom and authority could be properly balanced, not by allowing equal rights and obligations to all but by ensuring that the liberty and interests of the superior race were served by the natural submission of the inferior. We have tried however to demonstrate that such a conception of freedom is in any case nullified, even for the racial élite, by the implications of determinism and moral paralysis.

With regard to the racial dilemmas of our own time, Gobineau's mode of thinking would have vitiated any advice that he might have chosen to give. In the event, he felt simply unable to offer any political wisdom either to his contemporaries or to their potentially still more miserable descendants. Yet this does not reduce him to irrelevance. For the study of Gobineau and of his errors does retain great therapeutic value in relation to our contemporary racial difficulties, both domestic and global. This is not the place to launch into their examination. But we can note briefly that certain elements in an environment favourable to race-thinking remain, and that these are to a great extent bound up with the increasing contact and communication which Gobineau feared. Indeed the problem of race which he discussed in his major work –

however exotic the subject may have seemed in the 1850s – is now central not only to the practice of world politics but also to the question as to whether we wish to preserve intact what is best in that 'political tradition' upon which we in the West have prided ourselves.

It is in such a sense that, nearly a century after his lonely end in Turin, we must bear in mind Gobineau's prophecy that, 'I shall only come to be appreciated a hundred years after my death.'[5] Never in human history have prophets of doom had more scope for their speculations than today. And this is true particularly in regard to those whose predictions of disaster stem from analyses of racial confrontation. Despite the many paths of error along which Gobineau's thoughts meandered, it is striking to realize how often an isolated phrase of his still has great force and relevance. As daily are intensified the pressures towards making our world more truly one, we might recollect this remark in Gobineau's Conclusion to the *Essai*: 'Let us take it as axiomatic that the ultimate aim of the toil and suffering, the pleasures and triumphs of humanity is to attain, one day, supreme unity.'[6] In this thought are summarized the basic reasons for his profound pessimism. Yet, for those who have more generous conceptions of human freedom, dignity and justice than he, that same thought need not lead to despair. Rather, a century later, the encouragement of such unity provides them with their greatest moral challenge.

Appendix
The Structure of the 'Essai'

they subsequently formed through their mixtures. They are unequal in strength and beauty.

13 The human races are intellectually unequal; humanity is not infinitely perfectible.

14 Demonstration of the intellectual inequality of races continued. Different civilizations are in mutual repulsion. Mongrel races have civilizations equally mongrelized.

15 Languages, being unequal among themselves, are completely linked to the relative merit of races.

16 Recapitulation; respective characteristics of the three basic races; social effects of race-mixture; superiority of the white stock and, within this type, of the Aryan family.

Book Two
Ancient Civilization spreading
from Central Asia to the South-West

1 The Hamites.
2 The Semites.
3 The Maritime Canaanites.
4 The Assyrians; the Hebrews; the Choreans.
5 The Egyptians; the Ethiopians.

VOLUME II (1853)

6 The Egyptians were not conquerors; why their civilization remained stationary.

7 Ethnic connection between the Assyrian and Egyptian nations. The arts and lyric poetry are produced by the mingling of white and black peoples.

Book Three
Civilization spreading from
Central Asia to the South and South-East.

1 The Aryans; the Brahmins and their social system.
2 Developments in Brahminism.
3 Buddhism, its defeat; modern India.
4 The yellow race.
5 The Chinese.
6 The origins of the white race.

Book Four
Semitized Civilizations of the South-West

1   History exists only amongst the white nations. Why nearly all
    civilizations have been developed in the western hemisphere.
2   The Zoroastrians.
3   The autochthonous Greeks; the semite settlers; the Aryan-
    Hellenes.
4   The Semitic Greeks

VOLUME III (1855)

Book Five
Semitized European Civilization

1   The first peoples of Europe.
2   The Thracians; the Illyrians; the Etruscans; the Iberians.
3   The Gauls.
4   The aboriginal Italiot peoples.
5   The Tyrrhenian Etruscans; Etruscan Rome.
6   Italiot Rome.
7   Semitic Rome.

Book Six
Western Civilization

1   The Slavs; Domination by some pre-Germanic Aryan peoples.

VOLUME IV (1855)

2   The Aryan-Germans.
3   The capacity of native Germanic races.
4   Germanic Rome; the Romano-Celtic and Romano-Germanic
    armies; the German emperors.
5   The final Aryan-Scandinavian migrations.
6   The final developments of Germano-Roman society.
7   The indigenous Americans.
8   European colonization in America.

General Conclusion

References

Note on Abbreviations

AMAE   Archives du Ministère des Affaires Étrangères, Paris. References to these contain the further classificatory abbreviations:
     CC: *Correspondance Commerciale*
     CP: *Correspondance Politique*
     MD: *Mémoires et Documents*.

BNUS   Bibliothèque Nationale et Universitaire, Strasbourg.

EG   *Études Gobiniennes*

SPW   M. D. Biddiss (ed.), *Gobineau : Selected Political Writings*, London, 1970.
     Where quotations in the present volume are also to be found in the English text of the above collection then a further reference is made to the latter.

PART ONE: THE EMERGENCE OF SOCIAL PESSIMISM

1 : 1 The Early Years (pp. 11–14)

1   J. Puraye (ed.), *Les Mémoires du Comte Louis de Gobineau*, Bruxelles, 1955, p. 149.
2   *Ibid.*, p. 184.
3   BNUS, MS. 3537, item 4; reprinted in *EG*, 1967, pp. 109–29 (to which subsequent references are made).
4   To Comtesse de La Tour, 1 May 1883, BNUS, MS. 3533, item 55.
5   *Enfance et Première Jeunesse*, p. 118.
6   To Comtesse de La Tour, 7 Nov. 1882, BNUS, MS. 3531, item 41.
7   Wilfrid Nore in *Les Pléiades* (Livre de poche edition), Paris, 1960, p. 45.

8 To Comtesse de La Tour, 29 Oct. 1882, BNUS, MS. 3531, item 40a.
9 *Le Comte de Gobineau et l'Aryanisme Historique*, Paris, 1903, p. 6.

1 : 2 The Orleanist Monarchy (pp. 15–21)

1 BNUS, MS. 3530, f. 302a.
2 10 May 1836, BNUS, MS. 3518, item 9, quoted in *Enfance et Première Jeunesse*, p. 124.
3 To his father, 12 Nov. 1840, BNUS, MS. 3518, item 60.
4 *Ibid.*, 19 Mar. 1838, item 25.
5 *Ibid.*, 12 Jan. 1838, item 20.
6 A. B. Duff (ed.), 'Un Fragment inédit des *Souvenirs* de Diane de Guldencrone', *EG*, 1966, p. 61.
7 To Caroline, 16 May 1837, BNUS, MS. 3518, item 16.
8 *Ibid.*, 16 Jan. 1836, item 3.
9 To his father, *ibid.*, 20 Feb. 1839, item 36.
10 *Ibid.*
11 *Ibid.*
12 *Ibid.*, 17 Feb. 1840, item 49.
13 Chambord to Gobineau, 19 Oct. 1846, BNUS, MS. 3526, item 42.
14 BNUS, MS. 3518, item 111.
15 To Caroline, *ibid.*, 16 Jan. 1844, item 117.
16 To Caroline, 23 July 1877, in A. B. Duff (ed.), *Correspondance de Gobineau avec Mère Bénédicte, 1872–1882*, 2 vols, Paris, 1958 (cited hereafter as '*Corr. Bénédicte*'), vol. 1, p. 266.
17 'Opposition Royaliste', *La Quotidienne*, 14 July 1843.
18 *Ibid.*, 12 July 1843.
19 'Office des Royalistes dans la Société Présente', *ibid.*, 5 Dec. 1844.
20 *Ibid.*
21 'La Conscience Publique', *ibid.*, 29 Jan. 1844.
22 *Ce qui est arrivé à la France en 1870* in L. Schemann (ed.), *Nachgelassene Schriften des Grafen Gobineau*, vol. 2, pt. 1, Strassburg, 1918, p. 163. Some extracts from this work are included in *SPW*, pp. 203–9.

1 : 3 The German Situation (pp. 22–32)

1 'Capodistrias', *La Revue des Deux Mondes*, 15 Apr. 1841, p. 244.

2 *Études Critiques, 1844–8* (a collection of some of Gobineau's literary criticism), Paris, 1927, p. 96.

3 'L'Allemagne: la Lettre Patente du 3 février et l'Opinion Publique en Prusse', *La Revue Nouvelle*, May 1847, vol. 14, p. 420.

4 'Edgar Quinet', *L'Unité*, 5 Feb. 1843, vol. 1, p. 47.

5 *Ibid.*, p. 51.

6 *Ibid.*, p. 48.

7 'Études sur l'Allemagne: des Princes Médiatisés', *ibid.*, 29 Apr. 1843, vol. 2, p. 118.

8 'L'Allemagne: Institutions Politiques de la Prusse', *La Revue Nouvelle*, Mar. 1847, vol. 13, p. 418.

9 'Troubles de la Silésie', *La Revue de Paris*, 27 June 1844, p. 278.

10 'Institutions Politiques de la Prusse', *loc. cit.*, p. 418.

11 'Des Princes Médiatisés', *loc. cit.*, p. 118.

12 *Ibid.*, p. 120.

13 *Ibid.*, p. 121.

14 'Les Agitations Actuelles de l'Allemagne', *La Revue Nouvelle*, Dec. 1845, vol. 6, p. 40.

15 'Des Princes Médiatisés', p. 123.

16 'Allemagne: Tendances Nouvelles', *La Revue de Paris*, 30 May 1844, vol. 1, no. 12, p. 134.

17 *Ibid.*

18 'Agitations Actuelles', *loc. cit.*, p. 36.

19 'Institutions Politiques de la Prusse', p. 434.

20 *Ibid.*, p. 438.

21 'L'Opinion Publique en Prusse', *loc. cit.*, p. 419.

22 *Ibid.*

23 *Ibid.*, p. 401.

24 'Agitations Actuelles', p. 39.

25 *Ibid.*, p. 38.

26 'Troubles de la Silésie', *loc. cit.*, p. 278.

27 'Institutions Politiques de la Prusse', p. 449.

28 *Ibid.*, p. 456.

29 'L'Opinion Publique en Prusse', p. 426.

30 *Ibid.*

31 'Les Émigrations Actuelles des Allemands', *La Revue Nouvelle*, Mar. 1845, vol. 2, p. 5.

32 *Ibid.*

33 *Ibid.*, pp. 2–3.
34 *Ibid.*, pp. 6–7.
35 *Ibid.*, p. 44.
36 'L'Émigration Allemande', *La Revue de Paris*, 8 Apr. 1845, vol. 3, no. 146, p. 506.
37 *Ibid.*, p. 505.

1 : 4 Europe and Beyond (pp. 33–39)

1 'De l'Irlande', *La Quotidienne*, 30 July 1843.
2 'L'Émigration Allemande', *loc. cit.*, p. 505.
3 'Les Émigrations Actuelles des Allemands', *loc. cit.*, p. 3.
4 'De l'Angleterre', *La Quotidienne*, 20 Sept. 1843.
5 'Affaires de l'Afghanistan', *L'Union Catholique*, 31 Mar. 1842.
6 'De la Russie', *La Quotidienne*, 19 Aug. 1843.
7 To Caroline, 26 Mar. 1841, BNUS, MS. 3518, item 67.
8 'Capodistrias', *loc. cit.*, p. 270.
9 *Ibid.*, p. 271.
10 *Ibid.*
11 *Ibid.*
12 'Fragments de l'Histoire Moderne de la Grèce: Débuts du Ministère Colettis-Metaxas', *La Revue Nouvelle*, Jan. 1845, vol. 1, p. 99.
13 'Le Danemark et ses Provinces Allemandes', *La Revue de Paris*, 16 July 1844, vol. 1, no. 31, p. 363.
14 'Coup d'Oeil sur la Situation de l'Espagne', *La Quotidienne*, 13 July 1843.
15 *Ibid.*
16 *Ibid.*
17 *Ibid.*
18 *Ibid.*
19 'Institutions Politiques de la Prusse', *loc. cit.*, p. 416.
20 'Les Émigrations Actuelles des Allemands', p. 41.
21 *Ibid.*, p. 5.
22 *Ibid.*, pp. 36–37.
23 *Ibid.*, p. 1.

1 : 5 Literature and Society (pp. 40–46)

1 *La Revue Nouvelle*, May 1845, vol. 3, p. 106.

2 'Balzac', *Le Commerce,* 31 Dec. 1844.
3 To his father, 23 June 1838, BNUS, MS. 3518, item 31.
4 'Stendhal', *Le Commerce,* 14 Jan. 1845.
5 24 May 1841, BNUS, MS. 3518, item 70.
6 'L'Alviane', *L'Unité,* 13 May 1843, vol. 2, p. 176.
7 To Gobineau, 19 Jan. 1868, in L. Schemann (ed.), 'Une Correspondance Inédite de Prosper Mérimée', *La Revue des Deux Mondes,* 1 Nov. 1902, pp. 48–9.
8 *L'Abbaye de Typhaines,* Paris, 1922, p. 118.
9 *Ibid.,* p. 272.
10 *Jean Chouan,* Paris, 1846, pp. 6–7.
11 *Ternove,* Paris, 1922, pp. 82–83.
12 *Ibid.,* p. 146.
13 *Gobineau et l'Aryanisme Historique,* p. xxxix.
14 'Romantisme Allemand et Romantisme Français dans l'Oeuvre de Gobineau', Bibliothèque de l'Institut de France, Paris, MS. 5831, f. 3.

1:6 Religion and Morality (pp. 47–58)

1 8 Aug. 1843, in M. Degros (ed.), *Correspondance d'Alexis de Tocqueville et d'Arthur de Gobineau* (cited hereafter as 'Corr. Tocqueville' and being vol. 9 of J. P. Mayer's edition of Tocqueville's *Oeuvres Complètes*), Paris, 1959, p. 43.
2 To Caroline, 23 July 1843, BNUS, MS. 3518, item 104.
3 J. Lukacs (ed.), *Tocqueville: 'The European Revolution' and Correspondence with Gobineau,* New York, 1959, pp. 19–20.
4 To Caroline, 15 Apr. 1843, BNUS, MS. 3518, item 99.
5 To Gobineau, 5 Sept. 1843, *Corr. Tocqueville,* p. 45.
6 *Enfance et Première Jeunesse,* p. 121.
7 *Ibid.,* p. 118.
8 *Les Précurseurs: Arthur de Gobineau, Inventeur du Racisme (1816–82),* Paris, 1941, p. 43.
9 To Tocqueville, 8 Sept. 1843, *Corr. Tocqueville,* p. 49.
10 *Ibid.*
11 *Ibid.,* p. 50.
12 *Ibid.*
13 *Ibid.,* p. 51.
14 *Ibid.,* p. 52.
15 *Ibid.,* p. 53.

16 *Ibid.*
17 *Ibid.*, p. 54.
18 *Ibid.*, p. 55.
19 *Ibid.*
20 *Ibid.*, pp. 55–56.
21 *Ibid.*, pp. 54–55.
22 *Ibid.*, p. 55.
23 Letter to his father, undated (1847), BNUS, MS. 3519, item 22.
24 To Tocqueville, 16 Oct. 1843, *Corr. Tocqueville*, p. 64.
25 *Ibid.*, p. 65.
26 *Ibid.*, p. 66.
27 Published as Appendix I of *Corr. Tocqueville*, pp. 309–28, and cited hereafter as *'Histoire de la Morale'*.
28 *Ibid.*, p. 309.
29 *Ibid.*
30 *Ibid.*, p. 311.
31 *Ibid.*, p. 312.
32 *Ibid.*
33 *Ibid.*
34 *Ibid.*, p. 313.
35 *Ibid.*, p. 315.
36 *Ibid.*
37 Essay on *Bentham*, published as Appendix III of *Corr. Tocqueville*, p. 334.
38 *Ibid.*, p. 346.
39 *Histoire de la Morale*, p. 316.
40 Cf. generally the Appendices to *Corr. Tocqueville*.
41 26 Nov. 1843, in J. Gaulmier (ed.), 'Charles de Rémusat et Arthur de Gobineau', *Travaux du Centre de Philologie et de Littératures Romanes, Strasbourg,* vol. 2, no. 2, 1964 (cited hereafter as *'Corr. Rémusat'*), p. 72.
42 To Gobineau, 4 Oct 1844, *Corr. Tocqueville,* p. 74.
43 29 Apr. 1868, in J. Gaulmier (ed.), 'Lettres d'Arthur de Gobineau au Comte de Circourt', *EG*, 1966, pp. 103–38 (pt. 1) and *ibid.*, 1967, pp. 63–106 (pt. 2), this particular quotation being taken from pt. 2, p. 95. The letters are cited hereafter as *'Corr. Circourt'*.
44 Tocqueville to Gobineau, 22 Oct. 1843, *Corr. Tocqueville,* p. 68.

45 8 Aug. 1843, *ibid.*, p. 43.

1 : 7 Revolution and Reaction (pp. 59-69)

1   'Des Princes Médiatisés', *loc. cit.*, p. 118.
2   'Institutions Politiques de la Prusse', *loc. cit.*, p. 418.
3   'L'Opinion Publique en Prusse', *loc. cit.*, p. 426.
4   'Le Roi de Prusse et la Municipalité de Berlin', *La Quotidienne*, 20 Oct. 1845.
5   To his father, 26 Feb. 1848, BNUS, MS. 3519, item 28.
6   *Ibid.*, item 29.
7   *Ibid.*, item 38, undated.
8   26 Apr. 1849, *ibid.*, item 43.
9   Undated, *ibid.*, item 29.
10 June 1860, *Corr. Circourt* (pt. 1), pp. 117–18.
11 23 Nov. 1867, in *Briefwechsel Gobineaus mit Adelbert von Keller* (cited hereafter as '*Corr. Keller*') in L. Schemann (ed.), *Nachgelassene Schriften des Grafen Gobineau – Briefe I*, Strassburg, 1911, p. 54.
12 To Caroline, undated, BNUS, MS. 3519, item 44.
13 To his father, 29 Feb, 1850, *ibid.*, item 56.
14 *Ibid.*, 29 Apr. 1850, item 56.
15 Gobineau to Hercule de Serre, 10 Apr. 1850, transcribed by the latter in correspondence with Comte Walewski, 8 July 1857, to be found in AMAE, *Papiers d'Agents : Papiers Walewski*, Carton VIII, Dossier 'Divers'.
16 To his father, 10 Dec. 1851, BNUS, MS. 3519, item 84.
17 Letter of 16 July, in Mme. A. de Tocqueville and G. de Beaumont (eds.), *Tocqueville : Oeuvres Complètes,* Paris, 1864, vol. 7, pp. 289–90. In this edition, published in Gobineau's lifetime, the identity of Tocqueville's interlocutor is concealed.
18 BNUS, MS. 3502; the complete text has been published in P. Berselli Ambri (ed.), *Poemi Inediti di Arthur de Gobineau*, in *Biblioteca dell' "Archivum Romanicum"*, vol. 75, Firenze, 1965, pp. 125–213. This is cited henceforth as '*Poemi Inediti*'.
19 *Poemi Inediti*, p. 152.
20 *Ibid.*
21 *Ibid.*
22 *Ibid.*, p. 151.
23 *Ibid.*, p. 197.

24   *Ibid.*, p. 125.
25   *Ibid.*, p. 126.
26   *Ibid.*, p. 202.
27   Quoted in L. Schemann, *Gobineau : eine Biographie*, 2 vols, Strassburg, 1913–16, vol. 1, p. 244.
28   29 Nov. 1856, *Corr. Tocqueville*, p. 272.

1 : 8 Decentralization and Liberty (pp. 70–81)

1   Quoted in D. Bagge, *Les Idées Politiques en France sous la Restauration*, Paris, 1952, p. 315.
2   Letter of 3 July 1848, quoted in T. de Visan, 'Un Ancêtre du Régionalisme : le Comte Arthur de Gobineau', *La Revue Politique et Littéraire (Revue Bleue)*, vol. 49, no. 9, 26 Aug. 1911, p. 272.
3   Quoted *ibid.*
4   10 Apr, 1849, in M. P. Boyé and M. L. Concasty (eds), 'Autour de la *Revue Provinciale* : Gobineau et Gabriel Richard Lesclide', *EG*, 1967, p. 229.
5   Prospectus of *La Revue Provinciale*, Sept. 1848, p. 1.
6   'Études sur les Municipalités – II', *La Revue Provinciale*, Oct. 1848, vol. 1, p. 116.
7   'La Centralization devant l'Assemblée Nationale', *ibid.*, Nov. 1848, vol. 1, p. 174.
8   Prospectus, p. 2.
9   'Introduction', *La Revue Provinciale*, Sept. 1848, vol. 1, p. 3.
10   *Ibid.*, p. 8.
11   *Ibid.*
12   *Ibid.*, p. 9.
13   'Études sur les Municipalités – II', *loc. cit.*, p. 110.
14   A. B. Duff (ed.), 'Un Fragment Inédit des *Souvenirs* de Diane de Guldenecrone', *EG*, 1966, p. 64.
15   'Un Nouveau Livre de Gobineau : la *Troisième République*', *Le Gaulois*, 3 June 1907.
16   'Nouvelles Observations sur les Comités Provinciaux', *La Revue Provinciale*, Feb. 1849, vol. 1, pp. 412–13.
17   'Études sur les Municipalités – I', *ibid.*, Sept. 1848, vol. 1, p. 25.
18   *Ibid.*, p. 28.
19   'De la Politique Rétrospective', *ibid.*, June 1849, vol, 2, p. 251.
20   'Études sur les Municipalités – I', *loc. cit.*, p. 32.

21 *Ibid.* – II, pp. 110–11.
22 *Ibid.*, p. 118.
23 'Nouveaux Projets d'Organisation Départementale et Municipale', *ibid.*, Apr. 1849, vol. 2, p. 110.
24 'Études sur les Municipalités – II', p. 121.
25 'Du Renouvellement de l'Esprit Public', *ibid.*, Dec 1848, vol. 1, p. 255.
26 'Nouveaux Projets', *loc. cit.*, p. 123.
27 'La Centralisation devant l'Assemblée Nationale', *loc. cit.*, p. 164.
28 *Ibid.*, p. 167.
29 'De la Création de Comités Provinciaux', *ibid.*, Jan. 1849, vol. 1, p. 327.
30 *La Formation de la Pensée de Gobineau*, Paris 1967, p. 232.
31 'La Centralisation devant l'Assemblée Nationale', p. 168.
32 'De la Circonscription Cantonale', *La Revue Provinciale*, May 1849, vol. 2, p. 188.
33 *Ibid.*, p. 193.
34 'Du Renouvellement de l'Esprit Public', *loc. cit.*, p. 249.
35 'De la Création de Comités Provinciaux', p. 329.
36 'Nouvelles Observations', *loc. cit.*, pp. 414, 407.
37 'Nouveaux Projets', p. 125.
38 Prospectus, p. 3.
39 To his father, 29 Apr. 1850, BNUS, MS. 3519, item 56.
40 To Circourt, 4 Aug. 1688, *Corr. Circourt* (pt. 2), p. 103.
41 Quoted in L. Schemann, *Quellen und Untersuchungen zum Leben Gobineaus*, 2 vols, Strassburg, 1914 and Berlin, 1919, vol. 2, p. 310.
42 R. E. Park, 'The Nature of Race Relations', in his *Race and Culture: Essays in the Sociology of Contemporary Man*, London 1964, p. 116.

1:9 Diplomacy in Switzerland and Germany (pp. 82–92)

1 20 Aug. 1836, 'Voyage en Suisse', in J. P. Mayer's edition of the *Oeuvres Complètes*, vol. 5, pt. 2, p. 187.
2 Gobineau to Tocqueville, 11 July 1850, *Corr. Tocqueville*, p. 144.
3 24 Nov. 1851, BNUS, MS. 3519, item 83.
4 11 July 1850, *Corr. Tocqueville*, pp. 146–7.

5 Quoted in Boyé and Concasty, 'Autour de la *Revue Provinciale*', *loc. cit.*, p. 257.
6 Gobineau to Tocqueville, 24 Feb. 1850, *Corr. Tocqueville*, p. 107.
7 *Ibid.*, p. 109.
8 8 July 1853, BNUS, MS. 3519, item 113.
9 Gobineau to Tocqueville, 24 Feb. 1850, *Corr. Tocqueville*, p. 109.
10 *Ibid.*, p. 110.
11 *Ibid.*, p. 111.
12 *Ibid.*, 21 Feb. 1851, p. 163.
13 To Caroline, 9 June 1853, BNUS, MS. 3519, item 110.
14 To Tocqueville, 24 Feb. 1850, *Corr. Tocqueville*, p. 118.
15 *Ibid.*, 21 Apr. 1851, p. 168.
16 AMAE, *MD, Suisse*, vol. 87, 1850, no. 25.
17 To Tocqueville, 24 Feb. 1850, *Corr. Tocqueville*, p. 120.
18 *Ibid.*, p. 117.
19 AMAE, *CP, Suisse*, vol. 572, 7 Mar. 1853, no. 14, f. 201a.
20 *Ibid.*, f. 215b.
21 19 Jan. 1850, BNUS, MS. 3519, item 52.
22 AMAE, *CP, Suisse*, vol. 572, 7 Mar. 1853, no. 14, ff. 206b–207a.
23 28 Mar. 1850, *Corr. Tocqueville*, p. 128.
24 To Tocqueville, 24 Feb. 1850, *ibid.*, p. 118.
25 AMAE, *CP, Suisse*, vol. 573, 9 Apr. 1853, no. 31, f. 25b.
26 *Ibid.*, ff. 27b–28a.
27 To Tocqueville, 21 Apr. 1851, *Corr. Tocqueville*, pp. 171–2.
28 *Ibid.*, pp. 174–5.
29 AMAE, *CP, Suisse*, vol. 572, 7 Mar. 1853, no. 14, ff. 218b–219a.
30 *Ibid.*, *CC, Berne*, vol. 2, 1 Nov. 1850, f. 512a.
31 *Ibid.*, *CP, Suisse*, vol. 572, 7 Mar. 1853, no. 14, f. 211b.
32 To his father, 23 June 1851, BNUS, MS. 3519, item 73.
33 To Tocqueville, 30 June 1851, *Corr. Tocqueville*, p. 182.
34 AMAE, *CP, Hanovre*, vol. 70, 21 Aug. 1851, no. 2.
35 *Ibid.*, 6 Sept. 1851, no. 3.
36 17 Feb. 1853, BNUS, MS. 3519, item 106.
37 30 June 1851, *Corr. Tocqueville*, p. 185.
38 AMAE, *CP, Hanovre*, vol. 70, 7 Nov. 1851, no. 15; references are to the printed text in J. Mistler(ed.), 'Coup d'Oeil sur

l'Allemagne du Nord', *Revue Germanique*, vol. 3, no. 20, June
1929, pp. 481–94.
39 *Ibid.*, p. 483.
40 *Ibid.*, pp. 484–5.
41 *Ibid.*, p. 485.
42 *Ibid.*, p. 488.
43 *Ibid.*, p. 490.
44 *Ibid.*, pp. 490–1.
45 12 July 1854, *Corr. Tocqueville*, p. 215.
46 28 July 1854, *ibid.*, pp. 218–9.

1 : 10 The Assertion of Social Pessimism (pp. 93–100)

1 Introduction to *Corr. Tocqueville*, p. 18.
2 Prospectus, p. 2.
3 To his father, 20 Feb. 1839, BNUS, MS. 3518, item 36.
4 Prospectus, p. 2.
5 'Nouvelles Observations', *loc. cit.*, p. 406.
6 'De la Circonscription Cantonale', *loc. cit.*, p. 192.
7 15 Apr. 1843, BNUS, MS. 3518, item 99.
8 'Institutions Politiques de la Prusse', *loc. cit.*, p. 416.
9 'Études sur les Municipalités – II', *loc. cit.*, p. 121.
10 *Poemi Inediti*, p. 125.
11 'Troubles de la Silésie', *loc. cit.*, p. 278.
12 'Introduction', *La Revue Provinciale, loc. cit.*, p. 8.
13 'Nouvelles Observations', p. 407.
14 'Introduction', *La Revue Provinciale*, p. 7.
15 *Loc. cit.*, p. 242.
16 'Études sur les Municipalités – I', *loc. cit.*, p. 32.
17 'Institutions Politiques de la Prusse', p. 433.
18 'Du Renouvellement de l'Esprit Public', p. 253.
19 'Les Émigrations Actuelles des Allemands', *loc. cit.*, p. 1.
20 'Des Princes Médiatisés', *loc. cit.*, p. 118.
21 'Du Renouvellement de l'Esprit Public', p. 241.
22 BNUS, MS. 3519, item 66.

PART TWO: THE THEORY OF RACIAL DETERMINISM

2 :1 The Interlectual Context (pp. 103–111)
1 *The Origins of Totalitarianism*, 2nd ed., London, 1958
pp. 171–2.

L

2 Proposed second edition of *Ottar Jarl* (ca.1880), BNUS, MS.
   3530, f. 113a; relevant passage printed in L. Schemann,
   *Gobineaus Rassenwerk: Aktenstücke und Betrachtungen zur
   Geschichte und Kritik des 'Essai ... '*, Stuttgart, 1910, pp.
   475–7.
3 Book 1, ch. 15. In these notes all subsequent references to
   the *Essai* relate to Hubert Juin's one-volume edition, Paris,
   1967; where relevant we include an additional reference to
   SPW.
4 'The Influence of Anthropology on the Course of Political
   Science', *University of California Publications in History*, vol. 4,
   no. 1, 29 Feb. 1916, p. 11.
5 *Origins of Totalitarianism*, p. 469.
6 To Tocqueville, 8 Jan. 1855, *Corr. Tocqueville*, p. 222.
7 *Essai*, p. 30 (*SPW*, p. 42).

2 : 2 The Racial Theory (pp. 112–121)

1   To Caroline, 14 July 1851, BNUS, MS. 3519, item 74.
2   *Essai*, p. 39 (*SPW*, p. 42).
3   *Ibid.*, p. 29 (*ibid.*, p. 41).
4   *Ibid.*, p. 30 (*ibid.*, p. 42).
5   *Origins of Totalitarianism*, p. 171.
6   *Essai*, p. 47 (*SPW*, p. 53).
7   *Ibid.*, p. 53 (*ibid.*, p. 54).
8   *Ibid.*, p. 57 (*ibid.*, p. 58).
9   *Ibid.*, p. 43 (*ibid.*, p. 47).
10 *Ibid.*, p. 58 (*ibid.*, p. 59).
11 *Ibid.*, p. 59 (*ibid.*, p. 60).
12 *Ibid.*, p. 626.
13 *Ibid.*, p. 85 (*SPW*, p. 78).
14 *Ibid.*, p. 62 (*ibid.*, p. 64).
15 *Ibid.*, p. 110 (*ibid.*, p. 91).
16 *Ibid.*, p. 99 (*ibid.*, p. 84).
17 *Ibid.*, p. 209 (*ibid.*, p. 141).
18 *Ibid.* (*ibid.*, pp. 140–1).
19 *Ibid.*, p. 148 (*ibid.*, p. 107).
20 *Ibid.*, p. 145 (*ibid.*, pp. 103–4).
21 *Ibid.*, p. 155 (*ibid.*, p. 109).
22 *Ibid.*, p. 252.

23 *Ibid.*, p. 312
24 *Ibid.*, p. 208 (*SPW*, p. 138).
25 *Ibid.*, p. 206 (*ibid.*, p. 136).
26 *Ibid.* (*ibid.*).
27 *Ibid.*, p. 261.
28 *Ibid.*, p. 393.
29 *Ibid.*, p. 346.
30 *Ibid.*, p. 855 (*SPW*, p. 163).

2 : 3 The Historical Exposition (*pp. 122–131*)

1 *Essai*, p. 211 (*SPW*, p. 143).
2 *Ibid.*, p. 867 (*ibid.*, p. 168).
3 *Ibid.*, pp. 211–2 (*ibid.*, pp. 143–4).
4 *Ibid.*, p. 326.
5 *Ibid.*, p. 164 (*SPW*, p. 120).
6 *Ibid.*, pp. 672–3.
7 *Ibid.*, p. 245.
8 *Ibid.*, p. 269.
9 *Ibid.*, p. 755.
10 *Ibid.*, p. 868 (*SPW*, p. 168).
11 *Ibid.*, p. 790.
12 *Ibid.*, p. 698.
13 *Formation de la Pensée de Gobineau*, p. 406.
14 *Essai*, p. 759.
15 *Ibid.*, p. 869 (*SPW*, p. 170).
16 *Ibid.*, p. 681.
17 *Ibid.*, p. 760.
18 *Ibid.*, pp. 733–4.
19 *Ibid.*, p. 734.
20 *Ibid.*, p. 736.
21 *Ibid.*, p. 738.
22 *Ibid.*, p. 815.
23 *Ibid.*
24 *Ibid.*
25 *Ibid.*
26 'Edgar Quinet', *loc. cit.*, p. 48.
27 *Essai*, p. 72.
28 'Études sur les Municipalités – II', *loc. cit.*, p. 110.
29 *Essai*, p. 42 (*SPW*, p. 46).

30 8 July 1854, BNUS, MS. 3519, item 124.
31 *Essai*, p. 420 n.

2 : 4 The Method of Racial Determinism (pp. 132–8)

1   *Three Faces of Fascism*, London, 1965, p. 284.
2   *Race: a Study in Superstition*, revised ed., New York, 1965, p. 55.
3   'The Study of Man: a Debate on Race – the Tocqueville–Gobineau Correspondence', *Commentary*, vol. 25, 1958, p. 154.
4   *Essai*, pp. 507–8.
5   *Ibid.*, p. 873 (*SPW*, p. 176).
6   *Ibid.*, p. 313.
7   *Ibid.*, pp. 28–9 (*SPW*, p. 40).
8   'Critique Littéraire: les Oeuvres de M. Vitet', *La Revue Nouvelle*, Jan. 1846, vol. 6, p. 634.
9   *Essai*, p. 856.
10 *Ibid.*, p. 66 (*SPW*, p. 69).
11 *Ibid.*, pp. 566–7.
12 Gobineau to Pott, 9 Oct. 1854, in M. Lémonon, 'Les Débuts du Gobinisme en Allemagne', *EG*, 1968–9, p. 186.
13 *Essai*, pp. 771–2.
14 *Ibid.*, p. 674.
15 *Ibid.*
16 *Ibid.*, p. 644.
17 *Ibid.*, p. 645.
18 *Ibid.*, p. 181 (*SPW*, p. 134).

2 : 5 The Theory and the Modern World (pp. 139–150)

1   To Keller, 11 June 1872, *Corr. Keller*, p. 106.
2   *Essai*, p. 197.
3   *Ibid.*
4   *Ibid.*, p. 54 (*SPW*, p. 56).
5   *Ibid.*, p. 817 (*ibid.*, p. 154).
6   *Ibid.*, p. 744n.
7   *Ibid.*, p. 818 (*SPW*, p. 155).
8   *Ibid.*, p. 792.
9   *Ibid.*, p. 71 (*SPW*, p. 74).
10 *Ibid.*, p. 792.
11 *Ibid.*, p. 799 (*SPW*, p. 145).

12 *Ibid.*, pp. 800–1 (*ibid.*, p. 147).

13 *Ibid.*, p. 818 (*ibid.*, p. 155).

14 *Ibid.* (*ibid.*, pp. 154–5).

15 15 Jan. 1856, *Corr. Tocqueville*, p. 257.

16 *Essai*, p. 387.

17 *Ibid.*, p. 844.

18 *Ibid.*, p. 819 (*SPW*, p. 156).

19 'Plan d'une Nouvelle Organisation Municipale et Départementale', *La Revue Provinciale*, Mar. 1849, vol. 2, p. 20.

20 *Essai*, pp. 852–3 (*SPW*, p. 161).

21 *Ibid.*, p. 854 (*ibid.*, p. 162).

22 *Ibid.*, p. 848 (*ibid.*, p. 157).

23 *Ibid.*, pp. 848–9 (*ibid.*).

24 *Ibid.*, p. 849 (*ibid.*, p. 158).

25 *Origins of Totalitarianism*, p. 173.

26 *Essai*, p. 182 (*SPW*, p. 134).

27 20 June 1856, in C. Serpeille de Gobineau (ed.), *Correspondance entre le Comte de Gobineau et le Comte de Prokesch-Osten, 1854–76*, Paris, 1933, p. 92. This edition (cited henceforth as '*Corr. Prokesch*') contains frequent faulty readings and all quotations from it here have been checked against the original letters (BNUS, MS. 3524) and corrected accordingly.

28 20 June 1856, *Corr. Prokesch*, pp. 91–2.

29 *Gobineau au Jugement de ses Contemporains d'Outre-Rhin* (unpublished doctoral thesis of Paris University, typescript, 1961, conserved at the Bibliothèque Nationale, Paris), p. 389.

30 To Tocqueville, 20 Mar. 1856, *Corr. Tocqueville*, p. 260.

31 27 Dec. 1865, *Corr. Keller*, p. 28.

32 30 July 1856, *Corr. Tocqueville*, p. 267.

33 To Tocqueville, 1 May 1856, *ibid.*, p. 263.

34 'Rapport sur l'Ouvrage de M. de Gobineau . . . ', *Bulletin de la Société de Géographie*, Mar. 1857, p. 240.

35 'De la Civilisation Moderne', *La Revue des Deux Mondes*, 1 Nov. 1858, p. 38.

36 Maury's unpublished journal, Bibliothèque de l'Institut de France, MS. 2649, p. 142 (quoted in J. Gaulmier, *Spectre de Gobineau*, Paris, 1965, p. 32).

37 Renan to Gobineau, 26 June 1856, in J. de Lacretelle, 'Gobineau contre Renan' in *Idées dans un Chapeau*, Monaco, 1946, pp. 89–90.

38 To Tocqueville, 20 Mar. 1856, *Corr. Tocqueville*, p. 260 (*SPW*, p. 182).
39 To Gobineau, 17 Nov. 1853, *ibid.*, p. 203 (*ibid.*, p. 178).

2:6 The Question of Race, Religion and Morality (*pp. 151–5*)

1   *Essai*, p. 727.
2   *Ibid.*, p. 849.
3   *Ibid.*, pp. 40–1 (*SPW*, p. 44).
4   *Ibid.*, p. 592.
5   *Ibid.*, chapter-heading, Book 1, ch. 7.
6   *Ibid.*, pp. 89, 90 (*SPW*, p. 81).
7   *Ibid.*, pp. 81–90.
8   *Ibid.*, p. 180.
9   *Ibid.*, pp. 379–80.
10 *Ibid.*, p. 379.
11 *Ibid.*, p. 27 (*SPW*, p. 37).
12 To Prokesch-Osten, 20 June 1856, *Corr. Prokesch*, pp. 93–4.

2:7 The Search for Social Order (*pp. 156–163*)

1   *Essai*, p. 739.
2   *Ibid.*, p. 415.
3   *Ibid.*, p. 89.
4   *Ibid.*, p. 858.
5   *Ibid.*, p. 621.
6   *Ibid.*, pp. 53–4 (*SPW*, pp. 55–6).
7   *Ibid.*, p. 330.
8   *Ibid.*, p. 331.
9   *Ibid.*, p. 381.
10 *Ibid.*, p. 858.
11 *Ibid.*, p. 812.
12 *Ibid.*
13 *Ibid.*, pp. 812–3.
14 *Ibid.*, p. 786.
15 *Ibid.*, p. 754.
16 *Ibid.*, p. 750.
17 *Ibid.*, p. 675.
18 *Ibid.*, pp. 675–6.
19 *Ibid.*, p. 62 (*SPW*, p. 65).

20 *Ibid.*, p. 166 (*ibid.*, p. 122).
21 *Ibid.*, p. 174 (*ibid.*, p. 128).
22 20 Oct. 1854, BNUS, MS. 3519, item 129.

2 : 8 The Disruption of Society (pp. 164–172)

1   *Essai*, p. 776.
2   *Ibid.*, p. 157n.
3   *Ibid.*, p. 282.
4   *Ibid.*, p. 340.
5   *Ibid.*, p. 171.
6   *Ibid.*, pp. 254–5.
7   *Ibid.*, p. 339.
8   *Ibid.*, pp. 450–1.
9   *Ibid.*, p. 800 (*SPW*, 145).
10 *Ibid.*, p. 158 (*ibid.*, p. 112).
11 *Ibid.*, p. 834.
12 *Ibid.*, p. 87 (*SPW*, pp. 69–70).
13 *Ibid.*, pp. 67–8 (*ibid.*, p. 71).
14 Quoted in Boyé and Concasty, 'Autour de la *Revue Provinciale*', *loc. cit.*, p. 257.
15 *Essai*, p. 589.
16 *Ibid.*
17 *Ibid.*, p. 210 (*SPW*, p. 142).
18 *Ibid.*, p. 417.
19 *Ibid.*
20 *Ibid.*, p. 488.
21 *Ibid.*, p. 489.
22 *Ibid.*
23 *Ibid.*, p. 488n.

2 : 9 The Pessimistic Conclusion (pp. 173–7)

1   *Essai*, p. 163 (*SPW*, p. 118).
2   *Ibid.*, p. 171 (*ibid.*, p. 126).
3   To Tocqueville, 20 Mar. 1856, *Corr. Tocqueville*, p. 259 (*ibid.*, p. 181).
4   *Ibid.*, 15 Oct. 1854, p. 221 (*ibid.*, p. 180).
5   *Essai*, p. 727.

6 'Truth, Belief and Civilization: Tocqueville and Gobineau',
   Review of Politics, vol. 25, no. 4, Oct. 1963, p. 480.
7 16 Sept. 1858, *Corr. Tocqueville*, p. 297.
8 *Evolution and Society: a Study in Victorian Social Theory*,
   Cambridge, 1966, p. 62.
9 *Spectre de Gobineau*, p. 62.
10 *Essai*, p. 870 (*SPW*, p. 173).
11 *Ibid.*, p. 871 (*ibid.*).
12 *Ibid.*, p. 872 (*ibid.*, p. 175).
13 *Ibid.*, p. 873 (*ibid.*, p. 176).
14 *Ibid.*, p. 35.
15 BNUS, MS. 3482, 'Avant-Propos de la 2e Édition de
   l' "Essai"', f. 11a.
16 *Race: a Study in Superstition*, p. 61n.

PART THREE: THE TRIUMPH OF SOCIAL PESSIMISM

3:1 Diplomatic Horizons: Persia (pp. 181–9)

1 *Trois Ans en Asie*, Paris, 1859, p. 282.
2 To Gobineau, 12 June 1851, *Corr. Tocqueville*, p. 175.
3 Gobineau to Prokesch-Osten, 19 Sept. 1855, *Corr. Prokesch*,
   p. 44.
4 *Nouvelles Asiatiques* (ed. J. Gaulmier), Paris, 1965, p. 7.
5 20 Feb. 1856, *Corr. Prokesch*, p. 65.
6 'Memoire sur l'État Social de la Perse Actuelle', *Séances et
   Travaux de l'Académie des Sciences Morales et Politiques*,
   Oct–Nov. 1856, p. 256.
7 Gobineau to Caroline, 10 Sept. 1855, in A. B. Duff (ed.),
   Lettres Persanes, Paris, 1957, p. 25.
8 Gobineau to Tocqueville, 15 Jan. 1856, *Corr. Tocqueville*,
   p. 254.
9 *Trois Ans en Asie*, p. 288.
10 *Ibid.*, p. 80.
11 *Ibid.*, p. 410.
12 To Caroline, 20 June 1856, *Lettres Persanes*, p. 53.
13 *Trois Ans en Asie*, p. 411.
14 Gobineau to Prokesch-Osten, 1 June 1856, *Corr. Prokesch*,
   p. 88.
15 *Religions et Philosophies dans l'Asie Centrale*, Paris, 1957, p. 57.

16 'The Assassins', *Encounter*, Nov. 1967, p. 48.
17 To Tocqueville, 7 July 1855, *Corr. Tocqueville*, p. 232.
18 *Ibid.*, 5 Nov. 1855, p. 238.
19 To Mérimée, 20 Jan. 1856, in J. Gaulmier (ed.), 'Mérimée, Gobineau et les Bohémiens', *Revue d'Histoire Littéraire de la France*, vol. 66, no. 4, Oct–Dec. 1966, p. 685.
20 *Religions et Philosophies*, p. 318.
21 *Histoire des Perses*, Paris, 1869, vol. 1, pp. 265–6.
22 *Ibid.*, p. 511.
23 12 July 1866, BNUS, MS. 3520, item 45.
24 *Histoire des Perses*, vol. 1, p. 402.
25 *Ibid.*, vol. 2, p. 634.
26 *Essai* (Foreword to 2nd edition), p. 35.
27 *Trois Ans en Asie*, p. 482.

3:2 Diplomatic Horizons : Greece (pp. 190–6)

1 26 Dec, 1864, *Corr. Circourt* (pt. 2), p. 68.
2 *Ibid.*, 29 Apr. 1868 (pt. 2), p. 96.
3 In 'Le Royaume des Hellènes', a series of four articles published in *Le Correspondant* in 1878, as follows: (I) 10 May, vol. 111, p. 416–41; (II) 10 July, vol. 112, pp. 30–60; (III) 25 Aug., vol. 112, pp. 668–99; (IV) 10 Nov., vol. 113, pp. 471–504. The present quotation is from (III), p. 691. These articles were subsequently collected (with that on Capodistrias) as *Deux Études sur la Grèce Moderne*, Paris, 1905.
4 'Royaume des Hellènes – I', p. 430.
5 4 Aug. 1868, *Corr. Circourt*, (pt. 2), p. 103.
6 *Ibid.*, 8 July 1868, p. 101.
7 To Circourt, *ibid.*, 28 Aug. 1865, p. 75.
8 AMAE, *CP, Grèce,* vol. 90, 10 Aug. 1865, no. 60, ff. 341b–342a.
9 To Prokesch-Osten, 17 Dec. 1865, *Corr. Prokesch*, p. 282.
10 To Mlle. Marguerite Franck, 1 Aug. 1867, in R. Worms (ed.), 'Lettres Inédites de Gobineau à M. Adolphe Franck et à sa Famille', *Revue Internationale de Sociologie*, Aug–Sept. 1916, p. 432.
11 Quoted by Gaulmier in *Corr. Rémusat*, p. 99, n.2.
12 23 Mar. 1865, *Corr. Circourt*, (pt. 2), p. 71.
13 To Circourt, 24 Oct. 1867, *ibid.*, p. 86.
14 *Ibid.*, 4 Aug. 1868, p. 103.

15 'Royaume des Hellènes – III', p. 685.
16 9 Apr. 1867, *Corr. Prokesch*, p. 313.
17 19 Dec. 1867, *Corr. Circourt*, (pt. 2), p. 89.
18 31 Aug. 1868, *Corr. Prokesch*, p. 333.
19 'Royaume des Hellènes – I', p. 147.
20 *Ibid.*, IV, p. 504.

3 : 3 Diplomatic Horizons : The Americas (pp. 197–206).

1 *Voyage à Terre-Neuve*, Paris, 1861, p. 302.
2 *Ibid.*, p. 163.
3 1 Dec. 1862, quoted in J. Gaulmier (ed.), 'Arthur de Gobineau et le Ministre Baroche', *Travaux du Centre de Philologie et de Littératures Romanes, Strasbourg,* vol. 3, no. 2, 1965, p. 53, n.6.
4 To Prokesch-Osten, 15 Dec. 1859, *Corr. Prokesch*, pp. 208–9.
5 *Voyage à Terre-Neuve*, p. 170.
6 *Ibid.*
7 *Ibid.*, p. 305.
8 *Ibid.*, p. 45.
9 *Ibid.*, pp. 48–9.
10 *Ibid.*, p. 305.
11 7 Mar. 1869, in J. Mistler (ed.), 'Nouvelles Lettres Athéniennes', *Revue des Deux Mondes,* 1 Oct. 1954, p. 436.
12 17 Apr. 1689, *Corr. Keller*, p. 85.
13 AMAE, *CC, Rio,* vol. 16, 22 Sept. 1869, no. 5, f. 11a.
14 *Ibid.*, *CP, Brésil,* vol. 42, 23 July 1869, no. 15, f. 325b.
15 *Ibid.*, f. 326b.
16 *Ibid.*, *CC, Rio,* vol. 16, 22 Sept. 1869, no. 5, f. 13a.
17 *Ibid.*, *CP, Brésil,* vol. 42, 23 July 1869, no. 15, f. 320b.
18 'L'Émigration au Brésil', *Le Correspondant,* 25 July 1874, vol. 96, p. 355.
19 *Ibid.*, p. 376.
20 *Ibid.*, p. 354.
21 'L'Émigration Européenne dans les Deux Amériques', *Le Correspondant,* 25 Oct. 1872, vol. 89, p. 239.
22 *Ibid.*, p. 240.
23 *Voyage à Terre-Neuve*, p. 287.
24 29 Apr. 1868, *Corr. Circourt* (pt. 2), p. 96.
25 *L'Europe et la Russie*, BNUS, MS. 3505, ff. 11b–12a.

3:4 The State of France (pp. 207–224)

1 24 July 1870, in N. Méla (ed.), *Lettres à Deux Athéniennes, 1868–81*, Athènes, 1936, p. 142.

2 4 Mar. 1859, *Corr. Tocqueville*, p. 300.

3 10 Nov. 1862, BNUS, MS. 3524, item 103 (being part of a passage inexplicably omitted from *Corr. Prokesch*).

4 To Marika Dragoumis, 8 Oct. 1870, *Lettres à Deux Athéniennes* p. 154.

5 5 Nov. 1868, 'Nouvelles Lettres Athéniennes', *loc. cit.*, p. 423.

6 *Religions et Philosophies*, p. 317.

7 23 Jan. 1868, BNUS, MS. 3520, item 64.

8 26 May 1868, *Corr. Circourt*, (pt. 2), p. 97.

9 To Hercule de Serre, 1 Oct. 1854, transcribed in AMAE, *Papiers Walewski, loc. cit.*

10 11 Sept. 1866, *Corr. Keller*, pp. 38–9.

11 To Keller, 6 Mar. 1871, *ibid.*, pp. 95–6.

12 To Marika Dragoumis, undated (ca.1870–1), *Lettres à Deux Athéniennes*, p. 160.

13 *Essai.* pp. 115–6 (*SPW*, p. 96).

14 *Ibid.*, p. 116.

15 *Ibid.* It is to be noted that Juin's edition of the *Essai* wrongly prints '*nord-est*', in place of '*nord-ouest*'.

16 2 July 1864, *Corr. Rémusat*, p. 98.

17 6 June 1864, in M.L. Concasty (ed.), 'Gobineau Conseiller Général de l'Oise', *EG*, 1968–9, p. 226.

18 25 Apr. 1873, *Corr. Prokesch*, p. 372.

19 To Caroline, 16 Mar. 1871, BNUS, MS. 3520, item 160.

20 22 Mar. 1871, in G. Raeders (ed.), *Dom Pedro II e o Conde de Gobineau: Correspondencias Ineditas*, São Paulo, 1938 (cited hereafter as '*Corr. Pedro*'), p. 392.

21 28 May 1871, *Lettres à Deux Athéniennes*, p. 174.

22 12 Nov. 1870, *Corr. Keller*, p. 94.

23 *Ce qui est arrivé à la France en 1870, loc. cit.* (cf.1:2, note 22), pp. 81–2 (*SPW*, pp. 204–5).

24 *France en 1870*, p. 109.

25 *Ibid.*, p. 147.

26 *Ibid.*, p. 135.

27 *Ibid.*, pp. 138–9.

28 *Ibid.*, p. 146.

29 *Ibid.*, p. 110 (*SPW*, p. 208).

30 BNUS, MS. 3506, f. 117a.

31 To Jules Delpit, 7 June 1871, *Lettres de Gobineau à Jules Delpit*, Bilbiothèque Municipale de Bordeaux, MS. 1779, vol. 2, item 160.

32 To Dom Pedro, 11 Sept. 1873, *Corr. Pedro*, p. 454.

33 11 Feb. 1877, *Lettres à Deux Athéniennes*, p. 249.

34 *La Troisième République Française et ce qu'elle vaut* (ed. C. Serpeille de Gobineau), Paris, 1943, p. 128. The time and place of this publication are significant and the editor's *'notes actuelles'* are a pro-Nazi gloss. Some extracts from Gobineau's text are translated in *SPW*, pp. 210–8.

35 *Troisième République*, p.75 (*SPW*, p. 214).

36 *Ibid.*, p. 174.

37 *Ibid.*, p. 83 (*SPW*, pp. 215–6).

38 *Ibid.*, p. 94.

39 *Ibid.*, p. 180.

40 *L'Instinct Révolutionnaire en France*, Paris, 1928, pp. 84–5 (*SPW*, p. 225).

41 *Ibid.*, p. 75.

42 9 Oct. 1875, *Corr. Pedro*, p. 504.

43 *La Renaissance: Scènes Historiques* (ed. J. Mistler), Monaco, 1947, p. 108.

44 *Les Pléiades*, p. 248.

45 *The Nation*, 7 Dec. 1876 (BNUS, MS. 3541, item 26).

46 Comtesse de La Tour, *Les Dernières Années du Comte de Gobineau à travers mes Souvenirs et sa Correspondance* (BNUS, MS. 3568, '2e Copie Dactylographiée'), f. 164 (pagination of BNUS, not of the authoress).

47 9 Apr. 1874, in J. Gaulmier, 'Arthur de Gobineau et ses Amitiés Libérales', *EG*, 1968–9, p. 127.

48 To Dom Pedro, 24 Jan. 1879, *Corr. Pedro*, p. 555.

49 'Feuilles Éparpillées', BNUS, MS. 3542, item 11. Thiers died on 3 Sept, 1877.

50 16 June 1871, in *Lettres de Gobineau à Marika et Zoé Dragoumis*, Bibliothèque Nationale, Paris, Nouv.acq.fr., MS. 13788.

3 : 5 The Viking Inheritance (pp. 225–233)

1 25 May 1872, BNUS, MS. 3520, item 126.

2 To Dom Pedro, 16 Sept. 1872, *Corr. Pedro*, p. 420.

3   *Ibid.*, 16 Feb. 1873, p. 437.
4   26 July 1872, *Lettres à Deux Athéniennes.* p. 187.
5   6 Sept. 1872, in J. Boissel (ed.), 'Lettres de Gobineau à Jules Mohl et à Madame Mohl', *Revue de Littérature Comparée,* vol. 40, no. 3, July–Sept. 1966, pp. 357–8.
6   12 Sept. 1872, *Corr. Bénédicte,* vol. 1, p. 40.
7   To Prokesch-Osten, 23 Sept. 1872, *Corr. Prokesch,* p. 358.
8   16 Sept. 1872, *Corr. Pedro,* p. 421.
9   9 Mar. 1873, *ibid.,* p. 438.
10 'L'Instruction Primaire en Suède', *Le Correspondant,* 25 Feb. 1873, vol. 90, p. 674.
11 *Ibid.,* pp. 677–8.
12 16 Feb. 1879, *Corr. Pedro,* pp. 556–7.
13 11 Nov. 1876, in J. Buenzod (ed.), 'Lettres d'un Voyage en Russie, en Asie Mineure et en Grèce', *Études de Lettres,* Oct–Dec. 1961, p. 199.
14 To Comtesse de La Tour, 18 Oct. 1876, *ibid.,* p. 188.
15 *L'Ethnographie de la France,* BNUS, MS. 3504, f. 41a.
16 Quoted in M. Lange, *Le Comte Arthur de Gobineau: Étude Biographique et Critique,* Strasbourg, 1924, p. 210.
17 *Spectre de Gobineau,* p. 45.
18 14 Dec. 1879, *Corr. Pedro,* p. 581.
19 *Histoire des Perses,* vol. 1, p. 30.
20 *Ibid.,* vol. 2, p. 635.
21 *Ibid.,* p. 59.
22 *Histoire d'Ottar Jarl,* Paris, 1879, p. 16.
23 17 July 1869, in A.B. Duff (ed.), 'Sept Lettres du Comte Arthur de Gobineau à sa Soeur', *Revue de Littérature Comparée,* vol. 23, 1949, p. 551.
24 4 Jan. 1873, *Corr. Bénédicte,* vol. 1, p. 61.
25 26 Mar. 1875, *ibid.,* p. 163.
26 To Caroline, 15 Apr. 1874, *ibid.,* p. 123.
27 27 July 1872, *Corr. Pedro,* p. 417.
28 13 Feb. 1874, *Corr. Bénédicte,* vol. 1, p. 104.
29 *Dernières Années,* f. 227.

3:6 The Élite and the Masses (pp. 234–243)

1   *Ottar Jarl,* p. 284.
2   *Mémoire sur Diverses Manifestations de la Vie Individuelle* (ed. A.B. Duff), Paris, 1935, p. 33.

3 *Ibid.*, p. 48.
4 *Ibid.*, p. 218.
5 *Nouvelles Asiatiques* (ed. J. Gaulmier), Paris, 1965, p. 297.
6 *Ethnographie de la France*, f. 69a.
7 *Ibid.*, ff. 4b–5a.
8 7 Oct. 1872, *Corr. Prokesch*, p. 361.
9 *Les Pléiades*, p. 289.
10 *Ibid.*, pp. 29–30 (*SPW*, p. 187).
11 *Ibid.*, p. 31 (*ibid.*, p. 188).
12 *Ottar Jarl*, p. 299.
13 *La Renaissance: Scènes Historiques* (ed. J. Mistler), Monaco, 1947, p. 6.
14 2 June 1874, BNUS, MS. 3517, item 21.
15 17 Apr. 1873, *Lettres à Deux Athéniennes*, p. 200.
16 To Comtesse de La Tour, 8 June 1874, BNUS, MS. 3517, item 25.
17 *La Renaissance*, p. 10.
18 *Ibid.*, p. 314.
19 To Keller, 22 Oct. 1879, *Corr. Keller*, p. 159.
20 *Ibid.*
21 R. Thenen, *L'"Amadis' de Gobineau: Essai d'Histoire d'une Création Littéraire* (duplicated thesis, Faculté des Lettres, Montpellier, typescript, 1960, copy conserved at BNUS), p. 189. This work includes as an appendix (pp. 153ff.) the passages omitted from *Amadis*, Paris, 1887.
22 Undated (ca. Oct–Nov. 1883), BNUS, MS. 3481; quoted in *L'"Amadis' de Gobineau*, pp. 30–1, and in R. Thenen, 'Le Testament Spirituel de Gobineau', *EG*, 1966, pp. 223–4.
23 *Les Pléiades*, p. 34 (*SPW*, p. 191).
24 Quoted in A.E. Carter: *The Idea of Decadence in French Literature, 1830–1900*, Toronto, 1958, p. 9.
25 15 Apr. 1874, *Corr. Bénédicte*, vol. 1, p. 124.
26 8 Oct. 1868, *Lettres à Deux Athéniennes*, pp. 10–11.
27 *Ottar Jarl*, p. 287.
28 *La Renaissance*, p. 101 (*SPW*, pp. 199–200).

3:7 The Triumph of Social Pessimism (pp. 244–261)

1 11 Mar. 1873, *Corr. Prokesch*, p. 370.
2 *La Renaissance*, p. 312.

3   1 Feb. 1873, *Corr. Bénédicte*, vol. 1, p. 63.
4   *Ibid.*
5   *L'Histoire des Mérovingiens*, BNUS. MS. 3507 (pt. 1), f. 29a.
6   *Ibid.*, ff. 29b–30a.
7   To Dom Pedro, 10 July 1882, *Corr. Pedro*, p. 615.
8   8 Feb. 1882, *ibid.*, p. 613.
9   To Zoé Dragoumis, *Lettres à Deux Athéniennes*, p. 218.
10 2 June 1874, *Corr. Bénédicte*, vol. 1. p. 129.
11 To Comtesse de La Tour, 22 May 1874, in J. Mistler (ed.),
    'Lettres de Gobineau à la Comtesse de La Tour', *La Table
    Ronde*, Apr. (pp.36–46) and May (pp. 49–67) 1950, p. 38.
12 To Dom Pedro, 18 Aug. 1874, *Corr. Pedro*, p. 480.
13 Letter of 6 Aug. 1877, to Princesse de Wittgenstein, quoted in
    EG, 1966, p. 250.
14 *Essai*, p. 31 (*SPW*, p. 229).
15 *L'Ethnographie de la France*, f. 4a.
16 2 June 1874, *Corr. Bénédicte*, vol. 1, p. 128.
17 *Essai*, p. 33 (*SPW*, pp. 232–3).
18 'L'Émigration Européenne dans les Deux Amériques', *loc.
    cit.*, p. 208.
19 *France en 1870*, p. 144.
20 *L'Ethnographie de la France*, f. 33a.
21 *Ibid.*, f. 79b.
22 *Vues sur l'Histoire Générale*, BNUS, MS. 3511 (pt. 1), f. 9b.
23 3 July 1876, *Lettres à Deux Athéniennes*, p. 237.
24 To Dom Pedro, 14 Aug. 1878, *Corr. Pedro*, p. 545.
25 To Marika Dragoumis, 7 Apr. 1878, Bibliothèque Nationale,
    Paris, Nouv.acq. fr. MS. 13788.
26 To Dom Pedro, 26 Oct. 1878, *Corr. Pedro*, p. 550.
27 12 Sept. 1876, 'Lettres d'un Voyage en Russie', *loc. cit.*, p. 172.
28 9 Jan. 1879, quoted in C. Digeon, *La Crise Allemande de la
    Pensée Française, 1870–1914*, Paris, 1959, p. 93n.
29 *L'Europe et la Russie*, f. 46b.
30 2 Apr. 1881, *Corr. Bénédicte*, vol. 2, p. 207.
31 'Ce qui se fait en Asie', BNUS, MS. 3493, f. 8a (*SPW*, p. 235),
    We quote from the manuscript since the posthumously
    published French text (first appearing in the aptly-titled *Revue
    du Monde Latin*, vol. 6, 1885, pp. 397–418) reveals a number of
    variants. The German translation had appeared in May 1881,
    as 'Ein Urtheil über die jetzige Weltlage'.

32 11 July 1879, *Corr. Pedro*, p. 563.
33 'Ce qui se fait en Asie', f. 29a (*SPW*, p. 246).
34 *Ibid.*, f. 30a–b (*ibid.*, pp. 246–7).
35 *Trois Ans en Asie*, p. 482.
36 To Dom Pedro, 1 Dec. 1878, *Corr. Pedro*, p. 551.
37 To Comtesse de La Tour, 17 Aug. 1880, BNUS, MS. 3517, item 330.
38 *L'Ethnographie de la France*, f. 38b.
39 *Ibid.*, ff. 35b–36a.
40 *The Foundations of the Nineteenth Century* (tr. J. Lees), 2 vols, London, 1911, vol. 1, p. 266n.
41 *Mein Kampf* (tr. J. Murphy), London, 1939 (one-volume edition, unabridged), pp. 240, 242, 243.
42 *Les Pléiades*, p. 249.
43 1 Dec. 1872, *Corr. Pedro*, p. 430.
44 17 Feb. 1867, *Corr. Keller*, p. 44.
45 'Royaume des Hellènes – III', p. 668.
46 *Les Pléiades*, pp. 297, 298–9 (*SPW*, pp. 197–8).
47 *Ibid.*, p. 295 (*ibid.*, p. 195).
48 *Ibid.*, (*ibid.*).
49 Introduction to *Nouvelles Asiatiques*, p. lxxiii.
50 26 Mar. 1882, *Corr. Bénédicte*, vol. 2, p. 254.

CONCLUSION

1 *Origins of Totalitarianism*, p. 172.
2 *History of Western Philosophy*, London, 1962, p. 53.
3 BNUS, MS. 3511 (pt. 1), f. 7b.
4 *Historical Inevitability*, London, 1954, p. 68.
5 To Comtesse de La Tour, 26 Aug. 1873, BNUS, MS. 3517, item 8.
6 *Essai*, p. 870 (*SPW*, pp. 171–2).

Notes on Sources and
Further Reading

SOURCES

Much of the source material for this book has been already indicated, both generally in its Introduction and more precisely in the reference notes to its various parts. In the light of this, any full and classified enumeration of sources has been considered largely redundant. However, it will doubtless be helpful for the reader to know where certain useful listings of source material may be consulted and to have a check-list of the major works of Gobineau that can be found in volume form.

For manuscript materials the reader should turn first to the *Catalogue Général des Manuscrits des Bibliothèques Publiques de France*, vol. 47, *Strasbourg* (ed. E. Wickersheimer), Paris, 1923, pp. 610–23, where he will obtain an almost complete list of the holdings in the Gobineau Archives of the Bibliothèque Nationale et Universitaire (MSS. 3477–3569). The manuscript diplomatic reports are classified, with commentary, in the typed *Inventaire de la Correspondance Diplomatique du Comte de Gobineau*, 3 vols (eds. H. Miramon–Fitzjames & A. Outrey), which may be consulted in the Salle des Communications at the Archives du Ministère des Affaires Étrangères. The most convenient general bibliography is to be found in Janine Buenzod, *La Formation de la Pensée de Gobineau*, pp. 611–45. Though this naturally concentrates on the primary and secondary materials for the study of Gobineau until the time of the *Essai*'s appearance (being virtually complete from that standpoint), it also provides the best single list of broader commentaries and interpretations. It includes moreover (on p. 620) a useful enumeration of other Gobineau bibliographies. More information can be derived from the present author's Biblio-graphical Notes to *Gobineau : Selected Political Writings* and from his List of Sources appended to a doctoral dissertation on Gobineau conserved in the Anderson Room of Cambridge University Library. It must be added that the volumes of the *Études Gobiniennes* pro-vide continuing and invaluable aids regarding sources for every aspect of Gobineau scholarship.

We list below those works of Gobineau available in *book* form which we have used in the preparation of this study. The editions mentioned are those from which quotations (if any) have been made:

L'Abbaye de Typhaines, Paris, 1923.
Adélaïde and *Mademoiselle Irnois,* Paris, 1963.
Les Adieux de Don Juan, Paris, 1844.
Alexandre le Macédonien, in *Nachgelassene Schriften des Grafen Gobineau* (ed. L. Schemann), Strassburg, 1901.
Amadis, Paris, 1887.
L'Aphroëssa, Paris, 1869.
Ce qui est arrivé à la France en 1870, in *Nachgelassene Schriften* etc., Strassburg, 1918.
La Chronique Rimée de Jean Chouan et de ses Compagnons, Paris, 1846.
Essai sur l'Inégalité des Races Humaines, Paris, 1967.
Études Critiques, 1844–8, Paris, 1927.
Histoire d'Ottar Jarl, Paris, 1879.
Histoire des Perses, 2 vols, Paris, 1869.
Mémoire sur Diverses Manifestations de la Vie Individuelle, Paris, 1935.
Nicolas Belavoir, 2 vols, Paris, 1927.
Nouvelles, 2 vols, Paris, 1961.
Nouvelles Asiatiques, Paris, 1965.
Les Pléiades, Paris, 1960.
Poemi Inediti (ed. P. Berselli Ambri), in *Biblioteca dell' "Archivum Romanicum",* vol. 75, Firenze, 1965.
Le Prisonnier Chanceux, Paris, 1924.
Religions et Philosophies dans l'Asie Centrale, Paris, 1957.
La Renaissance, Monaco, 1947.
Scaramouche, Paris, 1962.
Souvenirs de Voyage, Paris, 1922.

Ternove, 3 vols, Bruxelles, 1848.
La Troisième République Française et ce qu'elle vaut, Paris, 1943.
Voyage à Terre-Neuve, Paris, 1861.

FURTHER READING

The following book-list notes simply the major general studies devoted to Gobineau:

BRION, Marcel: *Gobineau*, Marseille, 1927.

BUENZOD, Janine: *La Formation de la Pensée de Gobineau*, Paris, 1967.

CARTELLIERI, Alexander: *Gobineau*, Strassburg, 1917.

COMBRIS, Andrée: *La Philosophie des Races du Comte de Gobineau et sa Portée Actuelle*, Paris, 1937.

DREYFUS, Robert: *La Vie et les Prophéties du Comte de Gobineau*, Paris, 1905.

DUFRÉCHOU, Alfred: *Gobineau*, Paris, 1909.

FAURE-BIGUET, J. N.: *Gobineau*, Paris, 1930.

FOUQUÉ, Charles: *Défense et Illustration de la Race Blanche : à la Mémoire du Comte de Gobineau*, Lyon, 1958.

FRIEDRICH, Fritz: *Studien über Gobineau*, Leipzig, 1906.

GAULMIER, Jean: *Spectre de Gobineau*, Paris, 1965.

GIGLI, Lorenzo: *Vita di Gobineau*, Milano, 1933.

KAUFMANN, Josef: *Gobineau und die Kultur des Abendlandes*, Duisburg, 1929.

KRETZER, Eugen: *Joseph Arthur Graf von Gobineau : sein Leben und sein Werk*, Leipzig, 1902.

LACRETELLE, Jacques de: *Quatres Études sur Gobineau*, Liège, 1927.

LANGE, Maurice: *Le Comte Arthur de Gobineau : Étude Biographique et Critique*, Strasbourg, 1924.

RAEDERS, Georges: *Le Comte de Gobineau au Brésil*, Paris, 1934.

RIFFATERRE, Michael: *Le Style des Pléiades de Gobineau*, Paris, 1957.

ROWBOTHAM, Arnold: *The Literary Works of Count de Gobineau*, Paris, 1929.

SCHEMANN, Ludwig: *Gobineaus Rassenwerk : Aktenstücke und Betrachtungen zur Geschichte und Kritik des 'Essai ...'*, Stuttgart, 1910.

SCHEMANN, Ludwig: *Gobineau : eine Biographie,* 2 vols, Strassburg, 1913–6.

SCHEMANN, Ludwig: *Quellen und Untersuchungen zum Leben Gobineaus,* 2 vols, Strassburg 1914 & Berlin 1919.

SEILLIÈRE, Ernest: *Le Comte de Gobineau et l'Aryanisme Historique,* Paris, 1903.

SPIESS, Camille: *Impérialismes : la Conception Gobinienne de la Race : sa Valeur au point de vue bio-psychologique,* Genève, 1917.

SPRING, Gerald: *The Vitalism of Count Gobineau,* New York, 1932.

STREIDL, Rudolf: *Gobineau in der Französischen Kritik,* Würzburg, 1935.

THOMAS, Louis: *Les Précurseurs : Arthur de Gobineau, Inventeur du Racisme (1816–82),* Paris, 1941.

VALETTE, Rebecca M.: *Arthur de Gobineau and the Short Story,* Chapel Hill, 1969.

An item's inclusion above is in no way meant to mark approval of its contents – particularly as a number of the books are essays in tendentious misinterpretation. But no student of Gobineau who desired to understand also the nature of later Gobinism would wish to omit the travesties perpetrated by (for instance) Schemann, Spiess, Thomas and Fouqué. The two quite recent studies by Gaulmier and Buenzod are both valuable in their own way. The perceptive reader will however appreciate that some significant divergences of interpretation exist not only between these two works but also between each of them and the present volume. But, among those who cherish the vitality of Gobineau studies, this is a state of affairs that will encourage neither surprise nor dismay.

Index of Names

Index of Subjects